P9-EKE-969

Praise for *What They Don't Teach Teens*

"*What They Don't Teach Teens* is deep, impactful, and clearly conveys information about sexual and interpersonal violence that no young person should be without."—Patti Giggans, Executive Director, Peace Over Violence (formerly Los Angeles Commission on Assaults Against Women)

"*What They Don't Teach Teens* is a timely text that provides both parent and child alike with valuable information to identify and confront some of the most challenging teen issues of the day."—Justin Patchin, PhD, Professor of criminal justice, University of Wisconsin-Eau Claire and Co-Founder and Co-Director, Cyberbullying Research Center

"This book is like a cookbook; you keep referring back to it when you need the details for a specific recipe (or here, a topic)."—Tamberley M., parent of 16-year-old twins

"*What They Don't Teach Teens* is just bursting with compelling information about social media and the use of digital technologies that all young people coming of age today must know."—Terry Evans, CEO, Cybersleuth Investigations, Inc. and fellow with the National Cybersecurity Institute at Excelsior College

"Jonathan Cristall's background, experience, and writing style makes him relatable and gives his voice credibility that teens will listen to."—Kami Kosenko, Ph.D., Associate Professor, Department of Communication, North Carolina State University

"Easy to read and comprehensive on topics of safety, Cristall's volume is an informative read for teens and their parents, but may also prove to be a helpful text for a high-school level health class."—*Library Journal*

"A much better book than I thought it was going to be. I learned things that I thought I knew, but didn't really."—Bryan J., 11th grader

"*What They Don't Teach Teens* provides outstanding guidance on digital decision making and is written in a way to make it accessible to any person, of almost any age, who wisely chooses to pick it up."—Jedidiah Bracy, Editorial Director, International Association of Privacy Professionals (IAPP)

"*What They Don't Teach Teens* will help prevent sexual violence in relationships, friendships, peer groups, and communities."—Connie J. Kirkland, MA, NCC, CTTS, Director of Sexual Assault Services, Northern Virginia Community College

"*What They Don't Teach Teens* is an essential tool for young people, parents, and guardians in navigating the rocky terrains of street and digital safety, and sexual violence."—Bianca Fileborn, PhD, Lecturer in Criminology, University of Melbourne

"*What They Don't Teach Teens* is a wonderful way for school administrators and school counselors to start meaningful conversations with students. A book like no other that schools (and parents) have been longing for."—Ali Norman-Franks, Intervention Counselor, Beverly Hills High School

"I received this book as assigned reading from my wife. I had some hesitation, but within minutes of starting to read I was hooked. As a dad, I appreciated how comprehensive the book is."—Andy W., father to teens

"Jonathan Cristall provides not only great insight for how to best interface with the police, but is candid about racial injustice."—Dr. Cedric L. Alexander, Past National President of the National Organization of Black Law Enforcement Executives, CNN Law Enforcement Analyst

"Jonathan Cristall's book is designed to appeal directly to youth—to help them make healthy and safe choices, even when interacting with the police."—Elizabeth Englander, PhD, Executive Director and founder of the Massachusetts Aggression Reduction Center at Bridgewater State University

"*What They Don't Teach Teens* provides incredible guidance to young people on issues of contemporary importance like policing and sexual violence prevention. Jonathan Cristall does so in a way that's not only comprehensive and realistic, but sensitive to the diverse backgrounds of those who may read it."—Capri Maddox, Esq., Executive Director, Los Angeles Department of Civil and Human Rights

"Mr. Cristall's book exposes some of the most common methods perpetrators use to obtain child sexual abuse material by the exploitation of young people. His prevention techniques and tips are savvy, well explained, and will certainly keep tweens, teens, and young adults safer online and off."—Glen Pounder, Chief Operating Officer, Child Rescue Coalition, Inc.

What They Don't Teach Teens

Life Safety Skills for Teens
and the Adults Who
Care for Them

Jonathan Cristall, Esq.

Fresno, California

What They Don't Teach Teens

Copyright © 2020 by Jonathan Cristall. All rights reserved.
Interior design by Carla Green, Clarity Designworks.
Illustrations by Bintang Suhadiyono.
Cover design by @difrats.

Published by Quill Driver Books,
an imprint of Linden Publishing
2006 South Mary Street, Fresno, California 93721
(559) 233-6633 / (800) 345-4447
QuillDriverBooks.com

Quill Driver Books and Colophon are trademarks of
Linden Publishing, Inc.

Linden Publishing titles may be purchased in quantity at special discounts for
educational, business, or promotional use. To inquire about discount
pricing, please refer to the contact information above. For permission to use
any portion of this book for academic purposes, please contact the
Copyright Clearance Center at www.copyright.com.

ISBN 978-1610353-58-8

135798642

Printed in the United States of America
on acid-free paper.

Library of Congress Cataloging-in-Publication Data on file.

Contents

Part 1 / Dealing with the Police and Street Safety

Part 2 / Sexual Violence and Misconduct

Part 3 / Staying Safer Online

To my wonderful wife Lisa, for building a life with me that
I thought only existed in dreams.

To my sons, J, E, and B, who, in each of your own ways, have taught
me more about life and love than I ever could have imagined.

Preface for Teens and All Young People

I wrote this book for my three sons—two of them teenagers—so they can better understand what is expected of them as they transition from our home to the outside world. For them, and everyone coming of age today, there are new risks, expectations, and laws that didn't exist for previous generations.

Let's face it—going through adolescence has never been easy. But it can be more challenging today if you don't completely understand the ways a damaged digital footprint can alter your life; the statements or actions that amount to sexual harassment; the potentially severe consequences of underage sexting; the point a sexual interaction "goes too far"; the safest way to pull over when stopped by the police; and so much more.

While the subject matter in this book is serious and at times unsettling, my objective is not to scare you. To the contrary, I hope that understanding the fact-based information herein will bring you a sense of calm knowing that you're better prepared to handle the unexpected.

What to Know About Me

The most important things to know about me start with what I hold most dear: my wife, Lisa, and our three terrific sons.

I have the second-best job in the world as a veteran prosecutor for the City of Los Angeles. For many years, I've had the good fortune to supervise a team of prosecutors and support staff who work with great dedication to improve public safety throughout Los Angeles. (In case you're wondering, the best job to me would be playing for the Los Angeles Lakers.)

I'm also a trained and certified sexual violence prevention instructor at a large nonprofit in Los Angeles called Peace Over Violence—an organization you may know of from their annual, worldwide Denim Day event protesting sexual violence. For many years, this organization has performed impactful work in the greater Los Angeles area and far beyond, providing resources for victim-survivors of sexual violence. I am donating a portion of my book profits to Peace Over Violence because, unfortunately, they have way too much work to do.

Another activity that keeps me busy is teaching the topics in this book to parents and teens and at schools. I never anticipated that as I told people about the book I was writing, I'd be asked to teach these life skills to them in person. Fortunately, my voice seems to be resonating with many, and juggling my workshops with everything else is a real challenge. This is a good problem, I suppose.

Yet none of these or other accomplishments or, frankly, anything else in my life should have ever happened. I should be dead.

As a high schooler, I made countless bad choices that nearly cost me my life. I took unnecessary risks by riding fast motorcycles with no helmet, ingested things I shouldn't have, and went to dangerous places where I had no business. Adding fuel to the fire, I rarely attended school, found myself in an unhealthy intimate relationship, and had many police interactions, one of which led to my arrest for a property crime. To top it off, I often wondered whether my life was worth living and thought many times about ending it.

The backdrop to all of this isn't terribly surprising: my family was a mess. My parents were divorced, and their divorce was not amicable. My father wasn't present and neither, really, was my mother, who was rapidly deteriorating from a serious, debilitating disease. With no real boundaries or supervision, my life started to go in the wrong direction even though, at my core, I was a good kid.

Toward the end of my junior year in high school, as my life continued to unravel, my parents finally got on the same page and fully grasped the desperateness of my situation. Their intervention was to send me to a therapeutic boarding school. The two and a half years I spent there were exceptionally difficult, but the payoff was big: the school saved my life.

The contrast between my early life as a troubled teen and my ongoing career as a prosecutor is not lost on me. With the passage of time, I can now see that it is precisely my early life experiences that have given me the ability to better understand the challenges young people face today, and this, in turn, set the stage for me to write this book.

Introduction

Booksellers will put my book in the parenting category. I wish they wouldn't. You see, for it to be a true parenting book, I'd have to be some sort of parenting expert. I am not.

Thousands upon thousands of "parenting" books are in print. They offer many differing points of view about how to correctly parent, and I can't say who's right or wrong since nobody has all the answers. I simply think of myself as a parent who is fully aware that the laws and expectations for those coming of age today have changed dramatically.

The journey of writing this book started when my wife, Lisa, and I decided to teach our own sons about these laws and expectations. I searched everywhere for a single book or other comparable resource to make it a bit easier on us. I found nothing. Anywhere. Not even, ironically, in the parenting section of bookstores.

It was then that I knew that I *had* to write this book. I must confess that I didn't want to, but there was no choice. It had to be done and I believed I could do it.

> "I didn't have time to write a short letter,
> so I wrote a long one instead."
> —Mark Twain

The greatest challenge I faced writing this book was taking complex, nuanced subjects and distilling them into short, easy-to-understand chapters. In many ways, it would have been easier to write an entire book about each subject.

Although I do rely on the work of academics at times, I am not an academic and this book is not intended to read like a scholarly publication. One goal of this book is to be as straightforward as possible, direct, and accessible to anyone of nearly any age who might pick it up—parent, grandparent, guardian, caregiver, teacher, preteen, teen, young adult, or anyone else. To help in this regard, *the book is written as if the reader were a young person.*

The chapters can be read in the order presented or on an as-needed basis. Each is intended to be a mini-book in itself that covers the most important aspects of that topic in a way that is deployable if the situation calls for it. Collectively, the mini-books provide the reader with a comprehensive tool kit of essential life skills. For those readers who wish to dive deeper into any of the subjects and explore more than I have covered, additional information is certainly out there to be had.

Many, if not all, of the chapter topics in this book intersect with one another. For example, the chapter on sexual harassment touches on issues dealt with in the chapters on sexual consent, cyberbullying, and others.

One thread that can be pulled through every chapter of this book is impulsivity and the developing teenage brain. In short, until relatively recently, the conventional wisdom among brain scientists was that the teenage brain is identical to the adult brain. It is not. Dr. Dolly Klock, a board-certified family medicine physician who operates a consulting program on teen health and behaviors called Adolessons, explains that "We now know that the brain continues to develop until at least the age of 25 and the last part of the brain to fully mature is the prefrontal cortex."

The prefrontal cortex is the area of the brain right behind your forehead. It is "the executive center of the brain which controls things such as impulse control, organization, and the ability to foresee long-term consequences of today's actions. Meanwhile, other parts of the brain that drive risky, feel-good behaviors, especially around peers, are relatively more developed in adolescents. This may help explain why young people sometimes make more impulsive decisions than adults," says Dr. Klock.

I wanted all readers to know this little bit about brain science because I hear way too many young people beating themselves up over their mistakes (as parents, sometimes we pile on too). We all make mistakes, sometimes big ones, regardless of our age. There are simply some mistakes that young people can be more prone to make and the reason may involve a growing and developing brain.

Important Message to Teens and Young People: Find Your Person, Whoever That May Be

I spent over four years gathering, researching, interviewing, and writing this book. What's stuck with me now as I finish it is something that I saw over and over: the young people who seemed to be suffering the most were very often the ones who were trying to deal with what they were going through alone. In other words, they were suffering in silence.

I get it—I spent much of my adolescent years that way; I was deeply hurting inside, acting out and generally feeling lonely, desperate, and lost. I didn't talk to anyone about it, least of all my parents (though my best friend's dad would periodically check in on me). Looking back at my younger self, I wish I had reached out to a trusted adult. Who knows if talking to someone like that would have put me back on the "right" path—I do know that it certainly wouldn't have hurt.

Whatever may be causing you pain, please don't suffer in silence. When you do, the suffering isn't likely to stop . . . at least not anytime soon. If you don't have a trusted adult in your life, another good option can be talking to a peer, preferably one who is well functioning in life and might be willing to lend a hand, or an ear. Service organizations and agencies, both online and probably in your local community, also can often help (see appendix 1 for some leads).

Danielle Brooks is a licensed marriage and family therapist in Los Angeles and the founder of Brooks Psychological Group. Her busy practice specializes in the treatment of families, children, and teens. I met her when we were both speaking at a parenting event. Her message resonated with me, and I spoke to her about this recurring theme of young people suffering in silence.

The sage advice Brooks gives, in a nutshell, is: "As humans, regardless of age, we have to decide if we want to feel better. If you do, but are unsure how, seek out a healthy person who can potentially help you." She believes, as do I, that a parent is often best, but if not, "it can be a trusted adult, therapist, sibling, a peer, or anyone else who will understand you, support you, and not judge you. Who do you feel has the greatest chance of understanding you? Pick that person and reach out to them for support."

I summarize Brooks's advice like this: **Find Your Person, Whoever That May Be.** There is never any shame in asking for help, regardless of the reason. I wish I had known that growing up.

Book Terminology

My use of the words "teen" and "teenager" throughout the text is intended to include adolescents, preteens, tweens, and young adults.

My use of the word "parent" throughout the text is intended to include *any adult who cares for a young person*—whether or not they are biologically related. This includes married parents, single parents, grandparents, same-sex parents, stepparents, foster parents, extended family members, teachers, coaches, guardians, religious leaders, and other caregivers. I certainly understand the important role that many people other than birth or adoptive parents play in teenagers' lives.

The gender spectrum is vast and certainly goes far beyond narrow gender norms and terms such as "he," "she," "girl," "boy," "woman," and "man." I have done my very best to limit the use of these words throughout the text.

Parent Readers: Talking to Your Children and Having Them Talk to You

I wrote this book under no illusions about the intricacies of these concepts, let alone trying to teach them to the young people we care about. For those who are interested, appendix 6 has my top ten ways parents can gather the information *they believe* is most important in this book and pass it along to the teen in their life.

You'll also find in appendix 6 some important information about ways to get our children to start a conversation with us if they're struggling or suffering.

Disclaimer

The information in this book may not be effective in all situations, and the author and the publisher assume no responsibility for damages of any sort that occur as a consequence, directly or indirectly, from the reliance on and use and/or application of any of the material provided herein. It is always up to the readers to decide what the best course of action is under their circumstances. Whether you bought this book or not, we do not have an attorney–client relationship and I am not providing legal advice.

Every story in this book is true. However, unless the teen has chosen to share their story (rather than it finding its way to the press and being asked for comment), I've used fictitious names and even changed some locations depending on the egregiousness of the circumstances.

PART 1

Dealing with the Police and Street Safety

CHAPTER 1

Your Rights with the Police: You Probably Don't Know Them, but Should

KEY TAKEAWAYS

- There are only limited circumstances in which the police can perform lawful searches.

- Most police searches are lawful only because the subjects consent to the search.

- Other than perhaps identifying yourself, you do not have to answer questions posed to you by the police.

- The best way to stay out of the crosshairs of the police is by making good choices and following the law.

- Your rights are a tool to protect yourself and should never be used to help someone else who has done harm or intends to.

Chapter Highlights

Setting the Stage

The United States leads the developed world, by far, in the number of its citizens who are arrested—one in three Americans, regardless of race or gender, is arrested by the age of 23. This equates to someone in the United States being arrested every three seconds! In fact, the United States has as many people with arrest records as college degrees. To be arrested means to be taken into police custody and off to jail, usually in handcuffs, because of a crime the police believe you've committed.

Most arrests, I believe, are legally justified. Some are not. Good arrest or bad, all people who are arrested initially have the same thing: a criminal record.

Simply being arrested, even if you're immediately released without ever being charged or convicted of a crime, leaves you with a criminal record. In some circumstances, this can make it more difficult to fully function in society for years to come.

When I was 16, I became one of those one in three Americans arrested by the age of 23; I was arrested, rightfully, for a property crime. I was released soon thereafter, and the prosecutor didn't file criminal charges against me because of insufficient evidence. I thought that was the end of it, until decades later when the arrest showed up in a preemployment background check. Thankfully, I had the good fortune of being asked about it (rather than being eliminated outright) and still got the job. Many others in similar situations aren't as fortunate.

When I think back to the night of my arrest and many other police interactions I had as a young person, they were often nerve-wracking, and I had almost no idea what the police were allowed and not allowed to do. Did I have to answer their questions? Could they search me? My car? My home? Could the police lie to me? What were the "rules of engagement"?

Knowing your rights will enable you not only to answer these questions but to make informed choices when you interact with a police officer. Regardless of your country of origin and whether or not you're a US citizen, all people standing on US soil have the same rights.

For the record, I want to emphasize that, as the saying goes, if you do the crime, you

The answers to these and many other related questions come with knowing your rights.

should do the time. The point of this chapter is not to help young people escape justice or somehow cheat the system. Rather, my goal is to explain the rights we *all* have to help ensure that the criminal justice system treats you fairly.

What You'll Learn in this Chapter

We'll first cover what your rights are under the Fourth and Fifth Amendments to the US Constitution. We'll then transition to how and when we might choose to invoke those rights and, if we do, what we can expect the police to do in response. We'll also cover some other interesting things along the way.

Lots to cover here, so let's get to it.

The Basics of the Fourth and Fifth Amendments

The Fourth Amendment to the US Constitution

The Fourth Amendment guarantees a reasonable expectation of privacy, as it relates to a government agent, like the police, conducting searches of you, your car, your house, or pretty much anything else.

It states, in part, "The right of the people to be secure in their persons, houses, papers, and effects, against unreasonable searches and seizures." Put another way, police searches have to be reasonable. When it comes to searches of someone's home, it is "reasonable" for the police to do so if they are in possession of a search warrant signed by a judge.

The police can perform other reasonable searches without a search warrant. Some of the most common reasons for searching without a warrant are:

- when the police are in hot pursuit of a suspect
- when there are exigent (emergency) circumstances
- when evidence of criminality is seen in plain view
- when the police have probable cause (a reasonable belief supported by the facts) that evidence of criminality can (or might) be found in your vehicle
- when there is a reasonable suspicion that you may have something on your person that can hurt them, you can be patted down for weapons
- when you give the police consent to search, which is the grand-daddy of them all

There are a few other exceptions where the police don't need to get a search warrant, but the ones listed above are those most often utilized. As we'll discuss in greater detail below, most searches conducted by the police are performed by obtaining the person's consent.

The Fifth Amendment to the US Constitution

The Fifth Amendment states that no person "shall be compelled in any criminal case to be a witness against himself." Put another way, this amendment allows each of us to *choose for ourselves* whether or not to remain silent or to answer police questions.

Except for the Miranda requirement explained in the next chapter, which is triggered by police questioning after an arrest, the police *do not* need to inform you of your rights under the Fourth and Fifth Amendments. So understanding and exercising your rights is on you.

As a quick procedural overview, after the police make an arrest, they prepare an arrest report and submit it to a prosecutor (like me) for review. A prosecutor is a lawyer who represents the government and decides whether there is sufficient evidence to charge the arrested person with a crime. Defendants in criminal prosecutions are presumed innocent until proven guilty and the prosecutor must prove the defendant's guilt "beyond a reasonable doubt." If the accused cannot afford a lawyer, the government provides one at no cost to the individual.

When an arrest leads to a prosecution, a defense lawyer for the accused can challenge the admissibility of all incriminating statements and physical evidence recovered by the police that may have violated that person's rights. If the judge agrees, the evidence is likely to be made inadmissible and thrown out of court.

The Rules May Not Always Be the Same

The invocation of one's rights and the guidelines for safer police interactions (covered in the next chapter) may not always work as intended. This can be even truer for people of color, especially Black males, those who have disabilities, do not speak English fluently, identify as transgender or gender nonbinary (a gender identity that is not exclusively male or female), are poor, and certainly others—for some, these distinctions overlap.

During my workshops on police-related topics, it's not unusual for people of color, and sometimes others, to question whether there's any point to learning about their rights or safer police interactions. One young teen of color told me (and the entire class) that there was no use in learning this information because "the police do what they want to Blacks." It saddens me whenever I hear this sentiment, but who am I to tell him he's wrong?

Dr. Cedric L. Alexander, a mental health practitioner who spent decades in law enforcement, including as a chief of police and as the president of the National Organization of Black Law Enforcement Executives, says,

"What can you say to people who don't think the police will respect their rights and treat them with respect? In some cases they're absolutely right. Now you can't paint every police officer with the same brush, but if that's what they feel and if that's their experience, I'm not gonna try to get them to think otherwise."

The bottom line with *all* police interactions is that if you are being mistreated and/or your rights aren't being respected, that moment is not the time to get in a heated debate about it. You want to stay in control of your emotions. While mouthing off to an officer shouldn't subject you to harm, it certainly might if you interact with the wrong officer at the wrong time.

Gary Verge, senior lead officer for the Los Angeles Police Department (LAPD), believes that "everyone should know their rights. It's safer for you and the police." He understands as a Black man that knowing your rights does not mean that they won't be violated (he recounts some of his own off-duty police interactions in the next chapter). Officer Verge does offer a suggestion: "If you have a situation where an officer is doing something that is violating your rights, you can ask for a supervisor. Everybody reports to somebody, and many departments have a policy that if you ask for a supervisor, they need to send one out. If you don't get a supervisor, you'll be better able to make a complaint later on if you know your rights."

There is no shortage of information online about steps you can take after a police interaction in which your rights may have been violated and/or the police mistreated you. Some suggestions include making a written complaint about the officer(s) with their department (do your best to note names and badge numbers during the interaction), talking with a lawyer, or contacting an organization like the American Civil Liberties Union (ACLU).

Will Exercising My Rights Make the Police More Suspicious of Me?

Before we dig into the specifics of your rights and how you can invoke them if needed, I'd like to answer a question I get all the time: will invoking my rights make the police more suspicious of me? The answer is yes, it probably will. But *suspicion alone* does not give the police the legal authority to make an arrest or perform a search that they are otherwise not entitled to perform.

A common follow-up question I'm asked is: if I refuse to consent to a search or answer police questions, will it be used against me in court? The answer is far too complicated to possibly cover here.

In short, though, constitutional protections very often limit the government's ability to use your refusal to answer questions or consent to an unauthorized search as evidence in a criminal case. However, laws governing the admissibility of evidence are different in each state and change over time. Most importantly, though, as mentioned above, refusing to answer questions or consent to an impermissible search does *not* give the police the authority to make an arrest or perform a search that is not otherwise permitted by law.

The Fourth Amendment: Can I Say No to Warrantless Searches?

The short answer is yes, but as mentioned above, there's a difference between searches in which the police have a search warrant and those in which they do not.

When the police believe that they're likely to find evidence of criminality where someone lives, such as the person's house or apartment, in many instances they'll write out a search warrant.

The warrant requests a judge's approval to perform a search at a specific place, looking for evidence of criminality that the police believe will be found there. When the warrant is written, the officers must explain to the judge what evidence is in their possession to justify the issuance of the warrant and what evidence they believe will be recovered by the search. To adhere to the suspect's Fourth Amendment rights, the judge can issue the search warrant only if there is probable cause to perform the search.

Later, the defendant can challenge in court the probable cause justifying the issuance of the warrant and the manner in which the police executed the warrant. If the defendant is successful, the evidence will often be excluded from the case—perhaps the case even dismissed—and seized property returned to you (though not always). However, in real time, you cannot stop the search. You should ask for and receive a copy of the warrant, though.

> **Police are skilled at getting people to agree to consensual searches, even when the individual is in possession of something incriminating.**

In all likelihood, you will *not* be dealing with a police officer who's armed with a search warrant. Instead, the officer will likely be performing a consensual search. It's called consensual because the police seek your permission to perform the search.

Much of the time it won't seem like a request because the police are skilled at getting people to agree to consensual searches, even when the individual is in possession of something incriminating. You'll see some examples below. Later in court, your lawyer can argue that the consent should be invalidated because it was coerced by the officer—which makes it unlawful. However, it'll be an uphill battle because knowing you have the right to refuse consent is not necessary for a search to be found voluntary, and, as mentioned above, the police are not required to inform people of their rights.

Let's bring this to light by discussing the three places where the police will most frequently want to perform a warrantless search:

- you and your stuff, for example, your pockets, purse, bags, phone, personal effects, and so on
- your home
- your car

You and Your Stuff: Imagine the following scenario—you are attending a party at your friend's house and the party is broken up by the police. As you are walking out, an officer stops you and says something along the lines of "Do you have anything in your pockets I should worry about?" or "Let's see what's inside your backpack" or, in some circumstances, "Why don't you let me see your phone?"

If you hand over your backpack or your phone, you're likely consenting. As mentioned above, it may not seem like it, but the police officer is probably *requesting* a consensual, warrantless search. It can be difficult to differentiate between the two, but a police *request* is not an *order*. Tricky, right?

Let me be clear: no matter how a police officer words it, you are within your rights to refuse a request for a consensual search. If you are a teen or young adult, I'd suggest you say to the offi-cer: **"No disrespect, officer,**

Unless there's some sort of exigency (emergency), the officer will likely need a search warrant or consent to search this backpack.

but my parents (or uncle/grandma/guardian, etc.) told me not to con-sent to searches."

Variations to the language are fine; I just like this language because it's respectful and makes you seem like an obedient child, rather than a know-it-all smart-ass. Whatever language you use, though, always stay respectful and calm.

If the police tell you in response that you don't have a choice and to hand over the item, then it is *not* a consensual search. Rightly or wrongly, they believe a warrantless search is allowed by law and you'll need to com-ply with their order.

Your Home: Let's use the same scenario as above, but in this case, you are throwing the party and the police get a noise complaint. They show up at your door and want to be let in.

Therefore, it will probably be your decision whether to open the door in the first instance and, in the second, whether to allow them into your home (none of this will matter, though, if your friend answers the door and invites them in, which the police are very likely to accept and will lawfully enter). If you open the door and allow the police to come in, they

The police can enter your home if they: (a) have a search warrant, (b) believe there's a true emergency, (c) see evidence of a crime in plain view, or, most frequently, (d) receive consent or permission to enter.

can freely search any areas in your or anyone else's immediate vicinity for weapons, seize any contraband or possibly incriminating items they observe, and make arrests.

On the flip side, if you choose not to let them in and someone at the party is sexually assaulted, gets alcohol poisoning, and so on, you could have possibly prevented these events by cooperating with the police. Clearly, there's a lot to consider if you ever find yourself in this sort of situation. Knowing your rights comes with a great responsibility to think not just about your own well-being but that of others as well. We'll cover more about that shortly.

Your Car: The last scenario involves a search of your car (or any motorized vehicle). It begins when you've been pulled over for a minor traffic violation—such as making a wrong turn, rolling through a stop sign, or illegally changing lanes. At some point, the officer may ask if you have any drugs, guns, alcohol, or anything illegal in your car. If you answer no, they could then say something along the lines of "Then you don't mind if I search your car, right?" or "Great. I'll just take a look around. Okay?"

Not only can it be very difficult to say no under these and similar circumstances, but staying silent in response may be interpreted as consent to search or suspicious. Again, like above, you have the right not to consent to this search and can tell the police officer, **"No disrespect, officer, but my parents told me not to consent to searches"** or anything comparable.

However, keep in mind that if the police have probable cause that there's evidence of a crime in your vehicle based on what they see, hear, or smell, they can search it without a warrant *or* your consent (the automobile exception to the Fourth Amendment search warrant requirement mentioned earlier).

Even when the police have probable cause to lawfully search your vehicle, they'll likely still ask for your consent. The reason? Obtaining voluntary consent *always* makes a search lawful. Accordingly, if a judge later decides that their determination of probable cause was in error, the evidence won't be thrown out of court because you were the one who authorized the search.

If the police search your car and find something they

If the officer has probable cause that there's evidence of a crime in the trunk of this car, it can be lawfully searched.

believe to be incriminating, you will almost certainly be asked about it. They may say something like "Why do you have this?" or "Where'd you get this?" Answering these questions, as discussed in the next section, can result in your incriminating yourself.

The Fifth Amendment: Can I Stay Silent When Questioned by the Police?

The short answer is yes. Under the Fifth Amendment, you almost never have to answer questions from the police. Silence is an option.

However, in some instances, like during a traffic stop, you must identify yourself by providing your driver's license. When on foot, depending on the law in your state, if there is a reasonable suspicion that you've committed a crime, you may have to identity yourself to a police officer when requested (this happens when you're detained, as explained in greater detail in the next chapter).

As far as I'm concerned, regardless of the law in your state, if a police officer asks you to identify yourself, you should. However, if you are questioned about anything else, the choice is yours: you can either answer the questions *or* choose not to.

So now let's look at the practical application of all of this by using the scenario in which you've been pulled over for a traffic violation. During the interaction, the police look into the backseat of the car and see tools in plain view that are often used by burglars to break into homes. They then ask you, "Why do you have those tools?"

If you've done nothing wrong and the tools are being used for a legitimate purpose, you probably should just answer the question and explain why you have them. However, you do not have to—the choice is yours. For what it's worth, I've imparted two rules to my sons. First, if they've done something they shouldn't have, never answer questions. Second, if they

Your Rights Aren't the Same at School

Your Fourth and Fifth Amendment rights don't transfer entirely to your school life because your privacy interests are less compelling than the school's responsibility to maintain a safe place where students can learn. Your school can often perform searches without a warrant if administrators reasonably believe that you have evidence of criminality in your possession or have violated a school policy.

haven't done anything wrong, answer questions but stop if they believe the police suspect them of wrongdoing.

I speak to some parents who disagree with my perspective here and want their children to always talk to the police and answer questions, regardless of the circumstances. Since there's no "right answer" here, it's best if families discuss this among themselves and come up with a plan that fits their sensibilities.

If you choose not to answer questions from the police, you can simply stay silent. However, I think it's infinitely better to say something like **"No disrespect, officer, but my parents insist that I remain silent until I talk to them or a lawyer."**

The precise wording isn't critical as long as the message you are delivering is respectful and clearly conveys that you aren't answering questions. But again, I do like this language because it makes you seem like an obedient child, rather than a know-it-all. Just like not opening the door for the police may be uncomfortable, refusing to answer police questions can be similarly awkward, but you're within your rights if that is what you decide to do.

The Police Don't Give Up Easily and, Yes, They Can Lie to You

You should *never* try to talk your way out of police officers doing their job. If they suspect you have committed a crime, it won't work. This is what they do for a living, day in and day out, and by and large, they are really good at what they do.

It's one thing to remain silent in front of the police and/or not consent to searches, which is within your rights, but you should never lie to them—doing so may even be a crime. Ultimately, your lies won't work as you'd hoped and may only end up getting you into more trouble.

The police, however, can lie to you during an interaction and, in fact, are very skilled at doing so, as it helps them get dangerous criminals off the street. They are also good at pressuring people to get around the assertion of the very rights we have discussed above. They may say, "We're going to get a search warrant to search your car. You can save us both time by allowing us to search it now." In truth, the facts may not be enough to obtain a warrant—but the police don't need to tell you that!

If you become involved in a conversation with the police, such as the scenarios I've outlined above, they are not going to walk away just because you don't want to answer their questions or consent to a search. In fact, as mentioned earlier, their suspicions may very well be heightened. Either way, though, they are going to push back on you and say things like:

- "Why do you want to leave?"
- "Are your parents lawyers or something?"
- "Why won't you talk with me?"
- "What have you done?"
- "What's your rush?"
- "All I'm trying to do is have a conversation with you. What's the problem?"

Frankly, we should be grateful that the police keep pressing and aren't easily discouraged. The overwhelming majority of them are trying to make a positive impact on society, and they would be less effective at doing so if they gave up so easily.

When the police use these phrases and continue to pressure you, it is going to feel uncomfortable and you are going to want to start talking or consent to a search—which is exactly how they are trying to make you feel. As long as you have made up your mind that you are not going to consent to a warrantless search or that you are not going to speak to the police, you can always fall back on the phrases **"No disrespect, officer, but my parents**

Security Guards Are Not the Police

Although they often look similar (which is not unintentional on the part of security guards), there are far more differences than similarities between security guards and the police. Police officers are vested with governmental power to protect the safety and welfare of all people. Security guards are typically employed by a business or individual and assigned to protect its personnel or property. Security guards are ordinary citizens in a uniform who have no more power than you to search, interrogate, or make a citizen's arrest (which occurs under certain circumstances when a private person arrests another for a crime occurring in their presence).

told me not to consent to searches" or "No disrespect, officer, but my parents insist that I remain silent until I talk to them or a lawyer." If you start talking with the police, you can always stop at any time if you change your mind.

The Exception to the Rules

Despite the fact that there are situations where you may lawfully remain silent in the face of police questioning, it doesn't mean that you should. By way of example, let's say that a friend of yours told you about a sexual assault they committed. If the police want to question you about it, you should tell them what you know (perhaps with your parent or a lawyer in attendance).

Put in broader terms, don't invoke your rights if doing so allows someone else to get away with a crime or prevent timely police intervention. If either of these circumstances is present, stiffen your backbone, push out your chest, fire up your heart, and do the right thing. Remember, this book is about helping prevent bad things from happening to good teens, not helping good teens get away with bad things.

Always Your Best Option: Making Good Choices

The best way to stay out of the crosshairs of the police is by making good choices *and* following the rule of law. Although that is no guarantee that you will never have an uncomfortable interaction with the police, it certainly won't hurt.

Still, learning your rights will empower you with confidence and a greater sense of calm when a police interaction takes place—something that's beneficial to both you *and* the police. It's not ideal to start figuring out how you want to respond to the police once you're under the stress of an interaction.

Have a plan and discuss it with your parents in advance. If you do so, it is less likely that an interaction with the police will prompt you to do or say something that you don't want to.

What Three Things in This Chapter Matter Most to You?

We all take away different lessons from reading the information presented in this chapter. What resonates with one person may not be meaningful to another and vice versa. I certainly hope that you've learned a heck of a lot more than three things in this chapter, but if three things were all you learned, I still consider it a win. Even a single piece of information could be invaluable if it was just what you or someone you're with needs in a critical moment.

With the information from this chapter fresh in your mind, please take a few moments to write below the three things that you consider the most important.

1. _____

_____

2. _____

_____

3. _____

_____

What Would You Do if It Happened to You? (Question 1)

You are driving home after going to a movie with some friends. Suddenly, you see police lights flashing and you realize that you rolled through a stop sign. You carefully pull over and nervously wait for the policeman to approach.

1. Police: "Good evening. Do you know why I pulled you over?" You respond:

_____

2. Police: "Driver's license and registration please?" (You hand them to the officer, and after stepping back to his car for a couple minutes, he returns to your car.) "Where are you coming from?" How would you respond?

   _____

3. Police: "Have you been drinking?" How would you respond?

   _____

4. Police: "It smells like weed in your car. Have you been smoking any?" How would you respond?

   _____

5. Police: "Since you've got nothing to hide, then you don't mind if I search your car, right?" How would you respond?

   _____

Some Thoughts about "What Would You Do if It Happened to You?" (Question 1)

1. If you admit to committing the traffic violation, you won't be able to contest it later on in traffic court. However, if you admit to the traffic violation, there is a slight chance the officer might let you go without a ticket. I generally admit what I've done wrong. My rationale is that I'm probably getting a ticket anyway, so I might as well make this as fast as possible so the officer and I can get on with our day.

2. As you know, you don't have to answer this (or any other) question. You've done nothing wrong, so is there any harm in answering? Probably not.

3. If you haven't been drinking, is there any harm in answering this question? I don't think so. However, if you have been drinking, you may think it's best not to answer. That said, *you shouldn't be driving!*

Not only is it probably illegal under the circumstances, but it also can put your well-being and that of others at great risk of harm.

4. You haven't smoked any weed, but now you're getting really nervous. Why all these questions? What does he think I did? You can tell the officer either "No disrespect, officer, but my parents insist that I remain silent until I talk to them or a lawyer" or "No, officer, I haven't been smoking any marijuana." By the way, if you have been smoking, it is up to you whether you admit this to the police. *But you shouldn't be driving!*

5. If the officer detects the smell of marijuana, your car can be lawfully searched under the motor vehicle exception to the Fourth Amendment search warrant requirement. However, the officer wants your consent so that the search (and any recovered evidence) will hold up in court if a judge later rules that the police didn't have probable cause to search your vehicle; as mentioned earlier in the chapter, consent waives your ability to argue that the search was unlawful under the Fourth Amendment (except for a contention that the consent was coerced). If there is no evidence of criminality in your vehicle, some will consent to the search. Others won't for a variety of reasons, including the principle of wanting to maintain one's privacy, fear of an officer planting evidence, fear that a friend or previous owner of the car might have left something illegal in the car that you aren't aware of, or the fear that something in your car could be mistaken as evidence of criminality (go online and read Daniel Rushing's or Dasha Fincher's stories of their arrests and time in jail because glaze from a Krispy Kreme donut and cotton candy were mistaken by officers for the drug methamphetamine). There is no "correct" answer here except that you should do whatever resonates with you and your family values.

What Would You Do if It Happened to You? (Question 2)

In the following situations, answer whether you have to lawfully consent to the search.

1. Security at a basketball game wants to check backpacks as you enter the arena.   ☐ Y   ☐ N

2. Your principal is checking all students' cell phones for underage nudes.   ☐ Y   ☐ N

3. The security guard at the convenient store accuses you of shoplifting and demands to check your backpack.   ☐ Y   ☐ N

4. The police are breaking up a house party. They smell the odor of marijuana and ask everyone to empty their pockets upon leaving.   ☐ Y   ☐ N

5. A police officer pulls you over for speeding and asks you to open your trunk; he is responding to an amber alert of a kidnapping in the area.   ☐ Y   ☐ N

6. The police are at your door and want to take a look inside your house; someone called about hearing screams.   ☐ Y   ☐ N

Some Thoughts about "What Would You Do if It Happened to You?" (Question 2)

1. No: You don't have to consent to the search. Remember: the Fourth and Fifth Amendments apply only to government actors. Here the security guards aren't government actors, but you don't have a choice if you want to enter the venue.

2. Yes (probably): To maintain a safe learning environment, schools have the power to investigate reasonably suspected violations of law or school policy by students. This means that searches are permissible as long as they are not excessively intrusive in light of the student's age and gender and the nature of the alleged violation. So depending on the underlying facts, the school administrator might be able to lawfully search phones.

3. No: Security guards have no more power than you do. You do not have to let the guard search your backpack. However, that is not to say that the guard couldn't attempt to place you under citizen's

arrest for shoplifting if you don't show him or her that you haven't stolen anything. If you were shoplifting, resisted the citizen's arrest, and hurt the guard, you've likely committed additional crimes.

4. No: Under these facts alone, the police probably don't have the legal authority to search your pockets for drugs. If you empty them, you are consenting to the search.

5. Yes: You won't have a choice whether or not to open your trunk because of exigent circumstances. Regardless, though, why wouldn't you? Time is of the essence in kidnapping situations, and allowing the search will help the police eliminate you as a suspect and move on to other possible suspects. Keep in mind that once inside your trunk, anything incriminating in your trunk is now fair game.

6. Yes: The police can enter a private location without a search warrant to protect people who might be in danger (exigency). Here, with the report of someone screaming from inside, they may choose to do just that. Before entering, though, the police will likely ask you about it to see if there's a reasonable explanation and will evaluate other associated circumstances.

Final Thoughts

When I started writing this chapter, I wondered what the police officers whom I'm friendly with would say about it. Would they take offense that I was sharing the "tricks of the trade"? To find out, I asked a number of them to read this chapter with the question I'd posed to them in mind: "Does it bother you that I'm sharing this information?" I was surprised by their responses. Every officer who is a parent to tweens, teens, or young adults responded similarly: "No, it doesn't bother me. I taught my kids the same things."

Hearing their responses was reassuring to me. After all, if prosecutors like me and police officers teach their children the information in this chapter, it seems to me that it might be beneficial for others to know it too.

When I hold workshops on this topic, I start by asking the parents and/or teens how many of them know their rights under the Fourth and Fifth Amendments. Almost no hands go up and I find this startling. These rights were important enough that they have been the law of the land since 1781, but we cannot use them if we don't know them.

I've made clear to my own sons, who do know their rights, that if they ever invoke them, it doesn't mean that we won't later cooperate with the police investigation—because we absolutely will. However, the cooperation will happen once we know the full extent of what they've gotten themselves into.

In real time, it can be very difficult for anyone, particularly the young, to fully comprehend the situation they're facing. While I do not want my sons to escape justice if they break the law, I also don't want them to make their situation worse by answering questions or consenting to searches when they shouldn't—at least at that point in time.

Clearly, there's a lot to think about when it comes to our rights. As the saying goes: "With great power comes great responsibility." Now that you have the "great power" that comes with knowing your rights, I hope that you will act with "great responsibility" to do the right thing, even if it means pushing aside your rights to help bring someone to justice or help someone in need of timely police intervention.

Where Can I Get More Information?

This chapter contains the essentials of your rights with the police. For those who want to know more and dig deeper into this topic, a Google search is a good place to start and will deliver numerous resources, some with valuable information. Here are two you can start with:

- American Civil Liberties Union
    » a non-profit organization that defends the fundamental rights outlined in the United States Constitution and the Bill of Rights
    » 212-549-2500
    » www.aclu.org
- FlexYourRights.org
    » educates the public about how basic Bill of Rights protections apply during encounters with law enforcement
    » www.flexyourrights.org

Your Rights with the Police Quiz

Test your understanding of your rights with the police by taking this quiz. Hopefully, you'll get all of the answers correct because a single mistake could have real-world consequences if that answer contained the information you needed to stay safe.

Instructions: select the best answer from the available choices. Answers can be found in the back of the book.

1. Except perhaps to identify yourself, you never have to answer any other questions of the police.
   A. True
   B. False

2. If the police ask for your permission to search something in your possession (e.g., a backpack, your phone, etc.) you can refuse.
   A. True, but laws vary from state to state.
   B. True
   C. False, if police suspect you of a serious felony or you're 18 years old or younger.
   D. False

3. When questioning a suspect, a police officer can only lie if the crime being investigated involves violence.
   A. True
   B. False

4. If the police want to search your house, in most instances, they'll need to first obtain a search warrant.
   A. True
   B. False
   C. Depends on the seriousness of the alleged crime.
   D. Only if you're 18 or older.

5. Being wrongfully arrested for a petty offense and subsequently cleared of any wrongdoing may still leave you with a criminal record.
   A. True
   B. False

6. The best way to avoid the criminal justice system is:
   A. Choose your friends very carefully.
   B. Don't do things that are illegal.
   C. Cover your tracks whenever you do things that are illegal or immoral.
   D. Keep your friends close, but your enemies closer.

7. Your Fourth and Fifth Amendment rights apply equally in K–12 schools.
   A. True
   B. False

8. The Fourth Amendment guarantees an "absolute expectation of privacy."
   A. True
   B. False

9. The Fifth Amendment provides that we don't have to be a witness against ourselves.
   A. True
   B. False

10. The most common way that police conduct lawful searches is by obtaining your consent.
    A. True
    B. False

CHAPTER 2

Safer Police Interactions: Critical for Everyone Involved

KEY TAKEAWAYS

- When pulled over while driving, never reach for your license, proof of insurance, or car insurance until the officer requests them.

- Signing a traffic ticket is not an admission of guilt, and refusing to sign may be an entirely separate offense that subjects you to arrest.

- Don't argue with the police. The police have never lost an argument in the street. Arguments are for courtrooms.

- For an identical criminal act, 18-year-olds will often face more serious criminal consequences than their 17-year-old counterparts.

- Some police interactions can be ended if you ask the police, "Am I free to go or am I being detained?"

Chapter Highlights

Setting the Stage

If you read the last chapter about your rights during police interactions, you understand that no country on earth arrests more of its citizens than the United States. It gets worse because it's not just arrests that make the United States an outlier compared to other high-income countries, but also the frequency with which the police kill US residents—up to seventy times the rate of other high-income nations by some estimates.

Laying blame entirely on the police for this and other similar unsettling statistics would be erroneous; there are many reasons the United States is an anomaly here—which I cannot possibly cover now, but many academics already have. It is also worth recognizing that every year some of the brave men and women in law enforcement are seriously injured and killed in the line of duty.

My point here is that police interactions can be tricky business—for you, for the people you're with, *and* for the police.

There's a good chance that your first interaction with a police officer will be as a teenager or young adult, outside the presence of a parent. You might be pulled over in your car for a traffic violation or stopped on the street for an investigation, or you might have interfaced with officers who shut down a party you're attending.

Regardless of whether or not you've committed a criminal act, being stopped and investigated, questioned, or searched by a police officer can be downright scary. You may know that you pose no threat to the officer, but the officer does not. Everything police officers do starts and ends with ensuring their own personal safety. Therefore, they can react in a way that we don't want when they perceive a situation to be a danger to themselves (or to the public). At times, we can exacerbate such a situation by our own actions. However, despite the underlying circumstances, officers should be held accountable for using excessive force. Such accountability should include appropriate discipline, perhaps job termination, and at times, prosecution. All of which should be administered with transparency.

At the end of the day, following the law and the do's and don'ts in this chapter, knowing your rights, and not doing anything rash will help you *and* the police have a safer interaction.

What You'll Learn in this Chapter

We'll discuss what we should always do and what we should never do when interacting with the police. Along the way, we'll take a look at some of the things one would be wise to consider if arrested, how to possibly end a police interaction, and the many challenges of policing persons with disabilities.

There'll be other interesting things too, so let's get to it.

Ways to Safely Interact with the Police While Driving

There aren't many things that police officers do that are more dangerous than pulling people over. LAPD senior lead officer Gary Verge says, "It's life and death out there for the men and women of law enforcement. Every time we stop somebody, we don't know what we're walking into. Every single time."

The first minute of every police interaction is critical, because your goal is to quickly convey that you are not a threat. Here are my top ten ways to do that:

1. **Stay calm.** This may be easier said than done, I know. Still, take a deep breath and don't panic. If you're innocent, staying calm will make you seem less guilty. If you're guilty, staying calm will make you seem more innocent.

2. **Pull over when it's safe to do so.** Once the officer activates their siren and/or roof lights, be sure to stop at the side of the road where you won't be blocking traffic or putting your safety or the officer's at risk. If you can't pull over immediately, slow down, put on your hazard lights, and pull over the moment you can safely do so.

3. **Shut your engine.** You don't want the officer on edge thinking that you might speed off.

4. **Turn on your interior (dome) light.** Turning on your dome light when it's dark outside allows the officer to see more easily into your vehicle and is a smart way to help the officer quickly realize that you aren't a threat.

5. **Rest your hands on the steering wheel.** You want your hands to be seen as the officer approaches the car. The best way to do this is to place your hands on the top of the steering wheel. *Don't reach for your license, registration, or proof of insurance until you are asked.* Once you're asked for them, tell the officer what you're doing: "They're in my glove box. I'll get them now."

I wish I'd known this piece of information on the night of my arrest—which, as mentioned in the last chapter, was for a property crime. In the moments leading up to that unfortunate event, a handful of police officers had their guns trained on 16-year-old me and ordered me to get my hands up. In the heat of the moment and with a racing heart, I did not comply with their demands. Months

---

The Rules May Not Always Be the Same

As mentioned more broadly in the last chapter, I fully understand that many people, particularly those who are Black, believe that they wouldn't have been given the benefit of the doubt had they been in my situation the night of my arrest and would have been shot. They may be right.

Sadly, racial injustice can be found not just in policing and the excessive use of force, but also in many other aspects of the criminal justice system, such as the rates of incarceration, sentencing disparities, the granting of parole, and more. The criminal justice system, including policing, is in need of meaningful reform. In the meantime, my focus in this chapter is on the ways that *all* young people can increase their chances of staying safe during their police interactions.

---

later, my lawyer told me that the officers could have shot me because they were worried about what I was doing with my hands.

6. **Obey all orders.** It's very important that you closely follow the instructions you get from the officer, even if you believe them to be unwarranted because you haven't done anything wrong. The reality is that you don't know what the officer knows. The officer might be looking for someone dangerous who matches your physical description or whose car matches the one you're driving.

If you are ordered out of your car, you'll need to comply. If the officer tells you to put your hands behind your back so you can be handcuffed, you must. Under the circumstances, following the police commands is your best and only option.

7. **Don't argue or mouth off.** On the street, police win 100 percent of the arguments. Arguments are for courtrooms; starting one during a police interaction might escalate tensions to a level you don't want to reach.

While it's perfectly understandable to be angry or frustrated if you feel you were stopped unjustly or without reason, it is over-whelmingly in your best interest to bury those feelings for the time being and be courteous and respectful—even if you don't think the officer deserves it. You never want to be perceived as confrontational.

No matter how angry you are, mouthing off is not going to help your situation, and with some officers, it may hurt it significantly. If needed, take a deep breath, save your anger for later, and refer to them as "officer" (many prefer this) or "sir" or "ma'am."

Some officers may bully you and treat you disrespectfully. You know what you should do in that moment? Not a darn thing. Do not physically resist, yell at them, raise your voice, curse, make a threat, or use aggressive language. Officers expect their orders to be complied with, even those that the officers were wrong to give.

Dr. Cedric Alexander, introduced in the last chapter, says that if the police behave unprofessionally, "Cooperate and show citizenship with the police when you're out there. Get along. Don't try to fight them on the streets. It doesn't play to your advantage. However, if you feel that you've been mistreated or your rights have been violated, get names and badge numbers [which should be clearly visible on the officers' uniforms]. Write down the date and time and who the witnesses were. Deal with it later." As mentioned in the last chapter, some of the things one can do after the fact are to lodge a written complaint against the officer with the police department, talk with a lawyer or retain one, or contact a civil rights organization like the ACLU.

If you get out of your car without being told to do so by the officer, you will immediately be seen as a threat and the interaction may quickly escalate.

Dr. Alexander is certainly not the only person who gives this sort of advice. LAPD senior lead officer Gary Verge, also introduced in the last chapter, tells me, "As a Black man, I've been racially profiled and stopped by the police six or seven times." These stops happened to Officer Verge when he was driving in his personal vehicle and was off duty and, therefore, out of uniform. He was visibly frustrated when he relayed these incidents to me and understands how others feel who are treated similarly.

I asked Officer Verge whether he showed his badge and gave the officers a tongue-lashing. He said, "Nope. I was respectful. There are individuals in law enforcement who see Brown or Black and react to it. So when an individual of color thinks they've been profiled or discriminated against, what should they do in the moment?

Go along with it. Let it play out. Even if they stopped you on some bullsh*t, comply, be respectful, and take down their information like their name and badge number for a later complaint."

8. **Make eye contact.** Doing so is respectful and helps convey that you understand the seriousness of what is happening. However, don't stare them down—which conveys the opposite and can be perceived as confrontational.

9. **Stay in your car (unless instructed otherwise).** Unless you are ordered to get out of your car (words we never like to hear but are to be obeyed), don't exit your vehicle.

    Lieutenant Alisha Jordan, a veteran LAPD officer, says, "The biggest mistake that drivers make when getting pulled over is getting out of their car when they haven't been ordered to." As she makes clear, "If you get out of your car without being told to do so by the officer, you will immediately be seen as a threat and the interaction may quickly escalate."

10. **Don't touch.** You should never make any physical contact whatsoever with a police officer.

Don't Refuse to Sign the Ticket

Imagine that you get pulled over and the police officer writes you a ticket for running a red light. You don't believe that you ran the light and the officer asks you to sign the ticket. Should you sign? Yes, always! Signing a ticket is *not* an admission of guilt. Rather it's an acknowledgment of receipt of that ticket and/or that you'll appear in court. Refusing to sign it may be an entirely separate offense and permit the officer to arrest you on the spot.

Best Practices for Interacting with the Police When You Aren't Driving

Here's the scenario: It's 11 p.m., and you've just left a friend's house. As you're walking home, a police car's floodlight becomes trained on you. Moments later, two officers jump out of the vehicle and order you to stop. What should you do? In most ways, the advice provided above still pertains, but here are two add-ons.

1. **Keep your hands visible and away from your body.** Similar to the importance of keeping your hands on the steering wheel when getting pulled over while driving, don't reach into your pockets or put your hands behind your back. You want to hold your hands where the officers can clearly see them. Lieutenant Jordan says that not doing this is far too common and can make a police encounter potentially more dangerous. "Officers are taught that it's the hands that kill, and we want to maintain visibility of that weapon at all times."

2. **Don't run.** Guilty or innocent, don't run away. There's a widely held belief, and not just among police officers, that innocent people don't run. When you bolt, officers are automatically going to think you've committed a serious crime and might be armed—which will instantly and significantly escalate the situation.

Can I Film the Police?

Yes, you can film or record the police in public. There's a very thin line, though, between documenting something and interfering with the police as they carry out their duties—which you cannot do. If you feel the need to film the police during your own interaction or when witnessing another's, don't start making a show of it. Let the police do their job.

What Are My Rights If I'm Arrested?

The police need *probable cause*—a reasonable belief supported by the facts—to make a lawful arrest and are permitted to search you following the arrest. No matter what you did or did not do, good arrest or bad, *do not resist* or try to stop the search.

Some people escalate a relatively minor arrest into something far more serious by trying to run away, resisting, or not allowing the police to peacefully take them into custody.

Once you're arrested, which in some circumstances can occur before you've been handcuffed, if police want to question you about the facts of the arrest, they'll have to first read you your Miranda rights. These state that you have the right to remain silent and to speak to an attorney at the government's expense, and that anything you say may be used against you. After being read your Miranda rights, you can choose to waive them and speak to the police.

If police aren't going to question you about the facts related to the arrest, they *don't* have to read you your Miranda rights. If you just start talking (often in an attempt to explain your side of things, though no one has asked you to), the police don't have to stop you and anything incriminating you say will be noted and used against you later on.

What I've told my sons is that if they're arrested, they should not, under any circumstances, speak to the police without first speaking with a lawyer—with the exception of identifying themselves while being processed (or "booked") at the police station, where they'll be searched,

18-Year-Olds Face More Serious Criminal Consequences Than 17-Year-Olds

For many US youths, legal indiscretions such as crashing a party (illegal trespassing), disturbing the peace, engaging in petty theft, or getting into a scuffle are often handled with "kid gloves." You might just get a slap on the wrist or a warning in the juvenile court system rather than face charges in the far more serious adult court. The objective of juvenile courts is to rehabilitate minors (those under the age of 18), and the judge has more options available to keep minors out of jail or from even having a case prosecuted. Once you turn 18, though, you've reached "the age of majority," meaning you're an adult—now if you're charged with a criminal offense it will be in adult court with its accompanying severity.

Let me give you an example: say a 17-year-old and an 18-year-old each steal the same thing, at the same time, from the same store. The 17-year-old is likely to face far less serious consequences in juvenile court than the 18-year-old in adult court. (However, there are certain circumstances, often involving serious crimes, when minors are prosecuted as adults.)

photographed, and fingerprinted. They should respectfully advise the police that they won't be waiving their Miranda rights or answering any questions *and* that they'd like a lawyer. As I indicated in the last chapter, we will fully cooperate with the police. If my sons have done wrong, they will own up to it, but not before we first understand the allegations against them.

While they're waiting for me or their lawyer to arrive, I've instructed my sons not to sign anything presented to them by the police or to write out a confession. Even if they've started talking with the police, they can *always* change their mind and tell them that they now wish to remain silent and to see a lawyer.

No matter how great the urge to talk with the police to explain your point of view, there's nothing that anyone can say in that moment to improve their situation.

Interactions with the Police and Persons with Disabilities

Police interactions that involve individuals with physical and/or cognitive disabilities can be even more challenging for the police and potentially dangerous for the person with a disability. Having certain disabilities can cause irregular social interactions and difficulty following verbal commands.

These difficulties can be mistakenly perceived by the police as challenging their authority, suspicious, hostile, or a threat to the officer's safety. This can create a very dangerous situation for the person with the disability. Novelist Marie Myung-Ok Lee expresses this worry poignantly when speaking about her teenage son, who lacks cognitive ability: "My son does not understand the law. But more urgently, the law does not understand people like him." Marie's concern for her son is also felt by many other parents whose children live with disabilities.

Title II of the Americans with Disabilities Act (ADA) is a federal civil rights law that protects individuals with disabilities from discrimination. The law applies to any nonfederal governmental entity, like a local police department, and is meant to ensure that people with disabilities, as defined by the ADA, are not discriminated against in the criminal justice system.

Police departments, and many other public actors, must provide effective communication, reasonable modifications, and equal access to services.

William Goren is an attorney whose law and consulting practice, as well as his blog, focuses on helping his clients and others understand how to comply with the ADA and related laws. He is also the author of a book published by the American Bar Association entitled *Understanding the Americans with Disabilities Act*. Goren tells me, "The ADA is one hundred miles wide and thirty miles deep in every direction." In other words, it's complex.

Goren says, "The police have to reasonably modify their policies and procedures when dealing with people with disabilities, unless it would basically put the organization under the ground financially or turn their operations upside down." (Goren is referring to the legal terms "undue burden" and "fundamental alteration." The legal standard that courts follow is whether the person with the disability is given the ability to "meaningfully access" police programs, services, and activities.)

The ADA governs pretty much everything police officers do on the job, such as taking police reports, interrogating suspects and witnesses, making arrests, operating 911 emergency services, and enforcing laws prohibiting criminal conduct.

Some of the things that people with disabilities and police departments are doing to help ensure a safe interaction include the following:

- Some people with disabilities carry special ID cards that have their name, explain their disability, a parent's or caretaker's name and phone numbers, and any other information that could be helpful to the police. They give these cards to police officers when the need arises. People with disabilities also put signs in their vehicles (see image) or even wear T-shirts and/or bracelets communicating their condition.

I've seen cars driving around with this sort of signage on display.

- Caregivers bring individuals with disabilities, from a young age, to police stations to see and interface with police officers so both parties can become more at ease with one another.

- Police departments are providing additional training so police officers are better able to recognize and interface with the large population of people with disabilities. This training can include such things as de-escalation techniques and methods, revised use-of-force policies, effective communication (including for police dispatchers), when to send a mental health provider into the field, and much more. Mr. Goren says that getting the necessary police training on the rights of people with disabilities is very much a work in progress.

- Police departments are also making reasonable modifications in policing practices, policies, or procedures when necessary to avoid disability discrimination.

Many police departments "have a long way to go ... to meet their ADA responsibilities," says Goren. "It isn't easy because there's a zillion disabilities and they all have different needs." Goren, who has a hearing disability (he functions entirely in the hearing world with lip-reading and the use of advanced, powerful hearing aids), makes it clear that Title II of the ADA has been the rule of law for almost thirty years. Goren adds, "People with disabilities are fed up when our rights are not being respected. We're mad and we won't take it lying down."

Public entities, such as the police, that have fifty or more employees are required by the ADA to have an ADA coordinator (an individual designated to coordinate and implement ADA compliance activities) and an ADA grievance procedure. Public entities with fewer than fifty employees are still governed by the ADA but aren't mandated by federal law to have an ADA coordinator and a grievance procedure—though it is an excellent idea if they do.

If the police department in your jurisdiction is not meeting its legal obligations under the ADA, a lawsuit can be filed in an effort to force the department to make changes (in many instances, a parent must file the suit on behalf of a minor). Before filing a lawsuit, though, the person with the disability may first want to consider meeting with the ADA coordinator or filing an ADA grievance with the department—assuming these options are available. If they do not, it can still be a good idea to first meet with someone as high ranking as possible in the police department who has the power to implement change. It never hurts to have the meeting with a qualified lawyer by your side, if you can arrange it.

Formal complaints about a police department's failure to modify police practices and procedures can be filed directly with the Department of Justice (DOJ) at ADA.gov. Filing with the DOJ before proceeding to court is not mandatory under the ADA, and you do not need to be a lawyer to file. You can consult with lawyers who sue police departments and local governments for disability discrimination, sometimes without paying a fee. Depending on the circumstances, these lawyers may be willing to file a lawsuit on your behalf and recover their fees only if the case is won.

Please stay mindful, though, that claims should be pursued as soon as possible because there is a statute of limitations (the maximum time after an event within which claims must be initiated) that varies by state.

Can I End a Police Interaction? (Detentions versus Consensual Encounters)

Imagine you are on foot or in a vehicle and the police stop to question you. After a while, you haven't been arrested and want the interaction to end. Should you just walk or drive away if you haven't committed a crime? Of course not. Can the police keep you indefinitely without an arrest? No. So how are you supposed to know if you can leave? You ask.

As background, the police are allowed to detain you for investigation—which may or may not lead to your arrest—when they have *reasonable suspicion* that you may be engaged in criminal activity (and since I get this question all the time, if you're being pulled over for a traffic stop, yes, you are being detained). While being detained, you are *not* free to leave for as long as is reasonably necessary for the police to conduct their investigation.

Other times, the police suspect that you might have done something wrong, but they don't have the requisite "reasonable suspicion" needed to lawfully detain you for an investigation. So, in this situation, they chat you up to find out more. This interaction is known as a "consensual encounter." In these encounters, the police will try to get you talking to determine whether you've committed a crime. Consensual encounters can evolve into a detention or an arrest based on things the person says or does.

Consensual encounters (which are voluntary) and detentions (which are not) often feel identical because you don't know what the officer knows. The only way to find out whether it's a consensual encounter and you are free to leave is to ask: "Am I free to go, officer, or am I being detained?"

OFFICER, AM I FREE TO GO OR AM I BEING DETAINED?

If you're being detained, you cannot leave. Most often, the officer will tell you why you're being detained. If the officer doesn't, you can ask for the reason. The bottom line: unless you are being detained or arrested, you have a right to terminate an encounter with the police.

Although the officer cannot lawfully prevent you from leaving during a consensual encounter,

This teen is asking the right question, but can you see what she's doing wrong? Hint: where should she have her hands?

it is unlikely that you'll be released without some sort of push-back. The officer may say, "I'm just trying to talk with you" or "What's the problem? Have you done something that I should know about?" At that point, repeat the question, respectfully and patiently: **"Am I free to go, officer, or am I being detained?"**

What Three Things in This Chapter Matter Most to You?

We all take away different lessons from reading the information presented in this chapter. What resonates with one person may not be meaningful to another and vice versa. I certainly hope that you've learned a heck of a lot more than three things in this chapter, but if three things were all you learned, I still consider it a win. Even a single piece of information could be invaluable if it was just what you or someone you're with needs in a critical moment.

With the information from this chapter fresh in your mind, please take a few moments to write below the three things that you consider the most important.

1. _____

_____

2. _____

_____

3. _____

_____

What Would You Do if It Happened to You?

You're at a party hanging out with your friends. Although you're only 16, you have a beer. Your friend Spencer, 17, has had too many and is really drunk. He lives within walking distance from the party and you decide to walk him home. He's stumbling, slurring his words, and being too loud in a quiet residential neighborhood. Suddenly a flood light from a police vehicle is shining on you both. Spencer looks over and tries to run away.

1. Spencer only gets about twenty feet away before the officers catch up to him. While they sort things out, you are both handcuffed and sat down on the curb. What would you do?

   _____

2. The police ask you for your name. What would you do?

   _____

3. The police ask if you've been drinking tonight. They also ask you if Spencer has been drinking. What would you do?

   _____

4. The police take off your handcuffs and tell you that you can go. Spencer is arrested for being drunk in public. What would you do?

   _____

5. Spencer is taken to the police station and booked. A few hours later after sobering up, the police pull him into an interrogation room, read him his Miranda rights, and ask why he ran away. If you were Spencer, what would you do?

   _____

Some Thoughts about "What Would You Do if It Happened to You?"

1. Spencer has escalated this police interaction for *both of you* by running. When officers have to give chase, they become even more concerned for their safety and will see both of you as threats. This is also known more broadly as "guilt by association" (see more about this in chapter 11). As Spencer runs, you should put your arms up in the air, fingers spread wide to show that your hands are empty.

   Once you're in handcuffs on the curb, you can ask the police why they've put you in handcuffs, but I doubt you'll get an answer right then. You may be tempted to express your anger toward them since you've done nothing wrong. It's best to remain calm, or as least as calm as possible under the circumstances. The police will probably separate you both and start asking questions.

2. Give them your name and date of birth when asked. Not doing so may be a crime subjecting you to immediate arrest.

3. You've got three choices here. First, answer with the truth—that you've had one beer. The police probably won't believe that you've consumed only one, and regardless, any amount of underage drinking may come with legal consequences. Second, tell them that you've had nothing to drink. This, of course, isn't true and can, in some circumstances, be a crime in its own right. Third, respectfully tell them you aren't going to answer questions. They're also likely to ask you about Spencer's underage drinking, for example, "What was he drinking tonight?" or "How much did he have to drink?" Although you also don't have to answer these questions either, you should if it might help the police determine whether Spencer might need medical attention for possible alcohol poisoning (alcohol kills over 4,300 people under the age of 21 every year and sends tens of thousands to emergency rooms).

4. Should you argue with the police that they shouldn't arrest Spencer? No. No one can talk the police out of making an arrest, nor is it your business. The best course of action at this point is to leave and contact Spencer's parents (and yours) immediately and tell them what happened.

5. If Spencer answers this or any other similar questions, he is waiving his Miranda rights. He may choose to do so and be transparent with the police, or he can say that he won't answer any questions (respectfully) and would like a lawyer. This is what I would want my own kids to say, but you should respond in a way that resonates with you and your family values.

Final Thoughts

Please keep in mind the "win-win" of safer police interactions: they are good for the police and for you. Integrate the information in this chapter with knowing your rights and exercising sound judgment and you should be in good shape as you go about your life.

Where Can I Get More Information?

This chapter contains the essentials of safer police interactions. For those who want to know more and dig deeper into this topic, a Google search is a good place to start and will deliver numerous resources, some with valuable information. You can also refer to the two sources listed at the end of chapter 1.

Safer Police Interactions Quiz

Test your understanding of safer police interactions by taking this quiz. Hopefully, you'll get all of the answers correct because a single mistake could have real-world consequences if that answer contained the information you needed to stay safe.

Instructions: select the best answer from the available choices. Answers can be found in the back of the book.

1. The first minute of a police interaction is the most important for you.
    A. True
    B. False

2. In order to detain you for the purposes of investigating whether you've committed a crime, police need:
    A. Probable cause.
    B. Reasonable suspicion.
    C. Nothing—so long as they were acting under color of law.
    D. A hunch based on their training and experience.

3. In order for police to make a lawful arrest, they need:
    A. Reasonable suspicion.
    B. Clear and convincing evidence.
    C. An articulated hunch.
    D. Probable cause.

4. When you're arrested, the police are required to read you your Miranda rights.
   A. True
   B. False

5. If you're given a citation by a police officer for a moving violation (e.g., a speeding ticket) and the officer asks you to sign it, you can refuse because it can be deemed an admission of guilt.
   A. True
   B. False

6. In every state, when a police officer orders a minor out of their car, the minor can refuse for a reasonable period of time until a trusted adult arrives.
   A. True
   B. False

7. If you're pulled over by the police at night while driving, you should:
   A. Turn on your interior light.
   B. Start preparing to exit the vehicle.
   C. Grab your license, proof of insurance, and car registration by the time the officer walks to your car to speed things up for them.
   D. Keep your hands in your lap.

8. It is generally lawful to video-record a police interaction.
   A. True
   B. False

9. 17-year-olds and 18-year-olds are treated the same in the criminal justice system for petty crimes.
   A. True
   B. False

10. You may be able to end a police interaction by asking if you're being detained or free to go.
    A. True
    B. False

CHAPTER 3

Street Safety: Wherever Life Takes You

KEY TAKEAWAYS

- The most important aspect of personal safety, also known as street safety, is situational awareness.

- Relying on and listening to our gut instinct when someone or something "doesn't seem right" can keep us safe in the presence of danger.

- The first responders in many active shooting situations are the people on the scene, not emergency responders.

- If a robber wants to take a material item from you, give it to them. People are hurt and killed over items that can be replaced. You are irreplaceable.

- If a bad guy tries to force you into a vehicle or to take you with them, don't go. Run, scream, or fight at the point of contact.

Chapter Highlights

Setting the Stage

When I was 16, one of my close friends, Daladier—"D-Loc"—saved my life. We were at a large party in an unfamiliar area, and I was having a great time talking and flirting with my new friend, Jane. Without warning, D-Loc told me we needed to leave immediately. I told him I wasn't leaving. He looked at me with urgency, pulled me close, and said, "Those dudes over there have been 'mean mugging' you. I think one's her boyfriend. We gotta go."

For the first time, I noticed two guys standing across the room. Both were staring at us and were visibly upset—one of them in particular. I was instantly terrified and started looking for the nearest exit, which D-Loc had already found and was leading me out of. We made it to my car, and as I was fiddling for my car key, D-Loc was frantically looking around for the guys and begging me to hurry up. The moment I started my car and sped away, the angrier of the two guys ran up behind my car with a gun in his hand, pointing it our way.

Once we were safely away and collected ourselves, I asked D-Loc how he had noticed those guys at such a crowded party. His simple response: "Head on a swivel, JC. Head on a swivel!"

That night I not only learned about situational awareness from D-Loc, but also greatly benefited from it. As I would come to understand, maintaining situational awareness puts us in the best position possible to head off danger before it develops, whether it be a natural disaster or man-made.

The lessons in this chapter are, in many ways, the simplest to learn and implement of any in this book. They're straightforward and can be utilized over the course of an entire lifetime—no matter where we are or what we're doing. However, the obstacle that many face when it comes to learning about personal safety is their complacency: *they don't think that they'll ever be victimized*, so they overlook the importance of personal safety and lower their guard.

The reality is that most of us, thankfully, won't ever get caught in a situation in which our safety is in jeopardy and quick action is required to stay safe. Yet we all know that sh*t does happen and that no victim ever thought it would happen to them. (I certainly never thought I'd have an angry boyfriend(?) point a gun at me.) The tips and tricks in this chapter will keep not only you safer but perhaps someone you're with too, as D-Loc did for me.

Here's the bottom line: this information increases your odds of surviving any sort of incident that puts your life or well-being in jeopardy. No one can say how much of an increase but an increase nonetheless—so play the odds and really dig into this chapter. You'll walk away from it with greater confidence and peace of mind that you can better handle some of the things that we don't expect to happen but sometimes do.

> **Having situational awareness, or street smarts, is what puts you in the best position possible to head off problems before they develop.**

What You'll Learn in this Chapter

We'll kick off this chapter with the backdrop of personal safety: situational awareness. While this chapter offers a lot more than that, just learning about how to stay situationally aware can be a huge game changer. We'll then move into the power of our intuition to accurately sense danger, even when logically we fail to connect the dots. We'll also cover ways to stay safer from gun violence and street predators, and much more.

Let's get to it.

Situational Awareness

As you transition out of your parents' care during your teen years, your personal security becomes your responsibility. Situational awareness may be one of the simplest and easiest ways to keep yourself safe—wherever your travels take you. This is particularly important for young people because they suffer "very high rates of crime victimization," says Dr. David Finkelhor, a professor of sociology at the University of New Hampshire and the director of the Crimes against Children Research Center.

> Being situationally aware means relying on your eyes, ears, and intuition to know what's going on around you in your daily life.

Dr. Finkelhor goes on to say, "The exact numbers are hard to fully assess because crimes against children are more underreported than most crimes." Yet some research studies have found that "youth are more likely than adults to face a weapon-toting assailant and to experience a victimization-related injury."

Jason Hanson, a former CIA officer and the *New York Times* best-selling author of *Spy Secrets That Can Save Your Life*, provides specifics on why young people are more susceptible to street crime: "It's been my experience that the physical safety of teens, generally, is at greater risk than adults. This often has to do with maturity, limited life experience, and lack of situational awareness when they're buried in their phones. Predators are more likely to attack teens because they're more vulnerable and often not as strong as adults."

We're not just talking about street criminals because maintaining situational awareness enables you to better assess and then handle *whatever* gets thrown your way. It could be a careless electric scooter rider on the sidewalk, a rabid stray dog headed your way, a vehicle driving toward you too slowly or too quickly, someone approaching you who seems mentally unstable, walking across a busy intersection, and countless other potentially dangerous yet all too common scenarios.

Situational awareness is *not* about living in a state of fear by irrationally thinking that all sorts of bad things are going to happen. Rather, it's about having your "head on a swivel," as D-Loc taught me (sadly, he passed away a few years later). This makes you more mindful of what's going on around you and thus more difficult to harm. In fact, situationally aware people are calm and alert, knowing that their heightened sense of awareness will benefit them in the unlikely event that a threat exists. It's not about expecting bad things to happen but recognizing that bad things are a possibility.

> **Situational awareness gives you a two-second head start, which is a meaningful period of time.**

Practicing situational awareness gives us a head start—something everyone needs in a crisis. Seeing what is going on in real time, often *before* other people do, enables us to take swift action. As a former FBI director explained to his own kids, in dangerous situations, "Situational awareness gives you a two-second head start, which is a meaningful period of time."

Ignorance Is Bliss

Three people robbed a Billings, Montana, bar at gunpoint. Surveillance video shows a couple in the bar "making out" throughout the entire robbery and not once noticing what was happening around them. I guess love really is blind! Although everything turned out okay for these lovers, I point their story out because it is, essentially, the opposite of situational awareness.

Part of becoming situationally aware is making sure you limit your distractions. Don't go through the day buried in your own thoughts, continually looking down at your phone, and being distracted by your conversations.

Dangerous people often look for victims who are in this "unaware" state, since their attention is focused elsewhere, making them more vulnerable to attack. Instead, keep your head on a swivel by **periodically lifting it up and looking forward, backward, and side-to-side**. Does everything appear normal? It takes only seconds to make this assessment.

It can take a little practice in the beginning to maintain situational awareness, but you'll learn to do these assessments with ease and speed and enjoy the peace of mind that situational awareness provides.

The Power of Intuition

This young man is situationally aware with his "head on a swivel."

To help keep us safe from violence, humans have developed a superpower. This power, which should not be underestimated, is your intuition, also known as your "gut instinct."

Your intuition sends you warning signals of potential danger. Those signals include suspicion, nagging feelings, apprehension, anxiety, hunches, hesitation, and, most importantly, fear. Gavin de Becker is a famed security consultant and the author of the renowned book *The Gift of Fear*. He points out in his book that the feeling of fear is actually a gift of survival because it's a warning signal that "always rings in the presence of danger."

He explains that we often ignore these warning signals because they are usually only whispers and you probably don't have a "logical reason" for what your gut instinct is telling you. It's easier to rationalize, minimize, make excuses, or explain away disturbing behavior. This is called denial—a form of inattention and even blindness to certain realities. When we don't trust our intuition, we are inadvertently keeping ourselves in a potentially dangerous situation.

If You Only Learn One Thing from This Chapter . . .

Knowing the location of at least one additional exit—other than the one in which you entered—in *every* building you find yourself in is

one of the most important ways to stay situationally aware. Be it a nightclub, movie theater, restaurant, house party, or hotel, finding an emergency or secondary exit is easy to do when you first enter a building—not so easy to do amid widespread panic.

As you saw in the situation I was in with D-Loc, I went looking for the nearest exit only when we needed to leave—but he already knew where it was.

Another reason people don't listen to their intuition is that they don't want to be rude. This is particularly true for women and girls, who are disproportionally impacted by violence. They may worry that if an approaching man perceives them as rude, it can trigger anger and ultimately violence toward them. There can be sexist cultural expectations that girls and women are supposed to be "nice," particularly to a man who is being nice to them. If they don't respond in the way that some men expect, they may be perceived as rude, arrogant, or ungrateful.

Being polite is one tactic to rebuff unwanted advances. Being curt or rude is another, particularly if you have the slightest concern for your safety. **The ironclad rule is your safety first, someone's feelings second.**

John Torres knows firsthand about trusting the power of his intuition. He worked for thirty years with great distinction at the Bureau of Alcohol, Tobacco, Firearms, and Explosives (ATF) and is now the system-wide director of investigations at the University of California Office of the President. Before Torres retired from the ATF, we worked together closely on numerous investigations that targeted some of the most dangerous people and places in Los Angeles.

Over the years, I got an up-close-and-personal view of how Torres supervised the many ATF agents in his chain of command and his persistent emphasis on intuition as an important way to stay safe. Years later, I asked him about this and he said, "People underestimate the importance of intuition, but it is so important. I could give you countless examples, but one stands out. I was a new ATF agent working undercover trying to buy a gun from someone totally sketchy. I was alone with him in a hotel room and I just got a bad feeling about the deal. I can't say what it was specifically, but my 'spidey sense' was buzzing and things just didn't seem right."

As a new agent, Torres wasn't sure how his supervisors would react if he aborted the mission without a specific reason for doing so. Nevertheless, he trusted his intuition and got himself out of the hotel room. Later, Torres discovered that his intuition was right. The suspect was going to rip him off and could've hurt or killed him before his partners could intervene.

I get asked a fair amount whether I carry a gun or knife with me. I do not. However, since the pen is mightier than the sword (as the saying goes), I do always carry a tactical pen. First and foremost, the pen is a functional writing instrument that I write with all the time. It can also be a self-defense tool. Made of super-sturdy aircraft-grade aluminum or stainless steel, it has a very strong ballpoint tip (separate from the tip of the ink pen) that can be used against an attacker, to break through glass, and more. I carry the pen almost everywhere I go.

Torres advises all people but particularly teens: "Don't underestimate your intuition or 'spidey sense.' If you feel something's off, take a second look at it because a lot of the time there's a good reason you're feeling that way. Don't be afraid to be the one who says 'Let's move' or 'We need to get out of here.' To be that person can be really hard to do. Not just for young people, but for older people too. It's just one of those courageous decisions you need to make for yourself. Sometimes you make your own luck by removing yourself from potentially bad situations that others may not notice or are in denial about."

Remember, please: A few moments of discomfort or embarrassment are better than the possibility of permanent consequences caused by delay.

Women Fighting Back

Ellen Snortland, in her book *Beauty Bites Beast*, destroys the myth that women can't defend themselves against predators. She describes a very effective technique for women to better protect themselves: learning how to say and then yell "No!"

For many of the women she has taught, saying no was often difficult to do. Learning to yell "No!" was an even greater challenge. Snortland explains that no is a critical first line of defense. Yelling "No!" not only conveys a strong message of resistance to a potential attacker but also can provide the physical and emotional power to take action.

Surviving a Violent Encounter

Gun Violence in America

The United States is the most heavily armed society in the world. Americans are twenty-five times more likely to be killed by a gun than citizens in any other high-income nation. In fact, every day, on average, 109 Americans die from gun violence.

The leading cause of death among teenagers is accidents

(unintentional injuries). Within that category, automobile accidents are first, guns are second. When it comes to young people more broadly, 15- to 24-year-olds are forty-nine times more likely to die from firearm homicide compared to similarly aged people in other high-income nations. So a chapter on street safety would be woefully incomplete without a discussion about gun violence in the United States (driving safety is a topic you'll get when you learn to drive).

No One Is Tougher Than a Bullet—Walk Away from Verbal Harassment

When I was a teen there were, of course, bullies and tough guys we had to deal with. Those were the guys whom everyone knew not to mess with because they would give you a beating. If you happened to cross paths, though, win or lose, you'd live to fight another day. That world no longer exists because many people today would sooner shoot than throw a punch.

There are many scenarios in which you could end up in a confrontation with someone and you just don't know what they're capable of. Another driver may flip you off, honk, and yell at you because you accidentally cut them off. Someone may confront you over a perceived slight, such as

---

Ride-Sharing Safety

Ride-sharing apps like Uber and Lyft have great utility but have also made us way too comfortable jumping into the car of a stranger. There have been countless incidents of people, often female, suffering significant harm at the hands of ride-sharing drivers or those posing as ride-sharing drivers.

I'm not saying you shouldn't use ride-sharing apps, only that you should pay attention if you do. Here are some quick tips to keep you safer while using these services:

- Trust your gut and stay situationally aware. To help you do this, don't be on your phone when getting in the car and don't be buried in your phone during the ride.
- Do not get in the car unless your driver can answer one simple question: "What's my name?" Once you book a ride, the "real" driver will have your contact info, including your name. If they don't have it, they're an impostor.

accidentally bumping them at a crowded party and spilling their drink. You or a friend may be confronted by a jealous boyfriend or girlfriend. In all these situations, and so many others, the other person may be downright insulting and unfairly targeting you with disproportionate aggression.

> As mad as the other person may make you, you should always weigh the potential consequences that a confrontation may bring.

As mad as the other person may make you, you should always weigh the potential consequences that a confrontation may bring. Is this argument really worth possibly getting shot or otherwise hurt over? Keep in mind that there are more guns in the United States than people, and three million Americans carry loaded firearms with them every day (a lot carry knives too).

You should assume that anyone who wants to get or gets physically confrontational with you may have a gun and in a fit of rage might just use it. Not even to contemplate such a scenario as you go about your daily life is a mistake. Be the bigger person and walk away from a potential confrontation—even though there may be a part of you that doesn't want to.

- Verify the car. Make sure the license plate, make, and model of the car that shows up matches that in the confirmation notice you received when you booked the ride.
- Familiarize yourself with the safety technologies offered by the ride-sharing service itself. These are constantly evolving and often embedded in the app. For example, look for an emergency button, glowing signs on the approaching driver's car that flash in the color of your choosing, and the ability to easily share your trip details in real time with friends or loved ones so they can track you.
- Wait for your driver in a well-lit public place, hopefully in the presence of others, and, again, not with your face buried in your phone.
- Don't forget to wear your seat belt!

Mass Shootings

There is no one uniform definition of "mass shooting," "active shooter," "active shooting incidents," or other terms used to describe acts in which a shooter attacks more than one person. As such, for consistency, I use the term "mass shooting" broadly.

Although the information below about mass shootings is important for all of us to know, let me be clear again that it is exceptionally unlikely that you will be caught up in such an event.

Warning Signs of Impending Gun Violence

There is no one profile of mass shooters. However, they are overwhelmingly male and typically have a history of violence and/or stalking against their family members, wives, and/or girlfriends. In fact, in most mass shootings the shooter is targeting a family member or a romantic partner—most often a woman. School shootings generate the most headlines, but far more children are shot and killed every year in domestic or family violence incidents. (Also, women in abusive relationships are five times more likely to be murdered by an abuser with access to a firearm.)

Regardless of the underlying events leading to a mass shooting, most shooters obtain access to their firearms legally and methodically plan their attacks, making the crime a predatory, not impulsive, act. As elaborated below, planned incidents give a window of opportunity to intercede.

In the months leading up to the gun violence, individuals who carry out attacks typically experience multiple stressors in their lives and are going through inner turmoil that has reached an identifiable crisis point. Some of the stressors include:

- mental health (this is *not* synonymous with being diagnosed with a mental illness)
- financial strain
- job-related issues
- conflicts with their peers, friends, family, or intimate partners
- legal problems
- the death of a friend or relative
- school-related problems

Many mass shooters signal their intention to do violence well before they commit it. They often communicate their intention to do harm to a third party—family, friends, neighbors, coworkers, teachers, and classmates, whether online or via a personal interaction—and display concerning behaviors that, in many instances, are observed by these third parties and create some level of concern for them. The communication of an intention to do harm is called "leakage" and can signal the research, planning, and possibly the implementation of a shooting.

The means of the leakage varies and can include blog posts, online videos created/shared/liked, voicemails, letters, emails, social media posts, and certainly others. People who witness leakage and/or observe any of the concerning behaviors (see below) are given an important opportunity to seek an intervention or speak up before an attack.

In addition to leakage, pre-shooting behaviors that are cause for concern are almost always present and noticeable to some. These behaviors may include:

- threatening others
- feeling wronged
- holding a distorted sense of injustice
- expressing hatred
- committing domestic violence or teen dating violence (see chapter 7 for more on teen dating violence)
- violating restraining orders, stalking, and harassing
- displaying explosive outbursts of anger without provocation
- being bitter over bullying at school
- engaging in substance abuse
- exhibiting erratic behavior and severe mood swings
- suffering despair, depression, self-harm ideation, and self-harm

These and other behaviors *do not mean* that an individual will resort to violence. However, they may suggest a progression toward violence. **If you recognize worrisome behavior, don't ignore the potential significance of these indicators, even if you think they may not rise to the level of calling 911.**

If you observe warning signs that a person may resort to violence, take action by sharing your concern with an adult you trust, a school administrator, your local police department (if there's no imminent threat, you can call the department's nonemergency phone number—which can be found online—or go into the police station), or the Federal Bureau of Investigation (FBI). If they don't take you seriously, report it again or to someone else. If desired, you may be able to report the concerning behavior anonymously. Saying something is the first line of defense against mass shootings.

As we covered earlier, it's easy to rationalize someone's troubling behavior by telling ourselves that we're overreacting. Trust your instincts about the situation and report it. You aren't being a "snitch" (as so many young people are concerned about), but rather you are potentially saving lives. **The bottom line: if you see something, hear something, or know something, please say something and never ignore your intuition.**

Dangerous Weapons and Anger Problems: A Toxic Mix

Kevin Rodriguez, 19, was pulling into a Temecula, California, Walmart parking lot with his girlfriend to pick up some groceries for his father's birthday party. Kevin was described as a kind, well-liked teen who was hugely popular on Instagram with forty thousand followers. An already agitated driver in the parking lot almost hit Kevin's car and some sort of dispute between the two arose.

When Kevin and his girlfriend were making their way into the store, the man confronted Kevin and stabbed him in the chest with a six-inch folding knife. While Kevin lay in his girlfriend's arms dying, the attacker pulled out his cell phone and started recording. He then snapped out of his rage and tried to render first aid to Kevin. It was too late. The attacker was convicted of second-degree murder. For the record, Kevin should not be blamed for this ruthless attack, but this tragedy should be a reminder to us all: many people who may seem ordinary blend in among us every day but when provoked (as *they* perceive it) may respond with extreme violence.

Gun Violence Safety Tips

While gun violence can happen anywhere at any time, some of the most frequent places include commercial buildings, education facilities, open spaces, government buildings, residences, health care facilities, and houses of worship. Since no space in the United States is immune from gun violence, it's best to know some strategies to keep ourselves safer, wherever we may find ourselves.

Staying situationally aware, as you now should know, allows for faster and more effective decision-making. Keep your faculties intact, don't bury your face in your smartphone, and, again, always trust your gut instincts—they're rarely wrong and are one of the best survival tools in your arsenal.

Know the exits in the buildings you go to—not just the exits you normally use. This lesson is incredibly important. If you can't run because a shooter is blocking your path, think outside the box about potential exit points. Can you throw a chair through a window and jump out? You're more likely to survive cuts from broken glass or a fall from a second-story window than you are multiple bullets fired at close range. Is there a crawl space that you can escape through or hide?

Red Flag Laws

Red flag gun laws—which may also be referred to as extreme risk protection orders, gun violence restraining orders, or something else—are becoming increasingly utilized as a way to help prevent gun violence. Often they allow police or family members (perhaps even employers, coworkers, and schools) to seek a court order removing firearms from individuals who are deemed by a judge to pose a significant risk to themselves or others. The protections may also block gun purchases, though these laws vary by the jurisdictions that have them.

Mara Elliott, the city attorney in San Diego, whose office aggressively seeks these types of orders, is "convinced that having this powerful tool gives . . . communities the ability to step in and prevent some tragedies from happening." You can do a Google search to see if your jurisdiction has such a law. For those that do, it can make reporting your concerns as outlined above even more critical.

Taking action rapidly is the optimal way to increase your chances of survival. Doing a "mental rehearsal" can provide you with a head start if you ever become caught in a shooting incident. Remember, the body may not go where the mind has never been. One of the reasons people delay quick flight from the scene of a shooting is that they mistake gunshots for a firecracker, something heavy falling, or a balloon popping. While guns may sound differently from one another, you may want to watch a YouTube video in which guns are being fired safely to become familiar with how they sound.

If you need to take flight, don't bother gathering your belongings. This seems so obvious, but the brain can respond oddly in emergencies. Some people waste precious seconds going back to grab their wallet, purse, or other belongings—even in the midst of danger. Leave them and get out by running in the opposite direction of the gunfire. As you make your rapid departure, be quiet and stealthy. The majority of shooters act alone, but there could be a second shooter, so don't drop your guard as you escape the first.

Nothing is worse than inaction in the midst of danger. When we believe or suspect that something is wrong, we often look to other people for cues about what we should do. If they're unsure too, they may be looking to us—all of which wastes precious time and potentially establishes a false conclusion that everything is fine. Despite what people are doing or not doing, take action. In the face of danger, some will do nothing because they're in disbelief or frozen in fear.

Suicide: America's Biggest Gun Problem

Mass shootings get far more attention, but most US gun deaths are by suicide. Similarly, most suicides are by gun. Simply having access to a firearm in the home increases the risk of suicide. If you or someone you know is in crisis, please seek immediate help by talking to a trusted adult or calling the National Suicide Prevention Lifeline at 800-273-8255.

School Shootings

I've attended several different active shooter trainings in my career as a prosecutor. Whether hosted by the Los Angeles Police Department (LAPD), the FBI, the ALICE Training Institute, or others, the trainers don't completely agree on all the methods to counter active shooters. For example, some teach the "run, hide, fight" protocol ("run/escape if you can, hide if you need to, fight if you must"), others the shelter-in-place strategy ("locks, lights, and out of sight"), and others the ALICE method (Alert, Lockdown, Inform, Counter, Evacuate).

Since there isn't one go-to training method, schools understandably vary in what they teach students and staff. (Some schools don't hold active shooter drills for a number of reasons, including the legitimate concern that the drills can cause psychological trauma to the participants.) I'm going to tread carefully here to ensure that I don't conflict with the approach your school takes (assuming it takes an approach).

First and foremost, if your school has a plan of action, by all means pay close attention to what you are instructed to do. In the very unlikely event that there is a gun violence incident, knowing the school protocol can help you react more quickly.

Silence is golden. Stay quiet. Silence both ringer and vibration modes on your phone.

Concealment and cover are not the same. Concealment shields you from view but doesn't stop bullets. Cover may or may not shield you from view but will stop bullets. An example of concealment would be under a desk. You can't be seen, but most desks are unlikely to stop a bullet. Examples of cover include heavy concrete or steel barriers (which, potentially, may also provide some concealment).

Look for any potential weapons before hiding, time permitting. Everyday items within your grasp can be weaponized, including fire extinguishers, pens, scissors, chairs, glass items, or anything that has a sharp edge. In many instances, when all else has failed, unarmed civilians have ended mass shootings by attacking and restraining the shooter. However, this should be an act of last resort.

When the police arrive. The first officers who arrive on the scene of an active shooter incident are not there to attend to the wounded but to neutralize the shooter. They'll probably be shouting commands, so do your best to stay calm and listen. Keep your hands empty and your arms up with fingers spread and visible at all times. Don't make quick movements toward the officers or touch them. Remember, they probably don't know who the shooter is or whether there's more than one, so everyone they encounter might be a suspect in their eyes.

The Phone App That Can Save Your Life

When someone is being rushed into an emergency room, every second matters. A patient may be unable to communicate with hospital personnel and the hospital may not know the identity of the victim, how to contact their family, or their medical history. The wealth of information that can be found in their phone is useless when it's locked. Emergency room doctor Julia Thompson smartly reminds and encourages us to use Medical ID in the Health app included free on all iPhones (comparable apps may be found or downloaded to Android devices). Even though the phone is locked, Medical ID allows ER personnel to access the patient's information, such as name, date of birth, emergency contacts, medical conditions, blood type, organ donor status, and more.

The First Responder—You

In at least one comprehensive study, almost 70 percent of mass-shooting incidents were over *before* the police arrived, 36 percent were over in two minutes or less, and nearly 70 percent ended in five minutes or less. So no matter how fast emergency services get there, bystanders will be on the scene first and may have to make life-and-death decisions. Anyone, including you, might be a first responder. Your closest help is likely to be you.

Jason Ames is a detective in the Los Angeles County Sheriff's Department, a licensed emergency medical technician (EMT), a DHS (Department of Homeland Security) active shooter threat and tactical medical instructor, and an instructor of NAEMT (National Association of Emergency Medical Technicians) programs. Detective Ames tells me, "Victims who suffer uncontrolled bleeding, whether by bullet, a car accident, or any other cause, can bleed out very rapidly, in as little as thirty seconds." Therefore, "It's important for all of us to know how to stop free-flowing bleeding and to help someone in need—perhaps ourselves.

Of course, you should *never* render aid if the circumstances might make it unsafe for you to do so."

I was certified as a tactical emergency combat casualty care provider by NAEMT, and it was eye-opening. In that course, I learned firsthand the incredibly important and pretty simple-to-learn methods to stop uncontrolled, fast-flowing bleeding. My course instructor was Detective Ames. He taught me about the use of tourniquets, direct pressure, chest seals, wound packing, hemostatic agents (which cause bleeding to stop), and other tools and techniques to stop bleeding.

Anyone, including you, might be a first responder.

I highly encourage all readers to take a first-aid class that teaches how to stop bleeding. You can find a provider in your area with a Google search or by going to stopthebleed.org. If you're in the greater LA area, you can contact Detective Ames's training company, Swift Tactical.

Since I suspect many readers won't take such a class, I'd like to focus your attention on tourniquet use—the first "go-to" treatment for stopping fast, uncontrolled bleeding from an artery or vein in a limb. While direct pressure to an open wound can help stop a minimal flow of blood, a tourniquet is utilized when the bleeding from your legs or arms is too extreme for direct pressure to be effective. The device stops the flow of blood by compression.

A good tourniquet runs about $30 and is generally made of a sturdy nylon strap, a quick slide buckle, and an attached windlass (a stick used to tighten the strap over the artery or vein to such an extent that the flow of blood is stopped).

Use of tourniquets on injured civilians corresponds to a nearly sixfold decrease in death. Tourniquets save lives because

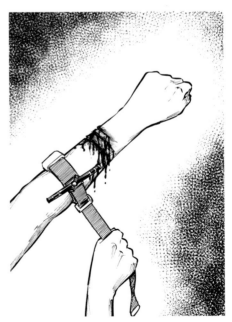

This tourniquet is in the process of being applied. It doesn't take long.

doctors can't treat gun or other trauma if the victims don't survive long enough to make it to the operating table. I keep tourniquets in my office and car and, while traveling, in my backpack. I certainly do not expect a shooting or other catastrophe to happen, but no one ever does.

The Department of Homeland Security, the American College of Surgeons, and their partners launched a national campaign called Stop the Bleed, which teaches civilians how to stop uncontrolled bleeding in emergencies before police and paramedics arrive on the scene. These skills are as important as knowing CPR and have become widespread. The Stop the Bleed website, stopthebleed.org, offers free classes, sells full bleeding control kits as well as tourniquets, and has instructional videos (and an app) about how to use the items. May has been crowned National Stop the Bleed month.

Also, importantly, if you don't have a tourniquet but need one, impromptu ones can be made with items you probably have on hand like a pliable cloth, large bandage, necktie, or shirt and a windlass in the form of a sturdy pen or stick, a carabiner (a small metal coupling link with a spring-loaded safety closure), or anything similar. There are good videos and other online instructions explaining how to make one.

Although a makeshift tourniquet can be a lifesaver, Detective Ames warns: "If you need a tourniquet, the lethal clock to stop bleeding is ticking fast. Spending time looking around for things to make a tourniquet may not be rapid enough to save the person. Think of bleeding injuries as leaking hoses and broken pipes. If you have a tourniquet, clamp the hose to stop the bleeding. If you do not have a tourniquet available, you must plug the broken pipe deep inside the wound. Do not leave a victim bleeding while you try to find components to improvise a tourniquet. Use any gauze or cloth material available and pack it tightly, deep into the wound. Apply firm direct pressure to the packed material to ensure the wound clots and the bleeding stops. Then, make an improvised tourniquet to add another layer of bleeding control."

Wrapping up this section, I want to mention that every state has a Good Samaritan law. These laws, which vary by jurisdiction, provide legal protections for persons who give reasonable assistance to a person in need at the scene of an emergency. The reason these laws are so widespread is to encourage bystanders to get involved in emergencies without fear that they will be sued or prosecuted if their actions inadvertently contribute to a person's injury or death.

What If a Robber Wants to Take My Stuff?

If a "bad guy" approaches you with a weapon in hand and demands your smartphone, wallet, laptop, purse, and so on, what would you do?

About a third of teens tell me that they'd refuse to give up their stuff. Wrong move. In countless incidents, people were seriously injured or killed because they didn't give a robber their material possessions or they gave chase after the item was taken. Moreover, some muggers or street robbers work in pairs, so if you challenge one, you're very likely to end up with an accomplice in your face.

In such a situation, nearly every parent would tell their child to give up their stuff without hesitation. Your stuff can be replaced, but you can't. I urge you to remember that you are loved by people who don't want to see you hurt, so give up material possessions if they're demanded by someone who could harm you physically—which could be just about anyone.

If you're being robbed for your wallet or other valuables, you want to make it clear to the assailant that you aren't resisting and are cooperative.

Robbery versus Burglary

Although the terms are often used interchangeably, burglary and robbery are quite different. A burglary is the entering of a building, such as a residence, with the intention to commit a crime. A robbery is when someone takes your property by the use of force, intimidation, or fear.

You want to keep the robber calm, and here are some ways that may help do that:

- Stay calm.

- Don't look directly at the robber, as he may think you're going to be better able to identify him to police (I say "him" because most street robbers and violent criminals are male).

- Whatever the robber has demanded, tell him, "No problem, you can have it." As you're reaching for the item, tell him what you're doing: "I'm reaching for my wallet to give to you. This is all I have."

- When it comes to how to best hand over the item(s) demanded, there are differing points of view about how exactly to do so. Some think it best to hand it over and then slowly start backing up. Others think you should throw your wallet or purse in one direction and run in the other. Former CIA officer Jason Hanson weighs in this way: "It's a case-by-case situation. If you believe the criminal really only wants money, give it to him. But if you believe he's going to kill you, definitely fight back and defend yourself."

  One seasoned ATF agent I spoke with about this (who didn't want to be named) summed it up well when she told me: "I don't think it really matters. You can plan all you want, but just give the money."

- Call 911 the moment you are safe. It's best to do so away from the scene in case the robber has decided, on second thought, to hurt you (or worse) so that you don't identify them to the police.

Material Possessions Can Be Replaced, Particularly When They Aren't Yours

Not only should you never fight over your material possessions, you shouldn't fight over someone else's! I was in a convenience store late one night and a young man walked in, grabbed a case of beer, and ran out. The clerk, who did not own the store, gave chase. Why? It wasn't even his beer! When the clerk exited the store, he was met with vicious blows from a baseball bat that was being wielded by the thief's accomplice. The clerk was seriously injured over a twelve-pack of beer. I called 911 and rendered aid as best I could.

What If a Robber Wants to Take Me?

It's an entirely different situation when a street mugger actually turns out to be a violent predator who is not interested in your possessions but rather in kidnapping you. As he's trying to steal you away, he'll say something like "Don't scream, or I'll kill you," "Get in the car," or "Don't resist and you won't get hurt."

At this point, you've got two choices, neither of them good: go with him or fight/flee. Generally, the better of the two options is the latter—refuse to be taken. Whatever that person wants to do to you, he can't do it there at the point of first contact. He needs time, isolation, and complete control over you in a secure, private environment. Obviously, there's no good outcome for a victim spending time with an abductor in that setting. Oklahoma State University veteran police officer Edward Welch says, "There's a 98 percent chance the assailant won't kill you if you refuse to go, but if you go with him, there's a 98 percent chance that you won't live."

Teen Fights Off Attacker

Marguerite, 16, from Washington State, was walking home at noon when she came around a corner to find a dark SUV parked with the motor running and a man standing outside the vehicle. Her intuition instantly told her something was wrong and she turned around to run away. The man grabbed her by the neck and pushed her into the vehicle and attempted to sexually assault her. Marguerite kicked at him and was able to knock him off. She then screamed as loud as she could and started honking the car horn trying to get someone's attention. He grabbed her again, and this time she scratched him in the face. As she was trying to flee, he grabbed her by her sweatshirt, but she was able to take it off. As she was trying to run away, the perpetrator grabbed Marguerite's foot, but her shoe came off and she was able to escape.

Please let this be a reminder to you that if you choose to fight an attacker, you very well might be able to save yourself by doing whatever it takes.

Acclaimed security consultant Gavin de Becker advises, and I echo, that if someone says "Don't yell," you should yell. The perpetrator is telegraphing that yelling would serve you but silence would serve him. We often go along with these kinds of demands. Why? Because we're afraid of getting hurt. Yet what do you fear more: injury sustained trying to escape or the attacker having total control over you?

Experienced police officers, self-defense experts, and other credible sources on the subject will often tell you the same thing: *never* go with the perpetrator. Instead, run, fight, bite, hit, scratch—draw attention to yourself by screaming. It may not be easy to muster the courage to fight back, but any risk is worth the price if it helps you escape.

In fact, your quick, strong resistance may surprise the attacker and he just may flee to find an easier target. As the famous boxer Mike Tyson said, "Everyone has a plan 'til they get punched in the mouth."

> Police and self-defense experts will often tell you the same thing: *never* go with the perpetrator.

The place of first contact is the best chance you have to escape—the last thing you want to do is to be passive. Risk everything to stop from being moved. Lousy options now are better than no options later. In these dire cases, many people are understandingly intimidated by a perpetrator with a gun. Yet if he shoots at you, particularly if you are a moving target (you're running away), it won't be surprising at all if he misses. As a point of reference, police officers, who constantly train on their service firearms, miss more than they hit when discharging their firearms in a real-world environment. One of the reasons for the surprising inaccuracy is stress. In most instances, I don't suspect a violent perpetrator would do any better.

By the way, if the perpetrator is willing to shoot you now, what do you think he was going to do when he got you alone?

Finally, never forget the best, first line of defense: avoid being a target. How? Situational awareness. Street robbers—and many other criminals—are opportunists who often strike people whom they perceive as vulnerable. We are less vulnerable when we stay situationally aware.

Street-Smart Safety Tips

Here are some other important safety tips when you're out and about:

- Keep your money and other valuables out of sight.
- Stay in well-lit areas, particularly when walking and parking your vehicle.
- There's safety in numbers, so travel in groups whenever possible. When leaving a public place alone, such as a restaurant, if you feel unsafe walking to your car, ask the manager to accompany you. Or you can just wait inside the exit doorway for a group going in the same direction as you are and join it.
- When at a party with your friends, make a pact to arrive together, stay together, and leave together.
- If you're on foot, walk facing traffic. Doing so makes it more difficult for a driver to follow you without being noticed or to push you into a car. Also, when walking, don't pass too close to shrubbery, dark doorways, and other places that might conceal a perpetrator.
- Don't wait until you arrive at your car or home to grab your keys. Have the right key in hand as you make your approach.
- Check the backseat of your car before getting in to make sure that it's empty. When you get into your car, lock the doors and drive away. Don't sit there on your smartphone once inside.
- Never get out of the car while talking on the phone or texting.
- Don't spend unnecessary time loading items into your car. This is a particularly vulnerable time for you. Get into your car and drive away as swiftly as possible.
- If you're jogging or even just walking around using headphones, keep one earpiece out so you can be more aware of your surroundings.
- Stay sober. Drugs, including alcohol, can impair your good judgment and your ability to stay situationally aware and defend yourself.

What Three Things in This Chapter Matter Most to You?

We all take away different lessons from reading the information presented in this chapter. What resonates with one person may not be meaningful to another and vice versa. I certainly hope that you've learned a heck of a lot more than three things in this chapter, but if three things were all you learned, I still consider it a win. Even a single piece of information could be invaluable if it was just what you or someone you're with needs in a critical moment.

With the information from this chapter fresh in your mind, please take a few moments to write below the three things that you consider the most important.

1. _____

_____

2. _____

_____

3. _____

_____

What Would You Do if It Happened to You? (Question 1)

You're walking late at night in a commercial area. You're looking down texting a friend (not being situationally aware) when out of nowhere a man jumps out, snatches your phone, and takes off running. How would you react?

Some Thoughts about "What Would You Do if It Happened to You?" (Question 1)

Many people's initial reaction would be to give chase. This is understandable because our smartphones are expensive and contain important information. It's inconvenient to be without them, but I urge you not to give chase. Although some people have successfully gone after a thief and recovered their property, others have been injured or killed doing so. It is far wiser to make your way to a safe place and call 911.

Vanessa, 15, was walking with her 7-year-old sister in Santa Ana, California, when a man snatched her iPhone and then jumped into the passenger seat of a waiting car driven by his accomplice. She had just gotten the phone a week earlier and promised her mom she'd take care of it. Vanessa chased after the robber and in the heat of the moment jumped onto the car as it was driving away. The car swerved and she fell off, hit her head, and was killed.

Victims like Vanessa are not to blame for the terrible acts of others, and we can all understand how emotions can sometimes get the best of us. Still, we can learn from her story (and countless others just like hers). For starters, it's always best not to walk down the street with your phone on display. Being glued to your phone not only is a distraction that limits your situational awareness of hazards, including robbers, but also lets robbers know that you have something of value on your person.

Also, if Vanessa had caught up to the robber, what would she have done? Fight him? Order him to stay in place until the police arrived? Demand he return the phone? Any of these scenarios might have worked, but the more likely outcome is that the robber (or an accomplice) would have physically assaulted her to avoid getting caught.

What Would You Do if It Happened to You? (Question 2)

A new kid at your high school, Tommy, has become a target of school bullies. Often the bullying is about how he dresses and how he looks, and happens in the presence of others. A school authority figure even walked by one of the bullying episodes and said, "Oh well, boys will be boys." One day, after some particularly mean bullying, as Tommy is walking by you he mutters under his breath, "I want to shoot those guys." Should you report this incident?

Some Thoughts about "What Would You Do if It Happened to You?" (Question 2)

This should be reported. Tommy didn't say that he was going to shoot them, but that he wanted to. Still, saying you want to shoot someone is very serious and should not be ignored.

I would urge you to tell a trusted adult at your school with decision-making authority, such as the principal or assistant principal. Perhaps you could do so anonymously. Of course, when doing so, it's important to also mention that Tommy is regularly being targeted by bullies and made the statement after one such incident. It's also appropriate to report what the school authority figure said. This person witnessed the bullying but didn't seem to realize how harmful bullying can be to a target.

In addition to reporting this incident, you could tell the bullies to knock it off, particularly if you are friendly with them. You could also say something kind to the target, either at the time or after the fact, such as "You didn't deserve that. Those guys are jerks." In countless situations, a simple kind word from an acquaintance or stranger has prevented someone from committing an act of violence. (We'll cover more about helping targets of bullying in chapter 10.)

Final Thoughts

I get asked a fair amount whether the world is more dangerous now than it was in the past. The answer—if there is one—really depends on whom you ask and how you look at things. Frankly, I don't like to entertain this question because the answer is irrelevant to me.

Today's world, like yesterday's, has risks that one of us might have to face at any given moment. That does not make the world unsafe but serves as a reminder to make good choices, hope for the best, and educate ourselves about how to best handle things if the unexpected happens.

Thinking about someone trying to hurt or kill us (or someone we care about) is unsettling. Burying our heads in the sand and pretending that bad things happen only to "other people" is unwise. Although it's somewhat counterintuitive, when we take these lessons to heart, we are safer and more confident knowing that we have actual things that we can do (or not do) in the unlikely event that things turn dangerous.

Where Can I Get More Information?

This chapter contains the essentials of street safety. For those who want to know more and dig deeper into this topic, a Google search is a good place to start and will deliver numerous resources, some with valuable information.

Street Safety Quiz

Test your understanding of the importance of street safety by taking this quiz. Hopefully, you'll get all of the answers correct because a single mistake could have real-world consequences if that answer contained the information you needed to stay safe.

Instructions: select the best answer from the available choices. Answers can be found in the back of the book.

1. Which is the most important way to keep yourself safe, regardless of where you are?
    A. Don't go out late at night.
    B. Carry weapons.
    C. Stay situationally aware.
    D. Don't trust anyone.

2. In every building you visit, the first thing you should do is:
    A. Locate an emergency exit.
    B. Text someone you trust letting them know where you are.
    C. Make sure your phone is charged in case you need to dial 911.
    D. Know exactly where you're going and the fastest way to get there.

3. Your intuition sends you:
   A. Mixed messages that can be confusing if you don't focus.
   B. Rarely anything because situational awareness is more important.
   C. Effective ways to rationalize potential danger.
   D. Warning signals of potential danger.

4. The targets of mass shootings are most commonly:
   A. Students
   B. Co-workers
   C. Wives, girlfriends, and/or other family members.
   D. Pets

5. Many mass shooters signal their intention to commit violence by:
   A. Leakage
   B. Displaying concerning behaviors to people who know them.
   C. Both A and B.
   D. Neither A nor B.

6. In the midst of a dangerous situation, you want to avoid:
   A. Inaction
   B. Not listening to your inner voice.
   C. Blaming someone without evidence.
   D. Both A and B.

7. The best way to stop uncontrolled bleeding from an arm or leg is:
   A. Apply a gauze pad.
   B. Put on a tourniquet.
   C. Prevent the person from going into shock.
   D. Apply indirect pressure.

8. You're walking home one night and simultaneously checking your Instagram feed on your phone. You look up and see a man about ten feet away who's approaching you with a knife in hand. He demands your phone. What should you do?

    A. If you're a fast runner, run the opposite direction, since ten feet is a meaningful head start.

    B. Tell him he can have it and either hand it over, toss it over, or put it on the ground and head the opposite direction.

    C. If you have cash, offer that to him instead of your phone.

    D. If you're definitely stronger than he is and/or trained in martial arts, kick his ass.

9. You're walking home under the same circumstances as the question above, but in this scenario the guy orders you to get in his car or he'll kill you. What should you do?

    A. Go with him to avoid getting hurt.

    B. Do not go and take all countermeasures needed such as running away, yelling, and/or fighting back.

    C. Offer him your phone and wallet instead.

    D. Ask him what went wrong in his life.

10. You're leaving a restaurant by yourself late at night and are nervous about it. You should:

    A. Make a run for it and don't slow down until you get to your car.

    B. Call 9-1-1 and ask them to talk with you on the phone while you're walking.

    C. Ask the manager to walk you out or wait until a group is leaving in the same direction as you and walk with them.

    D. None of the above.

PART 2

Sexual Violence and Misconduct

CHAPTER 4

Sexual Assault and Consent: We Must Do Better

KEY TAKEAWAYS

- Many myths about sexual assault mistakenly blame victim-survivors and excuse the acts of perpetrators.

- The perpetrator of a sexual assault is far more likely to be a friend or an acquaintance than a stranger.

- Asking for permission before a sexual interaction and verbally checking in with your partner throughout it is indispensable for the participants.

- Consent *cannot* be legally obtained in many circumstances, particularly when someone is drunk.

- There are numerous ways you can help prevent sexual assault.

Chapter Highlights

Setting the Stage

If you ask me, this chapter is the most important in the book. Why? Because not everyone will have an "experience" with some of the other topics, such as cyberbullying, sextortion, damaging one's digital footprint, and so on. Yet most readers, if not all, will sooner or later engage in sexual interactions.

The "standard" for obtaining sexual consent has evolved over the years. What my mother taught me (and what many other parents taught their children)—that "no means no"—is now woefully inadequate. We understand better today that there are many circumstances in which someone does not want to commence or continue a sexual interaction but does not say no.

The current standard of "affirmative consent"—asking for permission before and throughout a sexual interaction—eliminates what some might believe are certain gray areas in a sexual interaction. With affirmative consent there is no middle ground: either you have consent or you don't, and this is good for all the participants.

As I started to write this book, I wanted to know more about the causes and impact of sexual violence. That interest brought me to Peace Over Violence (POV), a large, impactful Los Angeles–based nonprofit focused on ending sexual violence. For many months, in both the classroom and "the field," POV professionals provided me with comprehensive, in-depth training in sexual violence prevention. The training was invaluable, and I ended up receiving credentials from them to teach sexual violence prevention.

"Sexual violence," as used here, is an all-encompassing term that refers to any nonconsensual sexual activity, such as sexual assault, child sexual abuse, some forms of domestic and dating violence, stalking, sexual harassment, and more. It can be physical, verbal, or visual (the latter two can also be accomplished digitally).

On this educational journey, I gained new insights and was astonished by the frequency with which sexual assault occurs not only in our country but throughout the world. For example, one in six women and at least one in thirty-three men will experience an attempted or completed rape in their lifetime. Take a moment to think about how many people that is. I certainly hope that this never happens to any of you readers or your loved ones, but unfortunately, the numbers suggest otherwise.

If we asked these individuals (the one in six and the one in thirty-three) at what age they were first sexually assaulted, the most frequent response would be between the ages of 12 and 34, when 70 percent of lifetime sexual assaults occur. This statistic and many others make clear that sexual assault disproportionally impacts young people. But the cold reality is that sexual assault can happen to anyone, no matter the age, relationship status, gender or gender identity (including persons who identify as nonbinary, trans, or asexual), race, sexual orientation, or economic status.

The frequency of sexual assault is worthy of our outrage, and all of us should be committed to ending it. Perhaps one of the most important ways to do this is by learning early on in life what true sexual consent is and what it is not. Doing so better allows us to prevent sexual violence in our relationships, friendships, peer groups, and community.

What You'll Learn in this Chapter

We'll kick things off by discussing sexual assault, examining damaging rape myths, and reviewing some troubling statistics that highlight the scope of this problem. We'll then transition to the different types of sexual consent, how to tell when you have it, and how to tell when you don't. Along the way, we'll also cover circumstances in which you *cannot* obtain consent from someone—for example, when they're drunk or high—even if the person in the moment says they want to have a sexual interaction. Finally, we'll go over some of the important ways you can help prevent sexual assault.

> **Victim-survivors of sexual assault are not at fault and should *never* be blamed.**

Once you understand the information in this chapter, you'll have a good understanding about what behavior is acceptable and what is not when it comes to our sexual interactions. In fact, you may end up finding yourself in a situation in which you use what you've learned to help someone in a time of need.

Before we dig in, let me be perfectly clear about something: victim-survivors of sexual assault are *not* at fault and should *never* be blamed. Whatever they may have been wearing, drinking, or doing is *completely and totally irrelevant*. What is relevant is that a perpetrator, probably someone trusted, chose to commit a terrible act against them.

Let's get to it.

A NOTE TO THE READER: I'll be using the term "victim-survivor" as it relates to people who have been sexually assaulted. Patti Giggans, the executive director of POV, has worked for decades in sexual violence prevention. She tells me, "The idea of using victim-survivor instead of victim is to acknowledge how much surviving goes on in the aftermath of sexual assault. In the actual attack, yes, you're being victimized, but people are amazingly resilient, trying to do the right thing to survive. The term survivor brings hope and aspiration and a path forward, saying that you don't always have to be a victim. You can heal and go from victim to survivor to thriver to warrior. But there is no one path there and it's different for everyone."

Sexual Assault

We can't understand sexual consent without first understanding sexual assault, which can include rape, attempted rape, anal sex, oral sex, fondling, forced kissing or touching, and many other acts that are committed by *force, fear, or coercion* (a tactic used to intimidate, threaten, trick, pressure, or manipulate someone to engage in sexual activity that is unwanted).

Sexual assault laws vary by state, age of the people involved, and circumstances, but the central component in every sexual assault is sexual contact *without consent*. Even if a behavior doesn't fully meet the legal definition of sexual assault in any given jurisdiction, that doesn't mean it's not just as harmful to victim-survivors as those behaviors that do. What is most important is to be ethical, regardless of what the law or a school code of conduct may or may not require.

As we're about to uncover, the best way to have an ethical, mutually desired, lawful, and wanted sexual encounter is to get explicit permission before engaging in any physical intimacy and to make sure we continue to have permission throughout the entire interaction.

The Numbers Are So Troubling
Did you know?

- Teen girls ages 16 to 19 are four times more likely than any other group to be victim-survivors of sexual assault. Males are assaulted too, sometimes by females but most often by other males, who, interestingly, primarily identify as heterosexual.

- Male college students ages 18 to 24 are five times more likely than nonstudents of the same age to be victim-survivors of sexual assault. Female college students ages 18 to 24 are three times more likely than women in general to experience sexual violence.

- Teens who identify as LGBTQ (lesbian, gay, bisexual, transgender, or queer/questioning) are three times more likely to be raped than their heterosexual peers. People of color, people with disabilities, people who are transgender, and gender nonbinary people also suffer higher rates of sexual violence.

- Alcohol is the substance that is the most used in drug-facilitated sexual assault.

Damaging Rape Myths Are Believed by Too Many
There are many myths about rape and sexual assault. These misperceptions are frequently believed by both young people *and* adults and perpetuate untruths that do further harm to victim-survivors. One of the

most common myths is the way many people envision the circumstances leading up to a sexual assault: a frightening, strange man, weapon in hand, sees and follows a woman out to a parking lot or an alley. By the time she's noticed him, he's pushing her into his creepy old van and shutting the sliding door.

In reality, that scenario is not the norm because 80 percent of sexual assaults are perpetrated by someone the victim-survivor knows—perhaps even an intimate partner—and are often preceded by consensual kissing. 60 percent of the time, sexual assault occurs in a residence. 50 percent of the time, the victim-survivor, perpetrator, or both were consuming alcohol.

I call these three factors the "80/60/50 rule." For the record, while alcohol may be present in many of these situations, *alcohol does not cause sexual assault.*

Here are some other myths about rape:

MYTH: Perpetrators choose their targets based on how they're dressed.

REALITY: Perpetrators choose people who are vulnerable and accessible to them, not based on how they dress or look. Rape is an expression of power and control.

MYTH: Rape that occurs on a date or in an intimate relationship isn't as serious as stranger rape.

REALITY: Non-stranger rape ("acquaintance rape" or "date rape") is just as traumatic as stranger rape—if not more so. Rape by stranger, partner, acquaintance, or "friend" is just that, rape.

MYTH: If we're both drunk, it's not rape.
REALITY: It is up to the initiator of sexual activity (or whoever tries to introduce a new sex act) to ensure that consent is present. Being drunk isn't an excuse, legally or morally, for actions amounting to sexual assault.

MYTH: Rape jokes, bragging about sexual conquests, and similar acts are just "locker room talk" and harmless.
REALITY: Bystander intervention, which we'll cover in greater detail later in this chapter, is not only about helping someone who's physically vulnerable in the moment. It's also about acting and intervening when you hear someone who objectifies others (which means to treat someone as a mere object of sexual desire), blames victim-survivors of sexual assault, trivializes rape, is sexist, or is oppressive in some other way. These acts are not harmless; research has shown that when members of peer groups hold rape-supportive attitudes, they can be less likely to intervene as bystanders and to report incidents of sexual assault, and are more likely to believe in rape myths.

MYTH: If someone is raped when they're drunk, they're partly to blame.
REALITY: Being drunk means you consented to one thing—to drink alcohol. Someone vulnerable isn't to blame for the wrongful acts of another. All people have the right to be safe from sexual assault, whether or not they're intoxicated. Blaming the assault on the victim-survivor is called "victim blaming."

> **Being drunk isn't an excuse, legally or morally, for actions amounting to sexual assault.**

Victim blaming happens when the victim of a crime or any wrongful act—rather than the perpetrator—is blamed in whole or in part for the harm that befalls them.

What Is Sexual Consent?

> Because there is no one uniform definition of sexual consent, it is most simply defined as knowingly agreeing to sexual activity based on a *free* choice.

Sexual consent means that no one is participating in sexual activity because they're feeling pressured, tricked, coerced, intimidated, or manipulated. An important way to make sure that you have consent from your prospective partner is to be certain they are *enthusiastic* about their decision to engage in sexual activity with you. To be clear, there are times when someone might be feeling a bit anxious about trying certain sexual activities but is still enthusiastic about trying them.

Contrary to what you may have been told, obtaining your partner's consent is not just a technicality to get out of the way prior to beginning sexual activity. Consent must continue *throughout* an entire sexual encounter and can be withdrawn *at any point* by either party—even once people are naked! So getting a yes from your partner in the heat of the moment isn't a blanket statement to keep going because they can always change their mind. At its core, consent is about treating a partner like an equal.

What Is Rape Culture?

"Rape culture" involves an atmosphere that normalizes sexualized violence and sexual coercion against women and other victim-survivors and blames them for it. Some examples of rape culture include:

- blaming the victim-survivor for inviting rape ("She was asking for it")
- slut or sex shaming ("She had sex with Adam? What a slut!")
- sexist or rape jokes, wisecracks, and threats ("I got raped by the salesperson when I bought my car")

The list goes on and on, but I hope you get the picture.

What can you do to combat rape culture? Here are just a few things:

Also, consenting to certain sexual activity on one occasion doesn't mean that your partner is okay with it or any other activity at another time; **a past relationship does not constitute consent.**

There are two types of consent: (1) implied consent and (2) affirmative consent.

Implied consent is consent that is not asked for verbally but implied by a person's actions or body language in response to the sexual activity. Implied consent relies on a "no means no" philosophy—meaning that unless someone says "No," "Stop," or something similar, sexual activity can be pursued. One significant problem with implied consent is that body language may not be reliable—particularly if participants are intoxicated.

I spoke about this with Dr. Kami Kosenko, an associate professor in the Department of Communication at North Carolina State University. She has spent much of her academic career studying sexual communication and tells me what her research (and that of others) has made clear: "Humans are surprisingly bad at interpreting nonverbal behavior, particularly when intoxicated."

Some believe that passivity and silence mean it's okay to proceed with a sexual interaction. In other words, the belief that the absence of a no means there is consent. Dr. Kosenko says, "This belief can be mistaken and dangerous since there are many situations in which a person may not verbally express a lack of consent but does not want the interaction."

- Don't objectify women or speak in a degrading way about them. For example, women are not a temperature, as in "She's so hot."
- If you hear someone tell a rape or sexist joke or otherwise trivialize rape, don't laugh—because it's not funny. If it's physically safe for you and you can muster the courage, speak up. An effective way to call out a joke can be to act like you don't get it and ask the person who told the joke to explain why it's funny. This can be a low-risk way to confront the behavior.
- Don't make sexual comments or obscene or sexual gestures to anyone, unless they are explicitly consensual and welcomed.
- Don't believe in rape myths or think someone is morally suspect because the person enjoys sex.

For example, if someone believes that they'll be physically harmed if they resist an advance, they may not indicate a verbal lack of consent like no. Or if the initiator of the sexual encounter uses force—by words *or* actions—the target may freeze and be too scared to say or do anything.

Another situation in which a person may feel unsafe or too scared or intimidated to rebuff a sexual advance can involve a significant imbalance of power between the individuals, such as between a teacher and a student or between an employer and an employee. A student or employee may not feel that they can decline these advances without possible retaliation, such as being unfairly disciplined or fired, getting a lower grade in a class, not receiving a well-deserved promotion, and so on. In fact, consent can be so difficult to determine when these and similar power differential dynamics are present that in some states it is against the law for a teacher to have sexual relations with a student, even one who is an adult. It may also be prohibited by school policy.

Affirmative consent occurs when a prospective partner is asked if they are okay with proceeding before each step of a sexual interaction. This is easily the best way to know that sexual consent is always present. We slow things down a bit and respect our prospective partner's answers and boundaries at all times. Affirmative consent is a great stepping-stone to positive, healthy sexual relationships.

Only a clear, authentic yes (or its functional equivalent such as "For sure!") makes it okay to proceed. The yes can be verbalized—which is always best—but could be nonverbal like a clear nod of the head or your prospective partner starting the very act you asked if they wanted to do.

Whether verbal or nonverbal, though, the most important thing is to make sure that you and your partner unequivocally communicate enthusiasm and willingness to participate in sexual activity. While we're at it, there's yes and then there's YES!—the latter being what you're looking for. **With affirmative consent, "yes means yes," and if it's not yes, then it's no.**

For decades, Connie Kirkland has worked at universities in sexual violence prevention. Countless times, she has taught, supported, and led investigations involving young adults related to sexual assault, dating violence, stalking, and other forms of sexual violence. There's not a lot that Kirkland hasn't seen.

She understands how "it can be very intimidating for young people especially to talk about sex out loud. If you're going to do something as intimate as have sex or have some kind of sexual activity, you should be able to talk about it together." Kirkland's point is a good one because so many people, of all ages, are more comfortable having sex than talking about it.

Kirkland also brings up another benefit of affirmative consent: "Most people love to hear that because it shows respect. It's an endearing quality by not just acting on your impulses but making the decision to ask. Affirmative consent not only helps individuals avoid situations that could lead to sexual violence but contributes to sexual and relationship satisfaction."

The Red Zone

The Department of Justice has identified the beginning of the fall semester through November as the stretch of time when college students face the greatest risk of being sexually assaulted (at least statistically). In fact, some studies have shown that more than 50 percent of sexual assaults in college occur during this stretch of time that has become known as the "Red Zone." The majority of these assaults occur between midnight and 6 a.m. on Saturday and Sunday mornings. With little drinking experience and few friends to watch out for them, freshmen can be particularly vulnerable to assault.

Why Don't More Victim-Survivors of Sexual Assault Come Forward?

Most victim-survivors of sexual assault do not report it. As a result, it is the most underreported crime. Here are just some of the reasons victim-survivors may not report a sexual assault:

- They fear that they won't be believed and will be the ones investigated rather than the accused.
- They don't want family or friends to know.
- They don't want to suffer additional pain and personal embarrassment by having to relay a traumatic experience.
- Even when a rape has occurred, some victim-survivors still don't consider it "serious enough."
- There's an outdated belief of some that "good women" and "real men" don't get raped. This causes victim-survivors to fear that they will be blamed (a form of revictimization). This blaming can sound like:
  - » "What were you wearing at the time?"
  - » "How much were you drinking?"
  - » "Why did you go up to their room?"
  - » "Why didn't you fight them off?"
- The belief that nothing will happen if they come forward.
- The social stigma that often and unfairly comes with being a victim-survivor of sexual assault. This can be particularly true for males, who may feel that their masculinity will be questioned after being assaulted by another male or a female.

Tips for Safer Sexual Conduct

Let's build on the foundation of what we've covered by going over some practical ways to make sure you've got authentic, enthusiastic consent for all of your sexual interactions and how, if needed, you might provide a helping hand to someone vulnerable to being sexual assaulted. Please remember, again, that violent behavior is always the responsibility of the person who perpetrates it, not the victim-survivor.

Ways to Tell You've Got Consent

It's easy to know when affirmative consent is present: permission is asked for at each step of the way and an answer to the question is obtained by listening, looking, or feeling how the other person reacts.

Whatever language you choose should be respectful and appropriate under the circumstances of the relationship, and how one person asks can be very different from how someone else does. Whether it's formal, such as "Are you giving me consent to do this?," or more casual, as shown in some of the examples below, use language that feels right to you.

> **How one person asks for consent can be very different from how someone else does. Use language that feels right to you.**

Here are some ways you might ask:

- "I'd like to _____. Is that okay with you?"
- "Is it cool if we _____?"
- "Do you like _____?"
- "Can we try _____?"
- "I love what we did last time. Want to do it again?"
- "How do you feel about _____?"
- "Would you like it if I _____?"

Sex Discrimination on Campus

Title IX of the Education Amendments Act of 1972 is a federal civil rights law that prohibits sex discrimination at all K–12 public schools and all public and private colleges and universities that receive federal funding. The purpose is to ensure that all students have equal access to an education free of sexual discrimination, and schools must be proactive in ensuring that this is the case. Sexual assault is considered a form of sexual discrimination. For more information, see the next chapter on sexual harassment.

How to Tell When There's No Consent

If you are unsure about whether you've got consent, you don't. Period. Full stop. The absence of no or some other protestation does not mean yes, nor is it the beginning of a negotiation. If someone says maybe, that too doesn't mean yes. Maybe always means no. Even in an established sexual relationship, a maybe or other unclear answer means it's time to stop.

In addition, just because someone is sexually interested, perhaps even aroused by someone else, doesn't mean the person wants to engage in sexual activity. The individual may be interested in some sex acts, like kissing or touching over clothes, but not others. Communication is key.

When consent is *not* present, a would-be sexual partner is likely to say any of the following or similar statements:

- "No."
- "Stop."
- "Maybe." (Remember, maybe always means no.)
- "Let's just cuddle."
- "I'm not sure."
- "Get off of me."
- "I just want to be friends."
- "I don't like that."
- "Can we just chill?"
- "I'm not really down."

Also, a sign that you might not have consent is your would-be partner's silence (many sexual interactions are not silent—particularly when a partner is enthusiastic about it).

Body language is another way to tell when consent may not be present. It includes what we see, feel, or hear from our would-be partner, such as:

- being rigid and/or not responding to sexual advances
- pulling away or pushing someone off
- trying to keep their clothes on
- squirming
- looking scared
- crying
- being drunk or under the influence of any drug

Sexual Coercion: When Yes Doesn't Mean Yes

Sexual assault can occur by physical force, fear, or coercion. Physical force or fear of the threat of physical force is a concept that should be pretty simple to understand. Coercion, on the other hand, is a bit more complex. As mentioned earlier, it's the sexually aggressive behavior of trying to get someone to engage in sexual activities that you know they aren't interested in doing. When sexual activity is coerced, consent is not present. Submission is not consent.

> **When sexual activity is coerced, consent is not present. Submission is not consent.**

Coercive sexual behavior includes:

- Social coercion: "You're a prude" or "I bought you dinner, so . . ."
- Intimidation: punching a wall when someone rebuffs your sexual advances
- Emotional coercion: "If you really loved me . . ." or "I'll leave you if you don't have sex with me."
- Threatening: "I'll spread false rumors about you if you don't . . ." or to "out" someone who's LGBTQ—"I'll tell everyone if you don't . . ."
- Intoxicated coercion: which involves the use of drugs or alcohol to lower the target's inhibitions: "Have another drink. It'll relax you."
- Coercion by authority: involves someone in a position of power over you, such as a boss or teacher: "If you want the work schedule you requested, you should sleep with me."

When Consent Cannot Be Given or Obtained

Some people cannot lawfully provide sexual consent—even if they say yes. For instance, someone who doesn't have the mental capacity for sexual decision-making cannot give consent. This includes people with certain disabilities or those incapacitated from alcohol or drugs, as further explained below.

Also, you must be a minimum of 16, 17, or 18 years old, depending on the state you live in, to legally consent to sexual activity. Two 16-year-olds may want to have sex, but if the age of consent in their state is 17 or 18, they cannot by law. By way of example, if the age of sexual consent in your state is 18, Sara and Billy, two 17-year-olds in a sexual relationship, are breaking the law because they are both incapable of giving consent.

However, the moment Sara, the older of the two, reaches adulthood, continuing her sexual relationship with Billy becomes a far more serious crime in the eyes of the law called statutory rape (sexual activity between an adult and someone under the age of sexual consent). Although Billy wants to give consent to Sara, he cannot give what he does not have the power to give by law. As a result, Sara, an adult, can, in the most extreme circumstances, be arrested, prosecuted, and sent to jail and ordered to register as a sex offender if she has sexual relations with Billy. (It is unlikely that this type of crime will draw the attention or interest of the police. However, it may if a parent makes a complaint to law enforcement.)

Because there's a difference between an older teen under the age of consent having sex with a young adult and adults who prey on teens, some states have passed what have come to be referred to as "Romeo and Juliet laws," named after Shakespeare's tragic teen lovers. These close-in-age exemptions apply to late adolescents and emerging adults, the specifics of which vary by the jurisdictions that have these laws. They generally provide that consensual acts between a person who's under the age of consent with someone their age or who's slightly older are not criminal offenses, or the severity of the penalties and punishment is lessened for such offenses. Unfairly, many Romeo and Juliet laws apply only to heterosexual relationships.

Another scenario where consent *cannot* be given is when someone is drunk (or under the influence of any drug). I get loads of questions from young people and adults asking for clarity about when it's okay to have sexual relations with someone if drinking is involved. These are not easy questions to answer.

The first thing I like to mention is that it is *always* a "best practice" not to have sexual relations if prospective participants have been drinking at all or using any other drugs. However, I'm just uncertain how practical that advice is. Drinking before sexual experimentation or interactions is not unusual, and it is certainly possible to have positive, consensual sexual experiences after some amount of drinking.

Much of the confusion is centered on when someone goes from drinking to becoming drunk and therefore is unable to consent to sexual activity. Here are three things I believe may bring some clarity:

1. If you ever find yourself making an assessment of someone to determine whether they're drunk and unable to have consensual sexual relations, the answer is as clear as day: they cannot. The mere questioning of their level of intoxication is your answer. Follow up on another, sober day. Please also remember that just because you haven't seen someone drinking, it doesn't mean they haven't been—some people start drinking before they head out to a party or other event (also known as "pregaming").

2. Usually it's pretty easy to tell whether someone is drunk when we pay attention to how they look, behave, and talk. While not an exhaustive list, some of the signs that someone is drunk (or otherwise highly intoxicated) can include:

   • an inability to communicate clearly

   • failure to completely understand what is going on

   • slurred speech

   • swaying, staggering, or stumbling

   • noticeable changes in behavior such as lowered inhibitions or becoming unusually aggressive

   • confusion

   • inability to be coherent

   • nodding off

   • passing out

   • crying or feeling sad

These and other similar signs are likely to mean that someone is drunk or otherwise too intoxicated and cannot lawfully give
consent.

3. I suspect you know not to drive with someone who's drunk. I take
    this a step further: don't have sexual relations with anyone you
    think *might* be too intoxicated to get behind the wheel of a car (or
    other moving vehicle). When we suspect, or know, that someone
    shouldn't or couldn't lawfully drive, for everyone's sake, *never* pro-
    ceed with any sexual activity. More succinctly, if you wouldn't drive
    with them, don't hook up with them.

I spoke with Ellen Friedrichs, a health and sexuality educator who
works extensively with teens and is the author of *Good Sexual Citizenship:
How to Create a (Sexually) Safer World*, about my advice here. She, like many
others working in this field whom I spoke with, agreed with it. However,

The Myth of False Rape Accusations

Another common rape myth is that many claims are false
accusations. Of course, there are false accusations; the myth is that
they are common.

At my sexual consent workshops, I often get asked by parents
of sons and by young men, "How do we prevent false rape
accusations?" I typically respond by explaining that research
studies make clear that rape is the least reported crime. So an
accusation, true or false, is unlikely. When someone does report
a sexual assault, false claims are no more frequent than the false
reporting of all other crimes. (Yet unlike the reporting of other
crimes such as a mugging, reporting sexual assault can lead to
great scrutiny and skepticism of the victim-survivor's recounting of
the underlying events.) For many, this response eases their concern
about false accusations. Other times, it does not.

Alec Rose is an attorney who has spent much of his career
specializing in legal cases involving sexual assault and gender
discrimination in schools. I spoke with him about this myth and
how commonly I get questions about false rape accusations.

she wisely adds, "We don't excuse drunk driving because someone has been drinking. Rather, we treat it as a serious crime. Overall, you don't need to use what you think is or isn't legal as a guide. Use what you think is morally right."

Taking a Stand: Bystander Intervention

Many times, the course of events leading to a sexual assault involves three people: the victim-survivor, the perpetrator, and the bystander. Yet in one recent comprehensive university study, only 23 percent of students who witnessed a drunk person heading for a sexual encounter intervened in some way. We must do better.

When we're around other people and see or hear something that seems wrong, we may not take action because we convince ourselves that someone else will. This is called the bystander effect: a phenomenon in which

---

Rose responded by saying, "I've been doing this job for decades— I've seen it all. It's very unlikely someone would be falsely accused if they do two things." Here's what he told me:

1. Don't have hookups when you or someone you want to have sex with has been drinking any amount of alcohol—even if they're not intoxicated. Around 90 percent of Rose's sexual assault cases involve the consumption of alcohol by the victim-survivor, perpetrator, or both.

2. Rose also advises to "be interactive with your partner, check in with them, and guide yourself on whether or not they're reacting and how they're reacting. Pay attention to how they respond." In other words, practice affirmative consent throughout all intimate activity.

I've incorporated the two points mentioned above in my response to questions about false accusations. My more comprehensive answer seems to alleviate much of the concern some parents and young men are feeling.

the more people who are present, the less likely it is that someone will help a target or victim.

When you see something that isn't right, trust your instincts and don't ignore the situation, especially if others aren't doing something to help. One courageous person speaking up or taking action makes it much easier for others to join in. Remember, courage inspires courage.

There is no one-size-fits-all to bystander intervention, and different circumstances may call for different approaches. The most important thing to remember is that when you see something that you know isn't right and if it's physically safe for you (and the potential target), do your best to help.

Connie Kirkland, introduced earlier in this chapter, says, "Just a few words can prevent sexual violence. The reality is that students are knowledgeable about things that are going on in their group, their party, their room, or wherever and could do something to stop someone from being harmed. They often don't know that they have that ability, but they do."

Here are four ways to help prevent sexual violence:

1. **Directly intervene.** Anyone can directly insert themselves in the moment to help prevent a problematic situation from starting or continuing. One method is to say something to one or both of the parties about the circumstances and why things don't seem right. This *entirely verbal technique* is especially useful when the bystander knows either the potential target or perpetrator.

   Ellen Friedrichs gives some good advice here: "So often we doubt what we are seeing, or we are so used to problematic behaviors that we don't see the need for intervention. Simply interrupting a situation by asking a potential victim whether they are okay can make a world of difference before a culminating event. A lot of people assume that bystander intervention means pulling an attacker off a victim. That rarely happens. What is most effective is typically preventing an assault during the lead-up."

   She continues: "Many people doubt themselves, so get others on board for backup. You can say all sorts of things, like 'Hey, does that look okay to you?' or 'Maybe we should say something together.' Remember, there's safety in numbers and you probably don't have to do this alone."

2. **Delegate.** This is when you get someone to assist you with an intervention or get them to do it because they're better situated to do so, such as a parent or other trusted adult, the person who's hosting or "in charge" at the location, someone you perceive as having more social standing than you, or perhaps the police who just showed up at the front door. This strategy allows someone to help without ever directly interacting with the potential perpetrator.

3. **Distract.** You can use a distraction technique to change the focus of a potential perpetrator or victim. This strategy can involve something as simple as starting an unrelated conversation with either of them. Distraction can be a good technique if the direct approach might be physically harmful to the target or the bystander.

   This is one of the techniques that Kirkland likes best. "You can go up to someone who you think is uncomfortable and say something like, 'Aren't you in my math class? I don't remember the homework. Do you know what it is?' It may sound corny, but it stops whatever is happening in that moment and gives the person the opportunity to leave. You may not be able to stop something forever, but you can stop it in the moment."

   After a recent school workshop I held on this topic, a student came up to me and told me that he used this technique effectively when his friends were "really wasted" and started to stumble upstairs to a bedroom. He told one of them a white lie: someone was breaking into his car. This got his friend distracted, and he and the other person "never hooked up."

4. **Delay.** If you aren't sure that intervention is warranted at that time, you can monitor the situation and intervene at a later stage, if necessary.

When none of these can be accomplished without putting yourself in harm's way, consider calling the police or telling a trusted adult as soon as possible. Please also remember these key points:

- Unless it's certain that immediate help is needed, check in with the person to see whether they want and/or need help. Sometimes the assistance will be appreciated, while other times it's not needed.

Moreover, the intervention shouldn't take agency away from the person who may be at risk of being assaulted. One of the most effective ways to do this is by being low-key and keeping the potential intervention, regardless of the method employed, fairly covert to avoid unnecessarily escalating the situation. Remember, intervention isn't about rescuing someone but rather about standing up for people who are vulnerable.

Bystander Intervention in Action

One evening, Stanford University graduate students Carl-Fredrik Arndt and Peter Jonsson were riding their bikes near a fraternity house when they saw a man on top of a half-naked woman behind a dumpster. That woman, Chanel Miller (self-identified), didn't appear to be moving at all, but the male on top of her was moving quite a bit. They knew something was wrong and asked the man on top of her, "What the hell are you doing?" The man then started to run away.

Not willing to watch someone get away with what looked like a sexual assault, Carl and Peter ran after the attacker, a freshman school athlete, tackled him, and pinned him down until authorities arrived. Eventually, the attacker was charged with and convicted of three counts of sexual assault.

At the trial of her attacker, Miller read a victim impact statement in court that told the man who assaulted her, "You took away my worth, my privacy, my energy, my time, my safety, my intimacy, my confidence, my own voice, until today." She went on to thank "the two men who saved me, who I have yet to meet. I sleep with two bicycles that I drew taped above my bed to remind myself there are heroes in this story. That we are looking out for one another. To have known all of these people, to have felt their protection and love, is something I will never forget."

Carl-Fredrik and Peter didn't know Chanel Miller, but they stepped in to protect someone who was being attacked because she was vulnerable. I'm not suggesting that you go around tackling people, but if it's physically safe, we all have an important role to play in stopping sexual assault.

- Angrily confronting a perpetrator can be bad for the intervener and the potential target.
- Look for warning signs of trouble and be prepared to intervene as early as possible. Some situations may look suspicious at first but end up being fine—it's better to find that out early than miss a chance to help someone in need. If a potential target is pulled aside by an intervener and it turns out they don't need help, most people will just be thankful that someone was looking out for them. In addition, if a would-be perpetrator sees that their target has people looking out for them, the person may choose to avoid a potential confrontation.

Again, perpetrators of sexual assault, statistically speaking, are unlikely to be strangers lurking in the shadows, armed with a gun or a knife. Instead, the would-be perpetrator might be well known, well liked, out in full view, with, perhaps, the only "weapon" in their possession being a cocktail or beer in hand. As we all keep a watchful eye out for—rather than turning a blind one to—people who are vulnerable to sexual assault, keep in mind that friends, peers, and people we care about are capable of being victimized and, at times, may be even capable of victimizing someone else.

Sexual Assault of Males

Male victim-survivors of sexual assault can have the same feelings and reactions as female victim-survivors, but often face increased pressure and challenges because of social norms about what it means to be masculine. These challenges can keep them from coming forward or seeking help.

Males are most often assaulted by another male but also by females. When I was in my early twenties, I was sexually assaulted by a woman I had been dating and had just broken up with. I kept this to myself over the years and disclosed it to only a small handful of people I was close to.

When I did share what happened that night, I always got the same reaction: laughter followed by remarks such as "How can a woman assault a man?" and "If you got an erection, you weren't assaulted." There are probably many reasons I have rarely disclosed what happened to me, but one of them was certainly this sort of reaction. Thankfully, the occurrence wasn't life altering for me. Such is not the case for many victim-survivors as the emotional damage of sexual assault doesn't end once the assault is over.

What my friends and many others do not understand is that when a man is made to penetrate another person, male or female, an erection or ejaculation does not mean it was consensual. These are normal physiological responses to stimulus that do not indicate that the man wanted, invited, or enjoyed the assault. The statistic quoted earlier warrants repeating here: conservatively, one in every thirty-three men has experienced an attempted or completed rape in his lifetime.

As I was wrapping up my last interview with attorney Alec Rose, I asked him if there was anything that I didn't ask that he wanted to mention. To my surprise, Rose responded, "We haven't discussed that males can be victims of sexual assault too. There are many people that think that a man can't be raped by a woman and when you tell them about it, they just laugh."

I was floored by his comment because just a few days earlier, for the first time after *many* previous drafts of this chapter, I decided to include my own experience. He continued, "Young men shouldn't assume that it can't happen to them, be it by another man or a woman. If it does happen, they should feel that they have a right to seek help. If it happens to one of their friends, they should support them. Making jokes about it is extremely detrimental to young men that this has happened to."

Things You Could Do for Victim-Survivors of Sexual Assault

It can be very difficult for victim-survivors to tell others about a sexual assault. If someone confides in you, here are some ways to be there for them:

- Be a good listener and don't question their story.
- Let them know it isn't their fault.
- Respect their privacy and confidentiality.
- Help empower them by not telling them what to do.
- Assist them in exploring and thinking through their options, like finding resources (see the end of this chapter).

It may not be easy to know what to say when someone tells you they've been sexually assaulted. **The most important thing is to believe them.**

A NOTE TO ANYONE WHO MIGHT BE A VICTIM-SURVIVOR: If you have or think you may have been sexually assaulted, please consider seeking support from a service organization (some are listed at the end of this chapter) and/or Find Your Person (see the "Find Your Person, Whoever That May Be" section in the Introduction).

What Three Things in This Chapter Matter Most to You?

We all take away different lessons from reading the information presented in this chapter. What resonates with one person may not be meaningful to another and vice versa. I certainly hope that you've learned a heck of a lot more than three things in this chapter, but if three things were all you learned, I still consider it a win. Even a single piece of information could be invaluable if it was just what you or someone you're with needs in a critical moment.

With the information from this chapter fresh in your mind, please take a few moments to write below the three things that you consider the most important.

1. _____

_____

2. _____

_____

3. _____

_____

What Would You Do if It Happened to You?

Your friend Pam's parents are out of town. She decides to host a big party where there is underage drug and alcohol use. After the party has been going a few hours, your friends, Wallace and Rebecca, who have both been drinking heavily, seem really drunk. As far as you know they have always just been friends, so you're surprised to see them starting to kiss each other as they dance. Soon, they start walking hand in hand to the bedrooms upstairs.

Do you think you should intervene? Why or why not?

Some Thoughts about "What Would You Do if It Happened to You?"

If you believe you wouldn't intervene, you should ask yourself why not? Do you think it's just not your problem? None of your business? Would you be scared of a physical confrontation? If any of the above is true, perhaps you can think of another way to intervene that would make you more comfortable and keep you safe.

Intervening in a situation like this or anything similar can be difficult and uncomfortable. It can be hard to confront a stranger, perhaps even harder a friend. If you're scared for your personal safety in any situation, you may choose not to intervene directly but may be able to intervene safely by delegating, distracting, and/or delaying. If needed, you can also contact the police or a trusted adult (perhaps anonymously).

Final Thoughts

Sexual assault happens with disturbing frequency, particularly for young people, and the impact on victim-survivors can be devastating and life altering. I hope you'll agree that understanding sexual consent is of paramount importance.

Arming ourselves with information about what is expected of us and what we can expect of others when it comes to our sexual interactions can be empowering. The essence of this empowerment is that you *always* have the right to decide for yourself, without pressure, if you want to engage in or continue with a sexual interaction.

I know that very few if any readers of this book would ever sexually assault anyone. You are all part of the solution, not the problem, and a large part of the solution is to keep a watchful eye out for one another, whether a friend, acquaintance, loved one, or anyone else.

Where Can I Get More Information?

This chapter contains the essentials of sexual assault and consent. For those who want to know more and dig deeper into this topic, a Google search is a good place to start and will deliver numerous resources, some with valuable information.

There are agencies and service organizations whose mission is to provide meaningful support for anyone in need of information and resources related to sexual assault. You can contact them about a specific concern you have for yourself, a friend, a loved one, or even a stranger. Often, if desired, you can stay anonymous. The ones below are a good place to start:

- Rape, Abuse & Incest National Network (RAINN)
    - » the nation's largest anti-sexual violence organization
    - » www.rainn.org
- National Human Trafficking Hotline
    - » connects victims and survivors of sex and labor trafficking with services and support
    - » 888-373-7888
    - » text: HELP to 233733
    - » www.humantraffickinghotline.org
- National Sexual Assault Hotline
    - » connects callers with a trained staff member from a sexual assault service provider in your area
    - » 800-656-HOPE (4673)
- National Sexual Violence Resource Center
    - » leading nonprofit in providing information and tools to prevent and respond to sexual violence
    - » www.nsvrc.org

- National Helpline for Men Who Were Sexually Abused or Assaulted
    - » helps men who have unwanted or abusive sexual experiences live healthier, happier lives
    - » www.1in6.org/helpline

NOTE TO THE READER: If you are a minor and make a complaint about sexual assault to certain people who work with children in their professional capacity, such as a teacher, they may be a "mandatory reporter." This means they are required to disclose suspected abuse or neglect of minors to law enforcement or child protective services.

Sexual Assault and Consent Quiz

Test your understanding of the importance of sexual assault and consent by taking this quiz. Hopefully, you'll get all of the answers correct because a single mistake could have real-world consequences if that answer contained the information you needed to stay safe.

Instructions: select the best answer from the available choices. Answers can be found in the back of the book.

1. Someone has to say "no," "stop," or something equivalent in order for it to be sexual assault.
   A. True
   B. False

2. Affirmative sexual consent is when you _____ permission to engage in a sexual act from beginning to the end.
   A. Imply that you have.
   B. Plead for.
   C. Assume that you have, if the facts warrant.
   D. Ask for and receive.

3. Adrian and Reese have had consensual sex numerous times. One evening, Adrian drinks way too much alcohol and passes out in Reese's apartment. Reese then has sex with Adrian. Has Reese sexually assaulted Adrian?

   A. Maybe. It depends on whether Adrian was planning to have sex with Reese that night.
   B. No. Adrian regularly has sex with Reese and there's no objective reason to think that they wouldn't be having sex again that night.
   C. Yes. Reese has committed sexual assault but only if Adrian remembers any portion of the sex.
   D. Yes. Adrian was unable to give consent to Reese for sex.

4. The "80" from the 80/60/50 rule relates to:

   A. Alcohol
   B. Location
   C. Someone you know.
   D. Age of consent.

5. If a woman dresses provocatively, dances sexually, drinks too much alcohol, and then gets sexually assaulted, she's (at least) partly to blame.

   A. True
   B. False

6. Pat and Billie have been casually dating and engaging in mutually enjoyable sexual activity every weekend for the past six months. In the midst of one of these encounters, Pat isn't feeling well and wants Billie to stop. Billie ignores Pat's requests for thirty seconds and then stops. Has Billie sexually assaulted Pat?

   A. No, because Pat had already consented to sexual activity with Billie and consent cannot be revoked once the participants are naked.
   B. Yes, because either party, at any point, can withdraw consent during a sexual encounter.
   C. No, because Billie stopped very close in time to Pat's request to stop and Billie may not have even heard it.
   D. No, if Pat and Billie are the same sex, because sexual assault can occur only between people of the opposite sex.

7. If, during a sexual interaction, you're not entirely sure you've got consent, you should:
    A. Slow things down a bit while you figure it out as quickly as possible.
    B. Keep going so long as you're objectively unsure.
    C. Stop
    D. Keep going, carefully, until you hear a no or something comparable.

8. Females between 16 and 19 years old are four times more likely than any other age group to be victims of sexual assault.
    A. True
    B. False

9. The drug referenced in the 80/60/50 rule is _____.
    A. GHB
    B. Marijuana
    C. Alcohol
    D. Barbiturates

10. If someone who's highly intoxicated wants to have sex with you, you should:
    A. Question them, slowly, to make sure that they're absolutely sure.
    B. Shoot a short video of them agreeing to in case they later change their mind.
    C. Ask them for consent.
    D. Refuse because they cannot provide you with consent.

CHAPTER 5

Sexual Harassment:
Daily Life for Many Students

KEY TAKEAWAYS

- Sexual harassment falls into three categories: physical, verbal (which can also be written), and visual. Both verbal and visual can also be done digitally.

- Anyone of any gender or gender identity can harass or be harassed.

- Title IX, a federal law that prohibits sexual harassment (and all other forms of sexual discrimination), governs all K–12 schools and colleges and universities that accept federal funding.

- Being a target of sexual harassment, or sometimes even witnessing it, can cause emotional harm.

- Many harassers don't realize the harm in their actions; if the target is able to do so, telling the harasser to stop can be effective.

Chapter Highlights

Setting the Stage

When many of us think about sexual harassment, adults in the workplace often come to mind. Yet sexual harassment at work is rarely the first time people have been the targets, perpetrators, or witnesses to it. Sexual harassment often begins in middle school, where almost all students will witness harassment; continues into high school, where 48 percent of students are harassed; perpetuates itself in college, where a majority of students experience harassment; and finally makes its way into the workforce.

School-based sexual harassment not only starts early on in our school careers but typically happens out in the open on full display to others. It's hardly surprising that many young people as well as adults have come to believe that behavior amounting to sexual harassment is a normal part of the school environment. This normalizing of the behavior (contributed to greatly by movies, TV, our culture, etc.) can lead people to believe that sexual harassment is not worthy of our outrage and can make witnesses less likely to intervene.

Sexual harassment is unwelcome sexual activity—verbal, visual, or physical. Both verbal and visual conduct can be done in writing or digitally. **Unwelcomed sexual activity is determined by the recipient of the behavior.** It is worth noting that definitions of sexual harassment vary by federal and state law and by school or school district.

I spend lots of time at schools talking with students about sexual harassment prevention. As they learn about what types of acts can amount to harassment, I can see the light bulb turn on when they better understand why this behavior can create an unhealthy school environment and hurt its targets—sometimes deeply.

One of the most effective ways to stop sexual harassment is by learning early on what it is, what it isn't, and how we can help stop it when it occurs in our presence. Similar to learning about sexual consent as we did in the last chapter, doing so helps us prevent this type of sexual violence in our relationships, friendships, peer groups, and school community.

What You'll Learn in this Chapter

We'll kick things off by explaining what sexual harassment looks and sounds like, the impact on its targets, and some damaging myths that can minimize and excuse the behavior. We'll then transition to various ways you might be able to end the harassment if you're targeted and how you can safely intervene when you witness harassment.

We've got some important ground to cover here, so let's get to it.

What Acts Constitute Sexual Harassment?

Here are some examples of acts that could amount to one of the different forms of sexual harassment:

Physical harassment includes any *unwelcomed* sexual touching such as butt smacking, intentionally brushing up against someone, invading someone's personal space, massaging, grabbing, pinching, and fondling. It can also include stalking and cyberstalking, which are more fully discussed in chapter 7.

Verbal (and written) harassment includes *unwelcomed*, inappropriate sexual comments on someone's appearance or body, whistling or catcalling, dirty or sexist jokes, intrusive sexual questions, "gender policing" (students are ridiculed for behavior outside of normative gender roles), "slut shaming" (a student is gossiped about as being sexually active or promiscuous), and unwanted sexual communications through phone calls, texts, emails, or social media comments.

Visual harassment includes the *unwelcomed* exposing of oneself (in person or digitally), creating/forwarding/displaying nonconsensual sexually explicit images or objects online or in person, making obscene gestures, or leering and staring.

To bring further clarity to acts that may amount to sexual harassment, below are some "real-life" examples:

- Maurice takes a picture of his genitals and texts it to Martina—who didn't ask for the picture.
- Beth writes on the girls' bathroom stall that her classmate Yoko is a "slut."
- Raleigh and Armani snap Jessica's bra strap as she's passing by the school lockers.
- Joey's classmates taunt him because in PE class he signs up for jazzercise instead of weightlifting.
- Rami posts sexual comments on Charlie's social media and catcalls her in real life.
- Paula walks behind Alejandro in the school cafeteria and grabs his butt.
- Yung is failing math and his teacher offers to give him an A for a nude massage.

- Oakley likes to tell jokes about blond girls not being smart.
- Coach John tells one of his wrestlers to "Man up."

Anyone of Any Gender or Gender Identity Can Harass or Be Harassed

Sexual harassment is often mistakenly believed to be limited to boys harassing girls. It's not. **A person of *any* gender identity who engages in unwanted sexual speech or behavior with someone of *any* gender identity, even the same gender as the perpetrator, is committing sexual harassment.** Also, persons who identify as nonbinary, for example, trans or asexual, can also perpetrate or be victims of harassment.

In the school environment, harassment can be carried out by students, school employees, and nonemployee third parties such as guest speakers. Perpetrators and targets can be anyone and of any

To avoid offending, I'll let the reader use their imagination as to what's being said in these four scenarios. I think you get the gist of it. The images look like bullying because sexual harassment is sexualized bullying.

race, socioeconomic status, or sexual identity. However, those who identify or are perceived as LGBTQ are targeted at even higher rates than their heterosexual peers.

Damaging Myths about Sexual Harassment

There are plenty of myths about sexual harassment. These misperceptions perpetuate falsehoods that further damage targets of sexual harassment. Let's clear some of these up.

MYTH: It's just flirting.
REALITY: Flirting and sexual harassment are nowhere near the same. Flirting is activity that both people choose to participate in based on mutual interest, and it feels good. Conversely, harassment is one-sided and makes someone feel threatened, uncomfortable, or unsafe. If you think that you are flirting with someone but they do not respond the way you want them to, STOP!

MYTH: People ask to be sexually harassed by the way they dress.
REALITY: Sexual harassment is not caused by the physical characteristics of the target or how they dress. People are harassed regardless of their appearance. As we covered in the last chapter, this is called "victim blaming."

MYTH: Most sexual harassment claims are made up.
REALITY: The least common response to sexual harassment is reporting it! Females rarely report harassment at work or school. Males do so even less frequently because of concerns about social stigma and cultural pressures not to identify themselves as the targets of unwanted sexual attention.

MYTH: I can't complain about the harassment because I've laughed at my harasser's acts in the past.
REALITY: The fact that you may have laughed or even flirted with the perpetrator in the past doesn't mean that it isn't sexual harassment. You may have been comfortable before but aren't any longer. Sometimes you might have laughed out of fear or not being sure how to react.

The Impact of Sexual Harassment on Targets

Sexual harassment is sexualized bullying, and just like bullying, it can cause significant emotional and physical harm to targets. Even simply witnessing severe or repeated harassment can be harmful, which is why sexual harassment laws and policies often provide relief to anyone who has to learn or work in such an environment. Interestingly, a target today may become a harasser tomorrow because students who harass other students are likely to have been harassed themselves.

> **Students who harass other students are likely to have been harassed themselves.**

One of the people I spoke with extensively about school and street-based sexual harassment is Dr. Bianca Fileborn, a professor of criminology at the University of Melbourne in Australia. Her research has shown that being the target of sexual harassment can be "incredibly harmful, even though it's often dismissed as being trivial, a joke, a compliment, or just 'boys being boys.' It actually has profound negative impacts on the people who are on the receiving end in a wide-ranging way."

The types of harm that sexual harassment can cause or contribute to include:

- **Emotional harm**: negative body image, anxiety, low self-esteem, hopelessness, depression, humiliation, fear, self-harm ideation and self-harm, isolation, confusion, sadness
- **Physical harm**: loss of sleep, loss of appetite, stress and stress-related disorders, not wanting to be touched, nightmares, inability to concentrate in class or at work

Am I Overreacting?

If you're uncomfortable with someone's sexual behavior toward you, you may start questioning what you did to deserve it. You may also think that you could be overreacting and wonder whether it is, in fact, harassment. Let me be clear: targets are never to blame for harassment and don't bring it upon themselves. We all deserve to be treated with dignity and respect. **If someone's actions are making you uncomfortable, you've got every right to have them stop.**

- **Behavioral harm**: skipping or changing schools, slipping grades, avoiding certain places or changing your route, changing how you dress, isolating oneself, acting out

Dr. Fileborn goes on to say that while both boys and girls are harassed, "The impact of sexual harassment and sexual violence can play out in a different way for females and trans people, particularly when it comes to street harassment. Those groups are often in real fear for their personal safety, and worry that the harassment may escalate into murder and sexual assault."

Sexual Harassment at School

Title IX of the Education Amendments Act of 1972, as supplemented by substantive guidelines issued by federal authorities, is a school-based federal civil rights law that prohibits all types of sex discrimination, including sexual harassment, at all K–12 schools and colleges/universities, public or private, that accept federal funding (including the accepting of federally funded school loans).

The law states, in part, "No person . . . shall, on the basis of sex, be excluded from participation in, be denied the benefits of, or be subjected to discrimination under any education program or activity receiving federal financial assistance."

The purpose of Title IX is to ensure that all students have equal access to an education free of sexual discrimination. Schools that are bound by this law must be proactive in ensuring that this is the case. Violation of Title IX by a school can impair its federal funding and in certain cases subject it to a lawsuit by the target of the harassment. (In most instances, a parent or other guardian must file the suit on behalf of a minor.)

The law prohibits all sex discrimination, which can include a surprisingly wide range of activities, including gender (sexual) harassment, sexual violence (such as sexual assault and rape), dating violence, stalking, and other similar discriminatory behaviors.

Title IX rules, definitions, regulations, and grievance procedures occasionally change. However, generally, when a school knows or reasonably should know about sexual harassment or unwelcome sexual contact that creates an environment that denies the target an equal opportunity to pursue their education, the school must do something about it—by law. The action must be reasonably calculated to eliminate the activity and, as appropriate, prevent its recurrence and effects.

> ## Quid Pro Quo and Hostile School Environment Harassment
>
> School-based sexual harassment (work-based too) falls into one of two categories: quid pro quo harassment (meaning something for something) and hostile environment harassment. An example of quid pro quo harassment could be when someone in a position of power, such as a teacher, offers something to a student, such as a good grade, for sexual activity. Another example could be when someone in a position of authority, such as a student government officer, pressures another student for a date in exchange for budgeting funds to their student organization.
>
> Generally, a hostile environment can exist when the harasser's actions are so severe and unwelcomed that the learning environment becomes toxic for targets and/or witnesses—who are unable to obtain equal access or benefit from the school's education programs. This type of harassment can occur from student to student, staff to student, or student to staff, or from a third party (such as a visitor) to a student.

The school itself can be sanctioned for violating Title IX—not the students. The students can be disciplined for violating the school's antiharassment policy or code of conduct, which must be in place at all Title IX schools. The most significant consequence that a student can receive from their school for violating the policy or code of conduct is to be expelled. However, the student can still face criminal consequences if the police get involved because the acts may amount to separate criminal offenses under state law.

Even schools that don't accept federal funds and are not bound by Title IX are still very likely to have some sort of written sexual harassment policy or code of conduct. However, the particulars of these policies are not uniform. Even in the absence of a written policy, though, *all* schools must take reasonable steps to ensure that the school environment is a safe place to learn. There may also be state laws comparable to Title IX that apply to a school (most often public schools) that accepts state funding.

Sexual Harassment Happens in Public Spaces Too

Sexual harassment certainly happens in places other than school or work, such as on the street, on public transportation, and in restaurants, movie theaters, and other public spaces. People start being targeted with street harassment around puberty, sometimes far younger. In fact, half of all harassed people report that they were harassed by the age of 17.

Street harassment can come in a variety of forms, including being cat-called, whistled at, honked at, followed, groped, and being subjected to sexual advances, sexually explicit comments, someone exposing themselves, gender policing, and many other unwelcome and threatening behaviors. All of these acts are fundamentally disrespectful. Moreover, they are forms of objectification and degradation and an expression of hostility. Targets report changing the routes they travel or the way they dress; feeling uncomfortable, disrespected, and demeaned; and, perhaps most significantly, fearing for their personal safety.

If you'd like to know more about the ill effects of street-based sexual harassment, ways you can help stop it, and how you can help someone who's being harassed (perhaps yourself), a good place to start is the resources at the end of this chapter.

Sexual Harassment and Homophobia

We've all heard it—"That's so gay," "She's a dyke," "What are you, queer?", "Don't be a girl." While seemingly mainstream, these are insults and the connotation is that being a girl, gay, or queer is somehow bad, which, of course, it isn't. The sad reality is that students are targeted for failing to follow norms that are typical for their gender, and this enforces unhealthy gender stereotypes. While Title IX does not directly address discrimination related to sexual orientation, these acts may be prohibited by other laws and school policies. Either way, they're just plain wrong.

Tips and Tactics for Addressing Sexual Harassment

Let's build on the foundation of what we've already covered by going over some practical ways to stop the harassment if you're the target and how to involve your school when needed.

Things You Can Do If You're Being Harassed

Option 1: Tell Them to Stop
If it's safe to do so and reasonable under the circumstances, targets of harassment can initially speak up for themselves and try to stop the harassment. Studies have shown that many students who harass others are trying to be funny or didn't think what they were doing or saying was a big deal. As a result, some harassers may not be aware of the harm they're causing, and speaking out can be an effective way to bring attention to and stop their behavior.

Remember, it may be difficult to speak out and advocate for oneself, but the price of speaking out is often not as high as the price of silence. Dr. Fileborn says that though it can be challenging to do, she encourages people to speak back to harassers. She notes, "It can be incredibly difficult and it's not always safe to do so." Still, "if you feel comfortable and able in the moment to challenge the person harassing you, by all means do whatever you feel that you're able to."

If you do choose to say something, one way to approach it is to firmly tell the harasser that the behavior makes you uncomfortable and that you want it to stop. Once you do so, don't engage in further back-and-forth with the individual, which can escalate the situation. Examples of things you can say are:

- "That's not cool. Please stop harassing me."
- "Stop doing that. It's harassment."
- "If you harass me again, I'll report it."
- "I don't like when you do that. Please don't do it again."
- "Maybe you didn't realize, but your words are hurtful."

If you are uncomfortable speaking to the perpetrator face-to-face, you can do it in writing. You should briefly describe the behaviors that make you uncomfortable and that you want to stop. You can hand-deliver a note or send an email to the harasser (keep a copy of whatever you write for your records). Asking the harasser to stop, in person or in writing, is the *target's choice* and should not be made mandatory by your school.

Omar's Story

Omar, an openly gay 17-year-old from Minnesota, felt uncomfortable when girls at his school touched him in an inappropriate way or asked which boys he thought were "hot" and which ones he thought wanted his "lovin'." He was bothered that these girls, some of them his good friends, thought it was okay to do these and other similar things with him because he was gay, and yet they didn't conduct themselves the same way with straight boys. Omar mustered up the courage and told the girls that he "didn't care for the way" they sometimes treated him. Not realizing the impact their actions were having, the girls stopped and even apologized!

Option 2: Get Your School Administration Involved

If you aren't comfortable asking the harasser to stop it, or if the harassment continues after you do so, you can seek help from your school. Some guidance on doing this follows, and further details can be found in appendix 2.

Please keep in mind that if you are a minor and make a complaint about sexual harassment to certain people who work with children in their professional capacity, such as a teacher, they may be a "mandatory reporter." This means they are required to disclose suspected abuse or neglect of minors to law enforcement or child protective services. Whether or not sexual harassment amounts to abuse or neglect depends on the facts at hand.

Making a complaint at your school, or in any other environment, can be nerve-wracking and intimidating. As indicated earlier, sexual harassment is rarely reported. Some of the reasons targets have for not reporting sexual harassment include the following:

- They think that doing so won't change anything.
- They won't be believed.
- They'll be blamed.

- They'll be retaliated against.
- They'll be socially ostracized for making an accusation.
- A school's intervention may make them even more uncomfortable, such as involving a face-to-face meeting with the harasser. (Incidentally, your school shouldn't require you to meet face-to-face with the perpetrator, though you may be able to request this option if you are comfortable with it and believe it might help.)
- Feelings of guilt about the punishment the harasser may receive.
- Their parents will find out.

These are just some of the reasons it can be so helpful to have a trusted adult by your side if you decide to speak up about it. Having a trusted adult with you also gives you another witness and may result in the school taking the situation more seriously.

When the Harasser Is in a Position of Power

Gabriella, a 17-year-old high school student in Maryland, was sexually harassed by a coach at her school when he said she "had a great rack." The coach made similar comments to other girls at her school. When Gabriella complained to her school principal, guidance counselors, and other administrators about what the coach was doing and what he said to her, the school scheduled a mediation between her and the coach—a power imbalance in favor of the coach that was inappropriate and unfair to Gabriella. In fact, this approach made her feel punished for reporting the coach's behavior. When she expressed dissatisfaction with the process, the school said it was her sole option, or she could cover herself up.

Gabriella could have chosen to take other steps to force her school to handle things better, but she was understandably discouraged and didn't feel believed. The ordeal changed her view of school. "I was a straight-A student, but I became scared to death to go to school every day."

If your school doesn't address incidents of sexual harassment the way it should, as was the case in Gabriella's situation, please don't give up. Sometimes it can take repeated complaints to get your school or school district's attention.

While the underlying facts and circumstances of harassment vary, there are numerous remedies that a school can enact. Before doing so, the school will typically first investigate the claim and make some sort of determination about its merits. The school's determination happens administratively, not in a court of law.

Ideally, your school should ask what resolution you believe is appropriate under the circumstances. For example, some targets of harassment only want the harasser to be advised to stop doing it, to understand that their conduct was hurtful, or to apologize. Nevertheless, in response to the complaint, some of the things the school can do are to suspend, expel, or move the student engaging in the harassment to another class or school. Alternatively, the reporting student can ask to be moved to another class or school. The school could also provide mental health and academic support services to the reporting student.

Joel Levin is the cofounder of Stop Sexual Assault in Schools (stopsexualassaultinschools.org), which provides resources and information about the right to an equal education free from sexual harassment. He tells me that over the last few years, high schools have gotten better in their enforcement

Sexual Harassment Happens at Work Too

Like school-based sexual harassment, work-based harassment is rampant. The viral spread of the culturally shifting #metoo movement against sexual violence, including sexual harassment and sexual assault, was triggered in part by people sharing their all-too-similar stories of how common sexual harassment is in the workplace.

The rate of teen employment in the United States is among the highest of any industrialized nation, so it shouldn't be surprising that significant numbers of teens experience sexual harassment in the workplace. Title VII of the federal Civil Rights Act of 1964 prohibits employers with fifteen or more employees from discriminating on the basis of sex (including sexual harassment), gender, race, religion, and more. The law is enforced by the US Equal Employment Opportunity Commission (EEOC). More information is available at www.eeoc.gov. Even if your employer has fewer than fifteen employees, there may be laws in your state that prohibit sexual harassment at work.

of sexual harassment school policies "but still have a lot of work to do." Levin also says, "Policies can lack transparency and clear procedures," and wants people to know that "they have an absolute right to learn in a school environment that is healthy and safe and free from sexual harassment."

If the school's designated Title IX coordinator—required by law at all schools bound by Title IX—or a school administrator at a school that is not bound by Title IX does not take meaningful action in response to a complaint, the parent or student may want to show administrators the Title IX law (if applicable), any state regulations, or the school and/or school district policies on sexual misconduct (which may be defined as "unwanted aggressive behavior").

In addition to taking steps that may be required pursuant to Title IX grievance procedures, if the complaining party still doesn't believe that they're getting school support, Levin suggests taking it to the school superintendent, the school board, the school district, or the state office of education—in other words, going up the chain of command. He has seen, repeatedly, that parent and student advocates have changed school policies to better protect targets and to hold harassers more accountable. Similar to many situations in our lives, **sometimes you have to make a stink to implement change**. It can be done.

Option 3: Go to the Police

There are limited circumstances when sexual harassment, in and of itself, will get someone arrested—street-based harassment where it is prohibited by law, for example. Yet sexual harassment can quite easily morph into a standalone crime that may subject the person to arrest. Examples can include threats of physical harm, actual physical harm, offensive sexual touching, stalking or cyberstalking, sexual assault, a property crime (someone damages or steals your personal property), and many others. The definitions of these and other laws vary by jurisdiction.

If someone's behavior makes you concerned for your personal safety, you should immediately go to the police and make a report. Of course, if you're in imminent danger, call 911. Additionally, let someone at your school in a senior administrative position, such as the principal or Title IX coordinator, know that you've gone to the police.

For some important ways to most effectively make a police report, see appendix 3. For information about protective orders related to stalking, physical, or sexual violence—including dating violence—and other crimes, see chapter 7.

Once Again . . . the Importance of Bystander Intervention

We discussed bystander intervention in the last chapter. It's worth mentioning again for those who did not read that chapter and because intervening in the context of sexual harassment can be different.

Much of the time, school-based harassment happens in the open, in front of other people—both students and staff. When school staff members witness harassment and don't intervene, they may be sending a message that the behavior is tolerated.

> When we're around other people and see or hear something that seems wrong, we may not take action because we convince ourselves that someone else will.

The presence of passive bystanders, students, or staff, can make targets of harassment feel that neither they nor their ordeal is important. From the harasser's perspective, inaction by witnesses gives the harasser the audience they often crave and will be construed as support for their actions.

When we're around other people and see or hear something that seems wrong, we may not take action because we convince ourselves that someone else will. This is called the bystander effect: a phenomenon in which the more people who are present, the less likely it is that someone will help a target or victim.

When you see something that isn't right, trust your instincts and don't ignore the situation, especially if others aren't doing something to help. If you are the courageous person to speak up, you'll make it much easier for others to join you. Remember, courage inspires courage. Oftentimes it takes only one or two people to shut down the harassment and can be just what the target needs in that moment. Depending on your comfort level, there's *always* something you can do to help! If you feel it's physically safe, the most important thing is not to stand by in silence when you witness harassment.

You have incredible power to help a target. Here are some ways to use that power:

1. At a bare minimum, *don't participate* in harassing behavior, directly or indirectly, by watching it, forwarding messages, laughing, or otherwise standing by idly. Even just the simple act of not watching or laughing at the harassment can help stop it, and if that's the extent of what you're willing to do to assist, so be it. That alone is a step in the right direction, and perhaps down the road your willingness to more directly intervene may change. For now, do what fits your comfort level.

2. Unless you're certain that immediate help is needed, before squaring off with the harasser, **address the target directly and ask if everything is okay and if your help is wanted**. Be low-key and keep the potential intervention fairly covert to avoid unnecessarily escalating the situation. This is particularly true if you don't know the target because speaking on their behalf can be disempowering to them in an already potentially traumatic and belittling situation.

3. If you know your help is wanted, stand up to the harasser in any way that is physically safe and comfortable for you. Some things you can do is to tell the harasser to stop and that what they're doing "isn't funny or cool." Or you can question them by saying something like "Why are you doing that?" Becoming aggressive may escalate things, so stay calm.

4. Since there's safety in numbers, try to get your friends and/or other bystanders to join you in whatever action you've decided to take to combat the harassment.

5. You can also report the harassment to your school, just as the target of the harassment can. Remember, simply being a witness to severe or recurring harassment can make the school environment feel hostile and impact your ability to learn. In some situations, particularly if you know the target, before reporting an incident you may want to talk with the person to see how they feel about it.

Helping Someone Who's Been Targeted . . . Even after the Fact

If you cannot intervene in real time, you can still support the target in a number of other ways, even after incidents of harassment. Don't underestimate how much a quick, kind, or thoughtful word can help the target feel better and stronger.

Here are just a few ways to help:

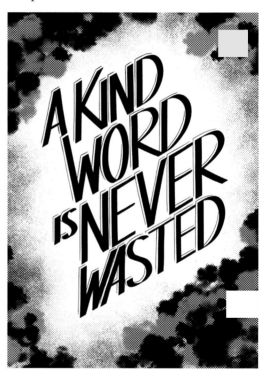

- Post or say something supportive to the target. For example, expressing that the person deserves to be treated with respect, that what was said is ridiculous and not true, and other similar sentiments can help the person feel less alone.

- You could report the harassment yourself. Title IX attorney Alec Rose, introduced in chapter 4, tells me, "I have a case right now involving a law student who was harassed in front of the entire class by her professor. She was too shocked to report the harassment when it happened, but one of her classmates did. The reporting student didn't use my client's name because she did not first ask her permission to do so, but she gave a detailed report. When my client was ready to come forward, she had the benefit of contemporaneous documentation of what happened to her."

- Encourage the target to talk to a trusted adult.

- Offer to help the target find more formal support, such as a school counselor. You can also offer to go with the target if they decide to report the harassment to school officials.
- Take screenshots of harassing digital messages, such as text messages and social media posts or comments, so that the targeted person will have evidence when they seek help.
- Show support, however you can. You may not know what exactly to do to help, and that's okay. Being someone whom the person can talk to can be invaluable. Saying something like "I'm here to help you. Whatever we can do we'll get through this together" can be incredibly comforting to the target.

What Three Things in This Chapter Matter Most to You?

We all take away different lessons from reading the information presented in this chapter. What resonates with one person may not be meaningful to another and vice versa. I certainly hope that you've learned a heck of a lot more than three things in this chapter, but if three things were all you learned, I still consider it a win. Even a single piece of information could be invaluable if it was just what you or someone you're with needs in a critical moment.

With the information from this chapter fresh in your mind, please take a few moments to write below the three things that you consider the most important.

1. _____

_____

2. _____

_____

3. _____

_____

What Would You Do if It Happened to You?

You are in gym class running laps and a quiet boy you don't know very well trips and hurts his ankle. It looks like he's tearing up, and another boy in your class yells mockingly, "Are you going to cry like a little girl? Man up!"

Would you laugh? What might you say to the boy who shouted? What might you say to the boy who was hurt?

Some Thoughts about "What Would You Do if It Happened to You?"

When we laugh at jokes that use gender (or sexual orientation) as an insult, we are reinforcing or normalizing damaging stereotypes such as girls/women are weak and that "real men" don't cry. Since these stereotypes are not true (and damaging to all), instead of laughing, you could say, "That's not funny," "I don't understand," or "Why is that funny?" If saying something feels risky, you could approach the target afterward and ask if everything is okay.

Final Thoughts

It's easy to grasp the potentially devastating aspects of so many of the topics in this book, such as sexual assault, dating violence, sextortion, cyberbullying, and others. However, for some, sexual harassment isn't taken as seriously and can be mistakenly thought of as insignificant. This is unfortunate because it can be just as serious.

I've spoken to many people who think that sexual harassment is overblown and people should just learn to take a joke. This misperception is one of the reasons sexual harassment is normalized and perpetuated. I hear this point of view from adults as much as, if not more often than, I do from teens. Sure, there are times when it's best to just let something roll off your back. Yet studies continually show that sexual harassment can be extremely harmful to targets.

Don't believe people who go around saying that "you can't even tell someone that they look nice without getting in trouble." This is total nonsense. Are you going to face school discipline if you earnestly tell someone that you like what they've done with their hair? Nope. Or that you think that the color yellow suits them well? Nope. How about, on a single occasion, respectfully asking someone out in your math class who turns out not to be interested in you? Not gonna get you in trouble either.

Harassment shouldn't be a part of growing up, yet it is. An important way we can all work to eliminate it is to become aware of our own actions and the actions of those in our peer group, and to do our best to intervene when harassment happens right in front of us.

Where Can I Get More Information?

This chapter contains the essentials of sexual harassment. For those who want to know more and dig deeper into this topic, a Google search is a good place to start and will deliver numerous resources, some with valuable information.

There are agencies and service organizations whose mission is to provide meaningful support to anyone in need of information and resources related to sexual harassment. You can contact them about a specific concern you have for yourself, a friend, a loved one, or even a stranger. Often, if desired, you can stay anonymous. The ones below are a good place to start:

- the Title IX coordinator for your school or school district
- Hollaback!
  - » a people-powered movement to end harassment
  - » www.ihollaback.org
- Know Your IX
  - » educates on Title IX and resources to empower students who look to stop sexual violence
  - » www.knowyourix.org

- Stop Sexual Assault in Schools
    - » educates students, families, and schools about the right to an equal education free from sexual harassment
    - » www.stopsexualassaultinschools.org
- Stop Street Harassment
    - » dedicated to ending gender harassment
    - » www.stopstreetharassment.org
- US Department of Education Office for Civil Rights (OCR)
    - » enforcers of Title IX of the Education Amendments Act of 1972
    - » www.ed.gov/ocr
- US Equal Employment Opportunity Commission
    - » enforcers of Title VII of the federal Civil Rights Act of 1964
    - » www.eeoc.gov

NOTE TO THE READER: If you are a minor and make a complaint about sexual harassment to certain people who work with children in their professional capacity, such as a teacher, they may be a "mandatory reporter." This means they are required to disclose to law enforcement or child protective services certain instances of harassment if they amount to suspected abuse or neglect of minors.

Sexual Harassment Quiz

Test your understanding of sexual harassment by taking this quiz. Hopefully, you'll get all of the answers correct because a single mistake could have real-world consequences if that answer contained the information you needed to stay safe.

Instructions: select the best answer from the available choices. Answers can be found in the back of the book.

1. Sexual harassment occurs only when there's unwelcome sexual advances by a male against a female.
    A. True
    B. False

2. Title IX of the Education Amendments Act of 1972 is a civil rights law that prohibits gender discrimination at every US school.
    A. True
    B. False

3. Violation of a school code of conduct prohibiting sexual harassment can result in school discipline, including expulsion.
    A. True
    B. False

4. Sexual harassment can be:
    A. Physical
    B. Verbal
    C. Visual
    D. All of the above.

5. Only students, not staff, can be punished for sexual harassment in the school environment.
    A. True
    B. False
    C. It depends if the staff member is a full-time employee of the institution.

6. Students who sexually harass others were likely sexually harassed themselves in the past.
   A. True
   B. False
   C. True, but only middle-school students.

7. Ollie's teacher offers an A in exchange for a nude massage. Might this be sexual harassment?
   A. No. Teachers aren't covered by harassment laws and regulations.
   B. Maybe. It depends on whether Ollie needed an A to pass the class.
   C. Yes, but only if Ollie gives the massage.
   D. Yes

8. Sexual harassment is essentially sexualized bullying.
   A. True
   B. False

9. Many people who sexually harass someone at their school:
   A. Are trying to be funny.
   B. Don't realize that their actions amount to sexual harassment.
   C. Both A and B.
   D. Neither

10. About 50 percent of students who are sexually harassed report it to a school administrator.
    A. True
    B. False

CHAPTER 6

Sextortion—Yes, It's Really a Thing

KEY TAKEAWAYS

- According to the US Department of Justice, sextortion is the most significant growing threat to anyone under 18.

- Perpetrators can be complete strangers *or* someone known to the victim such as an ex-boyfriend or ex-girlfriend.

- Sextortionists obtain "compromising" images of targets by threats, deception, and breaches of trust.

- There are effective ways to help protect yourself from sextortion.

- One of the most important things a victim of sextortion can do is to tell someone they trust about what they're going through.

Chapter Highlights

Setting the Stage

When it comes to the various topics in this book, many readers, to one extent or another, will know at least a little bit about them. Sexual consent, the importance of managing one's digital footprint, and sexual harassment, for example, are all things that many of you will have at least heard something about. Sextortion, not so much. It's a relatively new concern and very few people know what it is and how to best prevent it.

> Sextortion is online blackmail involving threats to expose sexual images of the target.

Sextortion is a uniquely twenty-first-century crime and a new form of sexual assault that can be done remotely. Sextortion affects the lives of countless unsuspecting people, many of them young. It can happen to anyone, though, regardless of age, gender or gender identity (including persons who identify as nonbinary, trans, or asexual), race, sexual orientation, economic status, or any other factor. (Also, for purposes of our sextortion definition above, "blackmail" means to force or coerce someone into doing something that they don't want to do.)

Amanda Todd, 15 years old, discovered the horror of sextortion firsthand. She shared what happened to her on YouTube in a video she posted that now has over 13 million views entitled "My Story: Struggling, Bullying, Suicide, Self-harm." In it, she tells her story of sextortion and cyberbullying by using flashcards and without uttering a single word.

Todd reveals that in seventh grade she'd go on her webcam to meet and talk to new people. She was flattered by someone who eventually asked her to flash him—which she did, quickly. Unbeknownst to her, he captured the image. A year later, out of nowhere, the man contacted her on social media and demanded "a show" or he would share her image. He knew Amanda's address as well as the names of her friends and family members.

This was just the beginning of Amanda's story, as relayed by her flashcards, and it continues with more twists and turns, each one seemingly

Amanda Todd from her YouTube video "My Story: Struggling, Bullying, Suicide, Self-harm."

more tragic than the last. I spoke to Carol Todd, Amanda's mom, who told me, "For a year he continued to relentlessly track and harass Amanda online and repeatedly shared the image, despite his promise not to." This contributed to "ruthless bullying" of Amanda by her peers, both online and in person.

After Amanda posted her YouTube video, Carol said, "Amanda felt really good about the video. She felt that a huge weight had been lifted off of her shoulders." Unfortunately, the feeling did not last. Amanda's sextortion victimization and bullying from her peers continued, and she tragically took her own life a month later. (The adult who is accused of sextorting Amanda did so from Europe. He is currently in prison as a result of the many other victims he sextorted and is awaiting a criminal trial in Amanda's case.)

These can be scary times in which we live, and Amanda's story is but one of countless others involving sextortion. According to the US Department of Justice, "sextortion is by far the most significantly growing threat to children…" and there are more victims per offender than all other child exploitation crimes. It happens in both the virtual world and the real one, and it's a crime that disproportionately victimizes young people—15 is the average age.

What You'll Learn in this Chapter

Stories like Amanda's and those of so many other girls *and* boys have helped illuminate ways that we can better protect ourselves from falling victim to sextortion. We'll cover many of these in this chapter. We'll first discuss the different methods that sextortionists use to obtain compromising images of their targets and the types of demands that they make once the image is in hand.

We'll then jump into safety tips and tactics to better protect yourself from the evils of sextortion. We'll also look at suggested actions you can take in the unlikely event that you are targeted by a perpetrator.

Before going any further, I must remind readers what we've covered in other chapters: **victims are not at fault for the predatory acts of another.** Sextortionists are often someone whom the victim completely trusted and who breached this trust in a terrible way. It can happen to anyone.

Let's get to it.

What Is Sextortion?

Sextortion Often Begins with a Sexual Image of the Target

Sextortion is a new form of sexual predation, and researchers are still learning about it. One of the pioneering researchers is Dr. David Finkelhor, the director of the Crimes against Children Research Center, introduced in chapter 3. He tells me, "Sextortion has largely slipped under the radar of the research community, yet we do know that sextortion revolves around threats to expose sexual images."

Perpetrators, who can be complete strangers *or* someone known to the victim such as an ex-boyfriend or ex-girlfriend, will acquire an image or video in which the target is nude, partially nude, engaging in sex acts, or wearing revealing clothing (all referred to as a "nude"). Once the nude is obtained, the perpetrator threatens the target with publicly sharing the

image electronically by posting the material on social
media and tagging the target's
friends and loved ones unless
their demands are met.

The demands include
meeting for sexual activity
(in person or online), sending
more images, paying money,
or having the victim return
to or not end an in-person
relationship.

How Do Perpetrators Get Nudes?

Sextortionists obtain nudes
through relationships (online
or in person), through computer hacks, and by threats. A
variety of techniques can be
employed, sometimes simultaneously, and can change based on the circumstances. Dr. Finkelhor describes some of the techniques as "elaborate
deceptions." Whatever the method utilized, sextortionists are looking for
someone who is vulnerable.

Here are some of the methods by which nudes are obtained:

Online relationships (the people involved have never met in person):

- Grooming is the process of finding and befriending a minor and
  developing an emotional bond with them. As the target's inhibitions are lowered and they begin to trust the groomer, the groomer/
  predator asks for a nude or to meet in person for sexual activity.
- Catfishing is the act of creating a fake online persona—for example, on social media or a dating site—to deceive someone into some
  sort of conversation. If the ploy works, the sextortionist develops an
  online relationship, which can lead to obtaining a nude.
- Offering a job (often modeling or acting), money, or drugs in
  exchange for a nude is a known tactic.

- Getting the victim to "flash" them quickly and capturing an image (as we saw with Amanda Todd) is another way perpetrators capture nudes.

These and other online sextortion schemes targeting young people are often perpetrated where young people are found, such as social media networks and apps, messaging apps, video voice call apps, adult sites, dating apps and sites, and gaming platforms.

In-person relationships:

- The target knowingly provides a nude to a partner ("knowingly," not "willingly," because a target may be forced or coerced into providing an image). Later on when the target wants to end the relationship or has done so, they're threatened with exposure of the nude if they don't stay in or return to the relationship.

Scams, hacking, and threats:

- Lying about already having a nude of the target can lead to obtaining one. For example, thousands of people are randomly contacted with a form email falsely claiming that their webcam has been hacked and images have been captured of them masturbating or walking around naked. Sometimes the perpetrator may include one of your old account passwords (probably purchased online from other hackers) in the email as an additional lure. Recipients are told that unless the perpetrator's demands are met, the nude will be released. Although no such compromising image is in the perpetrator's possession, recipients sometimes believe the claim and succumb to the demands.
- Impersonating someone whom the target knows and trusts (a type of catfishing), including a friend, boyfriend, or girlfriend, and requesting nudes.
- Getting targets to unknowingly download malicious software (malware) onto their digital devices that allows the perpetrator to access their digital files, photos, and videos; to track everything typed on their keyboards; and to take control of their webcam and microphone.
- Threatening self-harm (when the target cares about the perpetrator) or physical assault on the target, their family, or even pets unless they receive a nude.

- Threatening to create pornographic images of the target by photoshopping (or creating a deepfake; see chapter 8 for details) the target's face with another person's nude body if the demands for a nude are not met.

What Do Sextortionists Want?

After obtaining a nude, the perpetrator makes demands in exchange for not releasing the image—though they still might. These demands include:

- sending more sexual content
- insisting that the target stay in or return to an in-person relationship with the perpetrator
- meeting the target online or in person for sexual activity
- telling the target how to look or what to do sexually in pictures and videos
- delivering money (or goods of some kind)

Other times, or in combination with any of the above, the perpetrator wants to humiliate, harass, hurt, and/or control the target by getting them

---

Sextortion and the Law

Numerous states have laws that criminalize sextortion outright and the nonconsensual dissemination of nudes, though laws vary by jurisdiction. Some states also have other standalone laws that may apply in the context of sextortion. For example, when a sextortionist targets a child (anyone under 18 years of age) and persuades the person to send explicit images, the perpetrator may be engaging in criminal acts pertaining to the sexual coercion of a minor and child pornography (more accurately described in this context as child sexual exploitation material).

Sextortion can also involve various other crimes, such as extortion (generally, obtaining something by threat of violence), blackmail, computer hacking, sexual exploitation (defined, in part, by the World Health Organizations as any actual or attempted abuse of a position of vulnerability, differential power, or trust, for sexual purposes) sexual assault, stalking, and others.

in trouble at work or school or with the law; stalking them; physically hurting them, including rape or other physical harm; harming their family, friends, or pets; and reveling in the fear the victim is feeling.

Emotional Impact on Victims

When people knowingly share their nudes or seminude images, they don't expect them to be shown to anyone other than the individuals for whom they were intended and certainly not to be used as sextortion material. As such, the shock of being targeted with sextortion can be terrifying and overwhelming. It is a crime of unspeakable brutality, and the emotional effects can be devastating, traumatic, and lifelong.

Sextortion often leaves victims feeling isolated, fearful, embarrassed, helpless, and full of self-blame. Perpetrators know how to exploit these feelings in order to isolate their targets and make them afraid to seek help from family, friends, or law enforcement. As one 14-year-old victim explained, "The reason I didn't want to speak up is because I was afraid of what the adults in my life might think of me. I thought it was all my fault and I figured that's what they would tell me."

How to Recognize Sextortion

Although there are no hard-and-fast rules and the methods employed are constantly changing, sextortion may follow one of the following patterns.

Sextortion in Online Relationships

Boys and Sextortion

In one scenario, a would-be perpetrator presents as an attractive, young woman or man who connects with a boy on a mainstream social media site or on an adult (18 and over) site. The target is enticed to move the communication to an anonymous messaging app or video chat. During this private interaction, the perpetrator will disrobe and urge the target to disrobe as well.

Sextortion and Organized Crime

It's not just individuals who are committing these ruthless acts but also sophisticated, capable, and well-organized global crime syndicates that seek to financially exploit targets. With little upfront investment, low risk of getting arrested, and the potential for high financial gain, these groups run industrial-scale sextortion operations. There are no boundaries on the internet, and these cells are often based outside the United States but digitally reach US victims from across the world.

What the boy doesn't realize when he agrees to cybersex is that the video chat session is being recorded. The actual perpetrator may not even be the person they are viewing on-screen, as it can be more efficient for scammers to use a prerecorded video and type messages at the same time the woman or man in the video appears to be using the keyboard.

Once the image or video that the boy won't want shared publicly is obtained, the sextortionist then reveals their true intent: to post the image online if their demands—often for money—aren't met. Even if the initial demands are met, it's not unusual for the perpetrator to return with more demands.

Girls and Sextortion

Girls, who may be less likely to have cybersex with someone shortly after meeting them, are often sextorted in a different way. Often this involves grooming and catfishing. Before the grooming begins, would-be perpetrators may catfish the target by creating a fake online profile and presenting themselves as a teenager, a

This boy, who has partially disrobed, doesn't realize that he is being recorded. He will soon be threatened with sextortion.

celebrity, or a caring adult. In some cases, they might even assume the online identity of someone the target knows.

The fake profile will use someone else's image and share things on their timeline that didn't happen, but make the profile seem more authentic. To further entice targets, the perpetrator may add tidbits to their fictional profile of things that were discovered in the target's own social media presence to show that they have similar interests. (As mentioned in chapter 9, this is one of the reasons to limit the amount of personal information used in public online profiles.)

This girl thinks she's disrobing for her teenage boyfriend—whom she has never met in person. In fact, an adult sexual predator is catfishing her and will soon threaten her with sextortion.

The sextortionist contacts the target and attempts to befriend her by being friendly and nice and pretending to have things in common. As a

Sextortion's Cousin

As you'll see in chapter 11, image-based sexual abuse, more commonly known as revenge porn, is a close cousin of sextortion and there can be confusion about the two. Revenge porn frequently involves a former partner publicly posting nudes that were obtained during the course of a relationship as "revenge" for the breakup. While there is some overlap, generally, revenge porn is about spitefulness, anger, and trying to take someone down; sextortion is often about domination, power, and control.

friendship develops, the perpetrator may tell the girl that she is the only one with whom he can be himself, encourage her to talk to him about her school and family problems, and promise favors and gifts. (I say "he" and "him" because most sextortionists are male, though the characters they portray in their fake profiles might be female.) Over a period of hours, days, weeks, or months, the target starts to rely on this virtual friend for support rather than the people in her real life.

Once sufficient trust in the relationship is established, the sextortionist asks for a nude. If needed, the relationship will be used against the target. For example, the perpetrator may say that not sending a picture (or video) means that the target doesn't care about or trust them; or the sextortionist may threaten to end their friendship/relationship or to hurt themselves

A Prosecutor Going after Sexual Predators

Michael DeRose is a veteran prosecutor with the Los Angeles County District Attorney's Office who prosecutes violent sexual predators, some of them sextortionists. DeRose has seen firsthand how these perpetrators "employ multiple methods" to target victims. In one of his cases, the sextortionist, whom DeRose describes as a "pure predator," had multiple victims but was caught and brought to justice only when one of his targets told her mother.

The girl, 15 years old, had received a random message through social media from the perpetrator telling her that if she didn't send a nude, he'd kill her and her family. She was terrified because "this unnamed person knows her name, the names of her siblings, where she goes to school, and the way she walks home."

Frightened, the girl went straight to her mother, and they went to the police. The police department conducted a cyber investigation that led to the arrest of the perpetrator. Once he was in handcuffs, the police searched his devices and identified other sextortion victims, one of whom he had been sextorting for years. Thankfully, he was convicted and is going to prison. DeRose hopes that his case serves "as a cautionary tale that these sorts of perpetrators are out there and it's easier to fall into that net than you think."

He also wants victims to know that "it's not their fault what happened to them."

or others if an image isn't provided. After the target has sent a nude that meets the sextortionist's objectives, sooner or later, demands are made of the target.

Terry Evans, a cybersecurity consultant with a background in law enforcement who owns and operates Cybersleuth Investigations Inc., spends plenty of time tracking down sextortionists for private clients. He tells me that grooming involves "vulnerable targets" who can be exploited by perpetrators who "understand that everyone has a need to feel special and loved and they use this to trick and manipulate them. Their ruses are commonly known as social engineering, which involves manipulation to coerce others into actions they would not normally take."

Sextortion in Face-to-Face Relationships

Sextortion is also perpetrated in face-to-face relationships (as opposed to when people only know each other online and haven't met in person). The

perpetrator is typically a current or former partner who obtained a nude of the target during their relationship and subsequently threatens to publicly release the image. The perpetrator tags the target's friends and family if the target doesn't return to the relationship or if it is ended.

Dr. David Finkelhor says that although more studies are needed, preliminary research indicates that sextortion is more likely to happen in an in-person relationship as opposed to one online, which isn't surprising because "violence in general is more common in relationships than it is between strangers."

All is good in this relationship now, but things can change dramatically when one of them wants to end it or does end it.

Intimate Partners Sometimes Break Big Promises

Irma's boyfriend Lucas promised her that the nudes she sent him would stay private. They did—until she decided to break up with him. "He started threatening me with the nude photos," Irma said. Lucas threatened to post them to social media and send them to her place of work and all of her friends. Scared of what might happen if the photos were distributed, Irma agreed to get back together with Lucas. Irma said, "I was devastated. I was thinking that a million people could see my nude photos. And I had absolutely no control over it."

Irma finally broke up permanently with Lucas. However, she doesn't know what happened to her pictures or what might happen to them in the future. "They're still out there, and there's absolutely nothing I can do about it."

What Can I Do to Try to Prevent Sextortion?

While sextortion may be the fastest-growing form of child sexual exploitation, it can be the most preventable. Here are some ways to better protect yourself from sextortion:

- Keep all of your images PG rated and *never* disrobe online or send images with nudity or partial nudity or in provocative clothing—even if the person on the other side of the screen is someone you trust. Prosecutor Michael DeRose agrees with this advice but says, "Some teens won't listen to it." No doubt he's right, and it's also true that sending nudes can be done consensually between people age 18 or older as part of a healthy sexual relationship. He therefore urges people, regardless of age, "not to have their face or anything in the background that identifies them in the photo. This gives them an out and at the same time less leverage to the recipient if the recipient turns out to be a bad actor."

- Review and follow the many important recommendations for ensuring your digital data privacy in chapter 9.

- Always keep in mind that there are no truth monitors in the cyber world. Anyone can pretend to be someone they're not. It can be difficult to spot catfishing, but here are some possible clues:
  - » Google-search the person's profile image and other images they post to see if the images have been used other places online. This can show you whether the person is using stock images or an image that's taken from another person's account.
  - » Google the name that the person gave you and the user ID to see what you can discover about the person. Are they on other social media platforms? If so, are the profiles consistent?
  - » Cut and paste their messages into Google to see if they come up elsewhere online. Catfishers can be lazy and rip them from somewhere else online.
  - » How fast is your relationship moving? There's no one correct speed for how a relationship develops, but a relationship that is moving at breakneck speed can be a red flag.
  - » Ask for a picture of them doing something specific, such as two thumbs up or a hang-loose hand sign. Then, compare it to their profile picture. (Don't forget that images can be photoshopped.)

What Can I Do If I've Been Victimized?

If you or someone you care about has been sextorted or threatened with sextortion, some of your options are listed below. Remember, someone violated your trust. It is not your fault, and you should not be blamed by anyone. All of us have done something that we later regretted, particularly as a teen. It's what we learn from our mistakes that matters most.

- **Don't go through this alone.** Probably the most important thing for victims to do is to talk to someone about what is happening and not suffer in silence. There are service organizations (some listed at the end of this chapter) who are ready and willing to help anyone in need. Another option is to "Find Your Person" (see the "Find Your Person, Whoever That May Be" section in the Introduction).

Victims may not tell anyone about what's happening because they feel ashamed or embarrassed, are afraid of getting punished or being blamed, are LGBTQ and don't want to "out" themselves, or believe that they can handle it or that nobody can help. They may also be afraid that the perpetrator will inflict further harm if it is discovered that the person is seeking help. Dr. Finkelhor says that it may not always be easy to talk to an adult you trust about what you're going through, but "it is always the best option."

- It's not just victims who can talk to a trusted adult (or a resource provider) but also their friends who know about what is happening. I asked Carol Todd, Amanda Todd's mom, what the most important thing she'd like readers of this book to know about what tragically befell Amanda. She didn't hesitate: "If you know something, say something. Please talk to a trusted adult, particularly if there might be self-harm involved. Tell someone."

  Since some people think that doing so is "snitching," I'd like to clarify that snitching is about getting someone in trouble for something that is none of your business. Talking to a trusted adult about what you are witnessing a friend going through is about getting them help—a monumental difference.

- Cybersecurity consultant Terry Evans's advice is straightforward: **"End all communication immediately with the sextortionist.** Block all access to social media accounts, email addresses, and phones. Keeping victims in panic mode is a key tool used by these criminals to gain continued compliance. Closing all avenues of communication prevents the victim from being terrorized further."

- Report the sextortion to the website or apps where the contacts are occurring and ask that the image(s) be taken down and the perpetrator sanctioned. The person who took the picture (likely the victim) owns the copyright and its accompanying rights, which gives all the more justification to have the image(s) taken down. Because getting images removed and bad actors sanctioned varies by platform and evolves over time, I have not included how to do so herein. It's best to go to the site directly and follow the procedures outlined there.

- **Suspend any social media profiles through which the sextortionist contacted you** (even if you block the person, as mentioned above, the perpetrator can still create other user IDs to contact you). If you use multiple social media platforms using the same identifying information, you may need to suspend those accounts too.

- **Preserve or copy all relevant evidence** and keep it secure. More information about evidence preservation can be found in appendix 3 and in other parts of this book.

- Although every situation is unique, **I urge you not to give into the demands of the sextortionist** since the threats probably won't stop based on compliance with the demands. Michael DeRose says, "If

A Victim's Advice

Latanya, from Indianapolis, was 15 years old when she and a couple of girlfriends started chatting with strangers online one night using a webcam. The men they were chatting with dared her to flash them. Although it took only a second for her to raise her shirt on camera, that was all that was needed because one of the men, an experienced sextortionist, was ready and waiting to screenshot an image and turn that one second into a photo he could use to sextort her.

The sextortionist started cyberstalking Latanya. He found her on multiple social media sites and soon he obtained her mother's full name and address. He then used this to coerce Latanya into sending more nude photos and videos by threatening to show the original image to her mother.

Finally, it became too much for her to keep to herself. Latanya told her mother, and together they went to the police. Latanya says she wished she had gone to the police right away, as they were able to track down the offender and arrest him. The police were also able to connect him to nine other sextortion cases across the country.

Latanya has some advice for others who might find themselves victimized by a sextortionist: "Don't be driven by fear and don't let that person control you. You need to go and tell any adult, tell a parent, so it doesn't go on."

there's one thing I could impress upon young people it is that it's very hard to extricate yourself from the situation and compliance doesn't mean it's going to end."

- In some instances, victims have reported that they were able to get perpetrators to stop by confronting them, standing up to them, and not being intimidated—or at least pretending not to be. As one 19-year-old victim put it: "I told him I didn't care if my body got leaked to the world. I am not a celebrity so nobody will actually care. And . . . I bluffed, and said I was reporting him to the police, and they were tracking his IP address."

Going to the Police

Another option for victims of sextortion or someone threatened with it is to go to the police (appendix 3 has some effective ways to make police reports) or the FBI (the lead federal agency for investigating cybercrimes).

As we explore in chapter 11, creating, possessing, or distributing nude or partially nude images of minors, including of oneself, can be a serious crime related to child pornography. However, minors who share their nude images are rarely arrested, let alone prosecuted.

Still, some minors who are victims of sextortion worry that if they go to law enforcement to make a report, they might get in trouble for a nude they've shared. It's a fair question to ask, but it's unlikely they will because the minor is the *victim*, not the perpetrator. What the sextortionist is doing is far more serious than what the minor has done, and many police and prosecutors will see it that way.

DeRose says, "I struggle to see what incentive any law enforcement agency would have to do that. I really hope that that is not something that young people fear is going to happen to them." He added, "As prosecutors we're invested with some level of discretion. I can't imagine why we'd want to victimize the minor for a second time for a mistake that they're already paying for."

What Three Things in This Chapter Matter Most to You?

We all take away different lessons from reading the information presented in this chapter. What resonates with one person may not be meaningful to another and vice versa. I certainly hope that you've learned a heck of a lot more than three things in this chapter, but if three things were all you learned, I still consider it a win. Even a single piece of information could be invaluable if it was just what you or someone you're with needs in a critical moment.

With the information from this chapter fresh in your mind, please take a few moments to write below the three things that you consider the most important.

1. _____

_____

2. _____

_____

3. _____

_____

What Would You Do if It Happened to You?

You're on Instagram and see a notification. A girl you find attractive sent you a message! You check her profile and see that several friends from school follow her, but you don't know her personally. She thinks you're attractive and wants to chat with you more, maybe even exchange some private photos.

Would you keep chatting with her? Is there a way to confirm her identity?

Some Thoughts about "What Would You Do if It Happened to You?"
Just chatting may seem harmless, but if a predator is on the other side of that screen, the person could be subtly manipulating you to try to gain your trust. It's safer to simply ignore the message or to at least be sure the girl is who she says she is. Your friends could have been duped too. How might you check?

Ask your friends who follow her whether they know her in real life. If they do know her, show them the picture and ask them to confirm that it's her actual profile. To avoid these risks entirely, you could set your privacy settings so that no one can message you unless you're mutually following each other—and add new friends only when you're together in person. You can also try any of the techniques listed earlier for detecting catfishing.

However, you can worry a whole lot less about how to best handle this situation if you *never* get naked online and send nudes and if you cover your webcam when not in use.

Final Thoughts

It's hard to protect ourselves from harm if we aren't even aware that the harm exists. Lack of awareness always gives perpetrators the upper hand. Since I suspect that few readers knew much, if anything, about sextortion before reading this chapter, our first order of business here was to provide information about a crime that didn't exist until relatively recently.

In writing this book, I heard far too many accounts of sextortion than I care to reflect on, each heartbreaking in its own way. When I think about them, two commonalities among the victims come up: (1) giving in to the demands of the sextortionist and (2) not telling a trusted adult about what was happening. Again, the victims are not at fault, but we can learn from their experiences and do our best to resist a sextortionist's demands and not suffer in silence.

Where Can I Get More Information?

This chapter contains the essentials about sextortion. For those who want to know more and dig deeper into this topic, a Google search is a good place to start and will deliver numerous resources, some with valuable information.

There are agencies and service organizations whose mission is to provide meaningful support for anyone in need of information and resources related to sextortion. You can contact them about a specific concern you have for yourself, a friend, a loved one, or even a stranger. Often, if desired, you can stay anonymous. The ones below are a good place to start:

- Federal Bureau of Investigation (FBI)
    - » lead federal agency for investigating cyber crime, which includes its Violent Crime Against Children Program
    - » 800-CALL-FBI
    - » www.fbi.gov and www.IC3.gov to report (the FBI's Internet Crime Complaint Center)
- National Center for Missing and Exploited Children (NCMEC)
    - » resources pertaining to child victims of sexual exploitation
    - » 800-843-5678 for resources and reporting
    - » www.missingkids.org for resources and reporting
- THORN
    - » works to stop the spread of sexual abuse material
    - » text: THORN to 741741
    - » www.stopsextortion.com
- Child Rescue Coalition
    - » Works to stop the spread of sexual abuse material via decentralized file sharing networks and offers educational tips for parents
    - » childrescuecoalition.org

NOTE TO THE READER: If you are a minor and make a complaint about sextortion to certain people who work with children in their professional capacity, such as a teacher, they may be a "mandatory reporter." This means they are required to disclose suspected abuse or neglect of minors to law enforcement or child protective services.

Sextortion Quiz

Test your understanding of sextortion by taking this quiz. Hopefully, you'll get all of the answers correct because a single mistake could have real-world consequences if that answer contained the information you needed to stay safe.

Instructions: select the best answer from the available choices. Answers can be found in the back of the book.

1. According to the US Department of Justice, sextortion is the third-leading growing threat to anyone under 18.
   A. True
   B. False

2. Although there is no one definition of sextortion, it can be defined as online blackmail involving threats to expose sexual images.
   A. True
   B. False

3. Sextortion often begins when the perpetrator obtains an image or video of the target in which they're partially nude, engaging in sex acts, or wearing revealing clothing.
   A. True
   B. False

4. Sextortion happens:
   A. Only in the real world.
   B. Only in the virtual world.
   C. In both.

5. One of the most common things that sextortionists want from their targets is:

A. To return to a relationship.

B. To end a friendship.

C. To borrow money.

D. None of the above.

6. Catfishing is one way that a sextortionist uses to trick a target into sending them a nude image:

A. True

B. False

7. The lead federal law enforcement agency that assists minors who are victims of cybercrime involving sexual exploitation is:

A. ATF

B. DEA

C. FBI

D. There isn't one.

8. Giving into the demands of a sextortionist will likely:

A. Bring the sextortion to an end.

B. Escalate the demands.

9. Maintaining best digital privacy practices is an important way to protect oneself from sextortion.

A. True

B. False

10. Sextortion is a crime that disproportionately targets adults.

A. True

B. False

C. It depends on the state in which the victim lives.

CHAPTER 7

Teen Dating Violence:
It Happens in Every Zip Code

KEY TAKEAWAYS

- Dating violence includes physical, emotional, verbal, or sexual abuse, and stalking. Many abusive acts can be done digitally too.

- One in three adolescents will be physically, emotionally, or verbally abused by a dating partner.

- Teen dating violence can be minimized by adults as "puppy love" but should be taken as seriously as domestic violence.

- Targets of abuse often don't tell anyone about the abuse, but there are usually "red flags" that observant family members and friends can use to identify abuse.

- The ending of an abusive relationship is the most dangerous time for the target of the abuse because of the risk of breakup violence.

Chapter Highlights

Setting the Stage

No one thinks they'll be in an abusive relationship, since that is something that happens to "other people." As a result, abuse can be difficult to acknowledge in our own relationships, particularly because it's rarely on display when the relationship begins but creeps in over time. Such was the case for Lauren Astley, described as an energetic and talented 18-year-old. During her sophomore year of high school, she started dating classmate Nathaniel Fujita, who was regarded as quiet and kind. The two were in love and nearly inseparable. However, over time a pattern of abuse developed in which Nathaniel victimized Lauren.

Toward the end of their three-year relationship, Lauren and Nathaniel were constantly fighting and breaking up and then getting back together. On her 18th birthday, Lauren broke up with Nathaniel for good. She felt a huge sense of relief, but for Nathaniel the breakup started a downward spiral into depression, isolation, and substance abuse.

A month after the pair broke up, Nathaniel's mom became so worried about her son's well-being that she asked Lauren to go and talk with him. Lauren agreed and visited him that evening at his home. Nathaniel, alone in his house with Lauren, murdered her.

Sometime after Lauren's tragic death, her mother, Mary Dunne, was interviewed about the relationship. When speaking of red flags of abuse that might not have been seen, Dunne stated, "The signs, although I think they were there, were very, very soft. And I construed them as teenage behavior. And certainly there are things in retrospect that I would pay much more attention to."

For the record, Dunne is *not to blame* if there were red flags that she did not see; the responsibility for abuse lies with the choices and actions of the perpetrator. Moreover, Dunne is far from alone because *over 80 percent of parents* believe teen dating violence isn't an issue or admit they don't know whether it is.

> Teen dating violence is a *pattern of abusive behavior* where one partner seeks to gain *power and control* over the other. It isn't limited to physical abuse but also includes emotional or verbal abuse, sexual abuse, and stalking. Many abusive acts can be perpetrated digitally too.

Thankfully, it's uncommon for abusive teen relationships to end like Lauren and Nathaniel's. Yet it happens far more frequently than most realize. Violence in young relationships is not unusual because one in three adolescents in the United States will be physically, emotionally, or verbally abused by a dating partner. Teen dating violence exceeds all other types of youth violence and impacts millions of teens each year.

Both girls *and* boys (or anyone of any gender identity, including persons who identify as nonbinary, trans, or asexual) can be abused, and abuse can occur in any relationship, regardless of race, sexual orientation, or economic status. Abusers and their intimate partners do not have a certain look and can literally be anyone, including people like Lauren and Nathaniel.

Being aware of what dating violence looks and sounds like can make us better able to recognize what's happening and, if needed, to get help for ourselves or someone we care about.

My First Intimate Relationship

Like so many of the topics in this book, I have firsthand experience with this chapter's subject: my first intimate relationship, at the age of 16, was very unhealthy, and as I look back now decades later, it may have been abusive. To protect the innocent, I will talk only about my own actions and feelings.

My girlfriend and I dated for over a year, and like most relationships, it started out great. I don't remember when things started to change, but they did. I always thought that we were just going through the normal growing pains of "young love." Decades later, as I was going through my extensive sexual violence prevention training with Peace Over Violence (which included teen dating violence), I came to realize that the relationship was really unhealthy, perhaps even abusive.

I always wanted to know where she was, what she was doing, and who was with her. I would become desperate when we weren't together and always tried to get her to leave her friends and family so I could have her to myself. When things got heated between us, I remember saying things that were unkind.

I can't remember all the particulars of that relationship from over thirty years ago, but I do remember how I felt: confused, desperate, and lonely. I wish I had known then that our relationship wasn't just young lovers figuring things out and it was *not* how loving, healthy, intimate relationships should be.

What You'll Learn in this Chapter

There's no doubt that this is a serious book, and teen dating violence is a particularly serious subject that is not talked about often enough. It's unsettling to think about ourselves in such a relationship, but what if it's a friend or a relative? How can I help that person? How can I help myself? These are just a few of the questions we'll answer shortly.

We'll also cover some of the almost countless ways that abuse can look or sound by learning about the many different red flags of an abusive relationship. These red flags are often the easiest but not necessarily the only way to spot an abusive relationship. There'll be plenty of other things too, but enough talk.

Let's get to it.

What Is Teen Dating Violence?

Few relationships are perfect and there will always be bumps in the road, sometimes more often in some relationships than in others. A relationship may be unhealthy for either or both of the participants, but that doesn't necessarily mean it's abusive. Relationships can transition from unhealthy to abusive, and all abusive relationships, regardless of the participants' age, share a common thread: a *pattern of abusive behavior* (it's not a one-time thing) that is about *power and control* (one partner telling the other what to do, how to do it, when to do it, where to do it, whom they do it with, and whether to do it in the first place).

Abusers want power and control—to be able to pull all the strings. But as the reader will soon see, the strings can be cut.

Patti Giggans, the executive director of Peace Over Violence, explains, "Despite the ages of a teenage couple, what they are experiencing is just as problematic as domestic violence between adults. We simply use the term 'teen dating violence' because there are unique aspects to teen relationships."

February of every year is recognized nationally as Teen Dating Violence Awareness Month. The purpose is to help bring attention to the issue itself and to the differences between domestic violence among adults and teen dating violence.

The use of the word "teen" does not mean that only teenagers experience abusive relationships—these dynamics may also be present in relationships involving young adults and sometimes "tweens." Furthermore, "dating" is an inclusive term to cover the spectrum of adolescent intimate relationships, serious or casual, and may be described by the participants as just hanging out, crushing, hooking up, or seeing someone. Regardless of how a relationship might be classified, any can end up being abusive.

What's the Difference between Teen Dating Violence and Domestic Violence?

People often mistakenly think that intimate partner violence among adolescents is less serious than among adults. Although the types of abuse and experience of power and control are similar, there are reasons that teen dating violence and domestic violence are not, generally, used interchangeably. For example:

- Domestic violence is between adults, usually living together, who may have children together and mutual financial interests.
- The dangers of teen dating violence are often minimized by adults, and as a society, we've only recently started recognizing and paying closer attention to its ills.
- Teens have limited experience in intimate relationships and conflict resolution.
- Teen intimate relationships are more often affected by peer influence.
- Teens have less control over their lives and schedules.

A Note to the Reader: Even though some service organizations have names that only include the term "domestic violence," they may still provide services for teens in abusive relationships. Please don't be misled by the terminology.

Teen Dating Violence Often Flies Under the Radar but Shouldn't

Abusive teen relationships are far more widespread than many realize:

- Nearly 1.5 million high school students nationwide experience physical abuse each year. (Speaking of high schools and teen dating violence, schools have a duty to provide a safe place for students to learn. For more about this duty, generally, see chapter 5.)
- Teens who are abused by an intimate partner are more likely to experience depression, use alcohol or other drugs, have suicidal thoughts, and suffer other mental and physical health consequences into adulthood.

- More than 50 percent of *all* female homicide victims are killed by a current or former intimate partner (as opposed to a stranger), and one-third of all female homicide victims are under 30 years of age.
- Among college students, almost 60 percent said they didn't know how to help someone who's experiencing dating violence.

Jealousy Isn't Sweet

The media and one's peers can sometimes give the mistaken impression that jealousy is nothing more than a sign of affection. After all, if your partner freaks out about the idea of you with someone else, that's a sign that they really love you, right? Probably not.

Minor bouts of jealousy don't mean your relationship is unhealthy or abusive. However, jealousy that leads to possessiveness (we possess objects, not people) can be a sign that the relationship is unhealthy and potentially moving toward abuse.

Jealousy can be a normal emotion in a relationship, but it's how jealousy is handled that can be positive or negative. When a partner becomes possessive, they aren't thinking about you as an independent person but as an object that someone else is trying to steal.

Love is not about jealousy or control of another person—it's about respecting and admiring someone as a whole, separate person.

Negotiating Intimate Relationships Is Rarely Easy

Intimate relationships, at any age, can be difficult to navigate, and love can cloud one's judgment and ability to make good decisions. Giggans says, "For teens, intimate relationships are often more difficult because they are still maturing, developing, growing, and their brains aren't yet fully developed. They also don't have the experience of lots of practice in dealing with relationship issues that just comes with time."

The Different Types of Teen Dating Violence

Teen dating violence isn't just physical. The fact that someone doesn't have a black eye or swollen lip doesn't mean they aren't in an abusive relationship; there are many different forms of abuse. An abuser uses one, some, or all of the tactics listed below to exert *power and control* over their partner. Also, one act of abuse could overlap into multiple categories, for example, both physical and emotional.

Physical Abuse
Physical abuse is any intentional and unwanted physical contact (or putting the target in fear of physical contact) and includes:

- biting, scratching, pinching, hitting, pushing, pulling hair, slapping, punching, choking, or kicking
- assaulting one's partner with a weapon

Emotional Abuse Can Last a Lifetime

Emotional abuse, which doesn't show itself on the outside like some physical injuries, can last a lifetime and, for some survivors, is actually more damaging than physical abuse.

An abusive partner may make little comments about the target's looks or intelligence, putting the person down and suggesting that they're lucky that the abusive partner puts up with them. If no friends or family are around to counteract these negative messages, the target may start to wonder whether the put-downs are true. Eventually, the target's self-esteem may drop, and the person may believe that no one else could ever love them.

Even if the target breaks up with the abusive partner, those negative messages can stick around. They can become a part of the person's frame of reference and sense of self and can result in depression, anxiety, further isolation, and sometimes even self-harm.

- restraining a partner against their will, for example, stopping the person from leaving a room
- angrily throwing something at or near a partner
- driving recklessly with a partner in the car
- forcing drug or alcohol use

Emotional Abuse

Emotional abuse—also known as verbal or psychological abuse—makes the target of the abuse feel afraid, lowers self-esteem, and/or manipulates. This type of abuse causes emotional pain and can be a precursor to physical abuse. At times, the emotional abuse may be so severe that the target starts believing what the abusive partner is saying.

An emotionally abusive partner:

- has explosive outbursts of anger and sudden mood changes
- humiliates and/or intimidates the target of abuse

Kelsey Baker, a self-identified survivor of an abusive relationship, described her own experience of emotional abuse with a post to Facebook that went viral. She said, "Maybe he doesn't hit you, but he makes you apologize for getting upset after something he did to hurt you. Maybe he doesn't hit you, but you have to walk on eggshells every day to ensure he is satisfied enough to remain calm and happy. Maybe he doesn't hit you, but he steals your sense of comfort and security, leaving you paranoid and 'crazy.'"

Words can hurt. Sometimes for far longer than a physical injury.

- threatens to harm their partner, themselves, or pets, friends, and loved ones
- threatens to "out" the partner (who is LGBTQ)
- is extremely jealous or possessive
- acts with cruelty to their partner or to animals that the partner cares about
- gaslights their partner (manipulating by psychological means) by making comments that undermine the partner's sanity and self-confidence
- monitors the partner closely and tries to prevent them from doing things they like to do or pressure them to do something that the person doesn't want to
- isolates the partner from friends and/or family and prevents the person from being successful in school, work, or things that interest the target outside of their relationship

Digital Abuse

A subcategory of emotional abuse is digital dating abuse: the use of digital technologies, such as a phone, as tools of dating violence. The electronic world gives abusers another medium through which to abuse, even when the couple is physically apart. Because so many teens are spending lots of time on their digital devices, this type of abuse is common and can be more difficult for outside observers to detect.

Digital abuse can include:

- sending frequent or unwanted electronic messages
- monitoring online activities; for example, harassing a partner for liking someone's photos
- sending or posting threatening and/or harassing messages
- sharing or threatening to share embarrassing or private information or images
- checking the target's cell phone, email, or social media without permission, or with "permission" after exerting pressure
- posting false rumors or creating fake social media pages about a partner

- pressuring or forcing a partner to send nudes
- threatening to release sexual images of a partner unless the person stays or returns to the relationship (see chapter 6)

Emergency Protective Orders Can Save Lives

If you are being stalked, or if you are in an abusive relationship and have reason to fear for your physical safety, your local police station may be able to help you obtain an emergency protective order (an "EPO," which may be called something different in your jurisdiction). While laws and procedures vary, generally the target makes a police report about physical abuse/threats/stalking and requests an EPO. At that point, the officer should call a judge—who's often on call twenty-four hours a day—and relay the facts. The judge, in many instances, will issue the EPO, which goes into effect immediately. The order is of a limited duration, so the target will have to go to court later on to obtain a more permanent order—but first things first.

If an EPO is not an option, your local courthouse will offer a procedure for obtaining a temporary restraining order—which may be issued at the same time the required documents are filed with the court (again, this order will be of limited duration without later action on your part). Many courts have on-site clinics, websites, or information hotlines that can walk you through the process and provide the necessary forms. It may be best not to access the information (or to contact service organizations) from your own digital device in case the abuser is monitoring it.

The order, whether obtained from a police officer or directly from a court, prohibits the stalker/abuser from contacting or coming near you. Some jurisdictions even allow the police to seize firearms accessible to the stalker/abuser. Violation of the order allows the police to arrest the suspect on the spot.

Having said all this, it is often prudent for victims to first contact a domestic violence/teen dating violence/stalking service organization before seeking such an order for assistance in assessing if doing so may exacerbate an already volatile situation.

Sexual Abuse

Sexual abuse, known more broadly as sexual violence, refers to any type of sexual contact that is unwanted. Sexual abuse includes:

- nonconsensual sexual activity (see chapter 4 about sexual assault), including that which is painful or coerced, for example, using emotional blackmail or threats to obtain sex: "If you really loved me, you would" or "I'll break up with you if you don't"

- reproductive coercion, which includes forcing someone to get pregnant, tampering with birth control, stealthing (secretly removing a condom during intercourse), and controlling the person's choices while pregnant

Stalking

Stalking, which may also be referred to as civil harassment, is a pattern of willful, malicious behavior directed at a specific person that causes the person to fear for their safety. It frequently occurs with electronic stalking, also known as cyberstalking or cyberharassment. One in seven women and one in eighteen men are stalked by an intimate partner and report feeling very fearful during that time.

Stalking is a significant concern for young people between the ages of 18 and 24 because they experience the highest rates of stalking. Three in four people who are stalked know their stalker—a former boyfriend or girlfriend, or someone they declined to date. Stalking abuse includes:

- showing up unannounced or uninvited to places that the target frequents—in both the real and digital worlds

- making threats of physical or sexual violence

- making phone calls and sending letters and digital messages that are unwanted

- spying in person or via digital technologies, which the perpetrator can do by installing stalkerware, a form of malware (malicious software), on the target's digital devices to monitor the target's actions and whereabouts

- giving unwanted gifts

- waiting for the target without permission

- damaging the target's property

Anyone Can Abuse

As mentioned earlier, anyone can abuse or be abused. While every relationship is unique and possesses its own set of circumstances, many studies indicate that boys and girls report abuse about equally.

However, the relatively similar levels of overall victimization reported by girls and boys do not mean that there aren't significant differences by gender in the *types and effects* of the abuse; for example, girls and women are less likely to inflict serious physical injuries on boys and men and also suffer disproportionately from sexual abuse and death.

Both girls and boys can abuse.

Alex's Story

Alex Skeel (self-identified) and his girlfriend started dating when they were 16 years old. At first things were wonderful, but soon thereafter his girlfriend began telling him whom he was allowed to see and whom he wasn't and what to wear. She broke Alex's cell phone so he couldn't contact family or friends and started physically attacking him. For years, Alex was abused. It finally came to an end when a neighbor called the police to their home after hearing a loud argument. When the police arrived they discovered that Alex had severe, untreated burns to his arms and legs and had to be hospitalized. The police then discovered that his girlfriend had caused the injuries by throwing boiling water over him. With the help of others, Alex was able to end the relationship. He was interviewed on TV and gave advice to targets of abuse, whether male or female: "You're far more of a person if you speak out. You're only going to get better if you talk about it."

Troublingly, studies show that blame for the abuse is often placed on the abused person by both the abuser and the *target of the abuse*. This is certainly a mistaken belief because it is *never* the fault of the person being abused. We all have the right to feel safe in any relationship, and a healthy relationship never includes abuse. There is no excuse for abuse.

Why Don't All People Who Are Targets of Abuse Simply Leave the Relationship?

This question is not unusual and often posed by people who have never been in an abusive relationship. As a starting point, the person being abused wants the mistreatment to end but often not the relationship. Abusive behaviors usually aren't present at the beginning of a relationship. Rather, they creep in slowly and intensify over time. As such, *the target fell in love with the abuser before the abuse began and wants that person back.*

Many barriers can stand in the way of leaving an abusive relationship. Some of them are:

- Fear for one's personal safety, especially since abuse may not end when the relationship ends. **The most dangerous time in an abusive relationship is during the process of breaking up or just after having broken up.** This is often referred to as "breakup violence."

- Coercive control, a form of abuse in which one partner systematically dominates the other, particularly over an extended period, to gain complete control over the partner's life. Examples include preventing the target from having hobbies, friends, and access to money; dictating when the person sleeps; telling the partner when or what to cook and eat; and having sex on demand. It is essentially a form of caging, as the abuser can make it very difficult for the target to leave the relationship, having disempowered the person by placing significant restrictions over their freedom and access to resources.

- The cycle of abuse. Abusive relationships, like all others, start off in a honeymoon phase. Then, over time, tension builds in the relationship, which is followed by abuse. After abusive incidents, abusers almost always apologize, do something nice, ask for another

chance, make prom-
ises to seek counsel-
ing, and/or provide
assurances that they
will never do it again.
This often results in
the couple making
up and returning
to the honeymoon
phase—until the
tension builds again
and there's another
episode of abuse.

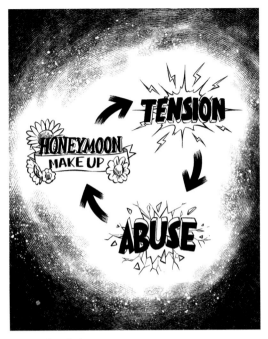

The cycle of abuse.

- Fear of not being
believed, including by
the police. Abusers
often have two per-
sonalities: a friendly
personality they show
to the outside world and the controlling, violent personality that only
the target of the abuse sees.

- Shame. It can be hard for someone to admit that they're being
abused, particularly if the person is fearful about being judged or
blamed by friends or family members for the abuse.

- Failing to understand that abuse is not part of a healthy, loving
relationship.

- Fear of being outed. If the relationship is LGBTQ and the target
of the abuse hasn't yet "come out," the person may fear being outed
when the relationship ends. Abusers may use the threat of outing
the partner to keep them in the relationship. Additionally, if they
come from a family or community that is unsupportive of their
sexual or gender identity, those identifying as LGBTQ may be less
likely to seek assistance or make a police report about the abuse.
For these and many other reasons, LGBTQ individuals can face
additional challenges seeking support.

Healthy Relationships

Everyone deserves to be in a healthy relationship in which one feels safe and respected at all times. When we're new to dating, it can be difficult to know what a healthy relationship looks like, particularly for those who witnessed an abusive relationship growing up.

Here's a quick rundown of some important features of healthy relationships:

Communication. You speak to each other honestly and respectfully—even when you're upset. You feel safe to say no to anything that makes you uncomfortable.

Trust. You have confidence in each other and feel safe, physically and emotionally.

Honesty. You can count on each other to speak the truth and not hide important information. You are able to express your wants and needs with each other.

Equality. You make decisions together, and when you disagree, you both offer compromises that feel fair and comfortable.

Sexual consent. You talk openly about what you like or don't like

These are just some of the attributes of a healthy, intimate relationship.

sexually and what you're willing to do or not do. You can take things at your own pace. No one is pressured, and consent is always present.

Respect. You are equals and treat each other as such. You recognize that you are separate people with unique feelings and opinions.

Boundaries. Creating good boundaries is a way to keep relationships healthy and secure. Boundaries can include everything from speaking up when you think you're being disrespected, advocating for yourself to do the things that are important to you, and owning the right to personal space, alone time, and ending the relationship if you choose to do so.

Please understand that abuse is a process of *disempowerment*, in which the target of the abuse is systematically isolated, often making it difficult to seek support. The fact that teen dating violence is often not talked about or not taken as seriously as warranted makes it that much easier for an abuser to convince the abused partner that no one will listen or help. The more we talk about this issue and assure our loved ones that we care, the less power abusers have.

How to Help the Targets of Teen Dating Violence

Observant Family and Friends Can Help

Only a third of teens who are in an abusive relationship ever tell anyone—and the confidant is normally a friend (rather than a parent or trusted adult) who is more likely to be on the scene than a parent when abuse may occur. There are many reasons so few targets of abuse speak out. Remember, abuse is about power and control, so the target of the abuse may be feeling powerless, isolated, ashamed, and fearful for their personal safety.

> Only a third of teens who are in an abusive relationship ever tell anyone.

Look for the Red Flags

One of the most important ways to help someone who might be in an abusive relationship is to know what the red flags of teen dating violence look like. The presence of red flags does not mean that a relationship is abusive, but can be an important first step in evaluating whether it might be. Some of the things you may observe are:

- unexplained physical injuries
- isolation from family and friends
- acting jumpy or nervous around one's partner
- a general lack of interest in activities
- feeling pressure to immediately respond to digital contacts from the partner
- dropping out of activities they previously enjoyed

- alcohol and/or drug abuse
- more than a three-year age difference between partners
- mood, behavior, and personality changes
- missing school and/or deteriorating grades
- self-harm ideation and the act of self-harm
- repeated attempts to break up, but the partner won't allow it, including threatening self-harm if a breakup occurs

---

Am I Being Abusive?

If you think that you *might* have abused your partner, the first and most difficult step is to accept that you may need help. Once you take responsibility for your actions, you should seek out professional counseling. You can ask yourself these questions, which might indicate that you have been abusive to your partner:

- Am I constantly checking up on my partner to see where they are and what they're doing?
- Is there a history of violence in my family? (Youth exposed to domestic violence are at greater risk of being in an abusive relationship as either an abuser or a target of abuse.)
- Am I possessive or jealous?
- Do I have an explosive temper that frightens my partner?
- Have I physically abused my partner?
- Have I pressured or forced my partner into sexual activities?
- Have I threatened to hurt my partner?
- Have I threatened to hurt myself, a pet, my partner, or anyone else if my partner breaks up with me or won't return to our relationship?

Listening Is an Act of Love

If someone you care about confides in you about relationship troubles and you recognize red flags of abuse, it's best not to question the person's story. Just talking to you is a huge step for the person. If you question the accuracy of their story, you can inadvertently send discouraging messages, such as no one will believe them, they're creating too much "drama" about it, or they are somehow at fault. No matter how good your intentions, this can cause the target to experience further, secondary trauma.

Some of these potentially damaging questions or comments can include:

- "I cannot picture her doing that at all. Really?"
- "You're so well educated and a strong person. How could this be happening?"
- "Did you say anything that got him so angry?"
- "Why would people believe you? It's your word against hers."
- "That's really hard to imagine. Why would he do that?"

Connie Kirkland, who works in sexual violence prevention in the university environment and was introduced in chapter 4, wants readers to know that "friends and family need to just accept what they hear as truth rather than minimizing or questioning what you're told." It's also important to listen with compassion, patience, and empathy and to "let your loved one know that they have rights, they have choices, they have control, and need to be respected for who they are. It is not their fault." Doing so will help them feel less alone and is an important first step in their seeking further help.

As much as we may want our loved ones to leave their abuser, it's best to refrain from telling them what to do. That decision can be made only by targets of the abuse—no matter how much you want them to break free. Their personal agency (their sense of free will and the power to make decisions for themselves) has been diminished by an abusive partner. Your objective is to help them get it back. If we try to make decisions for them, give them ultimatums about leaving the relationship, or try to keep them from seeing the abuser, our efforts may only further reduce their personal agency.

Try to validate the target's feelings and empower them to make decisions for themselves. A starting point can be to encourage the person to explore available public resources. You can even offer to research resources, call hotlines, and gather information on their behalf.

Patti Giggans notes that "service providers now have a lot of information about what can work to help the targets of abuse. We really do. So educating ourselves about what can be done is critical. There's lots of good information available online, by calling hotlines, or even making an appointment with an advocate to discuss the situation you or a loved one is facing. It's okay to not know what to do."

It is also important to remind the target of abuse that you will support them no matter what—even if the person decides to stay with the abuser. If we get upset with our loved ones for rejecting our help or for going back to the abusive partner, then the person may feel like there is now one less option for support and help in the future. This can further isolate the person and make them feel like the only person to rely on is the abuser. Targets of abuse need reassurance that we will always have their back, regardless of what they decide to do.

Aaliyah's Story

Aaliyah and her boyfriend Dylan started dating their freshman year of high school. After five months, their relationship started changing. Dylan started constantly texting Aaliyah, asking for her whereabouts, and got angry if she didn't respond immediately. If Dylan saw Aaliyah talking with a boy, he would accuse her of cheating. He would also yell at Aaliyah, grab her wrists, and throw things and punch walls in fits of anger. Aaliyah loved Dylan and begged him to change.

When she realized that Dylan wasn't going to change and the abuse continued, Aaliyah and her parents decided it'd be best if she left town for a while. Aaliyah moved away from Dylan, found support for what she was going through, and realized that Dylan had made her doubt herself and was a threat to her. When she decided to return home seven months later, Dylan began stalking her.

Aaliyah and her father went to the police station about their concerns and were told by an ill-informed officer that Dylan was "just being a boy." Thankfully, they were able to speak to a more knowledgeable officer who understood the danger of the situation, helped her file a police report, and obtain an emergency restraining order against Dylan. Since that time years ago, Dylan has been out of Aaliyah's life.

Aaliyah attributes her overcoming the abuse to a supportive father, a smart police officer, and the judge who issued the restraining order. She wants all teens to learn about teen dating violence and accept that it can happen to anyone.

It's best to be careful what you post online about a victim of dating violence. Pictures, locations, check-ins, and even brief statements can trigger abuse by the perpetrator. When you're not sure what's okay to post, you should ask. Also, don't confront the abuser or try to mediate the dispute. This can place you in harm's way and might even exacerbate the abuse. Remember, we can't fix the relationship, but we can and must support the people we care about.

Safety Plans for Breakups

Ending a relationship is difficult under any circumstances, regardless of age, but it can be far more challenging and potentially dangerous if your partner is abusive.

Abuse may not stop when the relationship ends, and what was mentioned earlier bears repeating: the most dangerous times in an abusive relationship are during the process of breaking up or just after having broken up. Lauren Astley's story mentioned at the onset of this chapter is just one example of breakup violence. It is also worth mentioning that the personal safety risk to targets is even greater when abusers have access to a firearm.

When breakups aren't mutual, the target of abuse is at significantly greater risk because the person is taking back power and control from the abuser. As such, anyone who is contemplating ending an abusive relationship should first empower themselves with a personalized and specific "safety plan" from a service organization.

A safety plan includes detailed ways to remain physically safer such as how to break up, where to break up, and how to follow through with it. A safety plan can help targets of abuse take power back and safely reconstruct one's life. They'll be able to figure out ahead of time whom to turn to for

A NOTE TO ANYONE WHO MIGHT BE A VICTIM OF TEEN DATING VIOLENCE: Please consider seeking support from a service organization (some are listed at the end of this chapter) and/or Find Your Person (see the "Find Your Person, Whoever That May Be" section in the Introduction).

help if they see their abuser at school, at work, or at home. It also provides targets with important information about how to protect their social media accounts and mental health.

Since many targets of abuse need ongoing support and resources throughout the process of leaving an abusive relationship, it's best to work with service organizations that will have experience preparing safety plans.

What If a Friend or Family Member Is the Abuser?

It can be hard to admit that a friend or family member might be an abuser. Staying silent, though, may encourage the behavior. While you can't change the abuser, you may be able to encourage the person to seek the help needed to stop the abuse.

Be mindful that it may be very difficult for an abuser to admit that their actions are wrong and must stop. Remember the saying: "The harder the truth to tell, the truer the friend who tells it." Try to help your loved one focus on what their partner may be feeling, rather than make efforts to justify the abusive behavior. Try to gently urge your friend to seek professional counseling.

What Three Things in This Chapter Matter Most to You?

We all take away different lessons from reading the information presented in this chapter. What resonates with one person may not be meaningful to another and vice versa. I certainly hope that you've learned a heck of a lot more than three things in this chapter, but if three things were all you learned, I still consider it a win. Even a single piece of information could be invaluable if it was just what you or someone you're with needs in a critical moment.

With the information from this chapter fresh in your mind, please take a few moments to write below the three things that you consider the most important.

1. _____

_____

2. _____

_____

3. _____

_____

What Would You Do if It Happened to You?

Your friend Ruben started dating Mia a few months ago. When the three of you and your other friends hang out, Mia is really funny and the life of the party. Like lots of your friends when they start dating, though, you begin to see less and less of Ruben. It hurts your feelings because he seems to be pulling away and to have forgotten your friendship. Finally, you ask him about it. Ruben gets emotional and says that Mia thinks you have a crush on him and is jealous. Ruben says that the last time he went to your house, Mia texted him every fifteen minutes and was really upset afterward, saying that if Ruben ever cheated on her or left her, she might hurt herself.

1. Do you see any potential red flags of abuse?

2. What would you say to Ruben?

Some Thoughts about "What Would You Do if It Happened to You?"

1. Do you see any potential red flags of abuse? Mia's behavior toward Ruben doesn't match how she's behaved with you and your other friends. This isn't a sign Ruben is lying—it's a potential red flag of an abusive relationship. Additionally, Mia is possessive, trying to isolate Ruben from his friends, and is threatening to harm herself, all other red flags.

2. What would you say to Ruben? It can be scary when a friend is in that kind of situation. It's up to you to decide what you might say, but from this chapter we've learned that the best thing to do is validate and empower. You might validate Ruben by telling him that it's not okay for someone to threaten to hurt themselves because of what their partner does and that Mia is responsible for her own actions. You could empower Ruben by offering to look up some resources for him on how to deal with a partner who is mistreating you. You could also encourage him to tell a trusted adult about Mia's behavior. Finally, you can remind Ruben that you will always be by his side, no matter what, and you don't blame him for hanging out with you less.

Final Thoughts

I'm not exactly sure why, but some of the teens and adults who attend my workshops on this topic seem to feel disconnected to it—like it won't happen to them. Most of them are right, because statistically it won't. However, we know that some people will be in abusive relationships and no one can say with certainty who that will be.

Part of the reason for this disconnect is that we so often think about domestic violence and teen dating violence only in terms of visible bruises and black eyes. While physical injury is part of what may be going on, you now know that there is much more to abuse than that.

I hope that at least every February, during Teen Dating Violence Awareness Month, you'll do what you can to spread the word about this issue. Even sharing some of this information with a single person could end up making a world of difference in their life . . . you just never know when it will.

Where Can I Get More Information?

This chapter contains the essentials of teen dating violence. For those who want to know more and dig deeper into this topic, a Google search is a good place to start and will deliver numerous resources, some with valuable information.

There are agencies and service organizations whose mission is to provide meaningful support for anyone who needs information and resources related to teen dating violence and domestic violence—and may not distinguish between the two. You can contact them about a specific concern you have for yourself, a friend, a loved one, or even a stranger. Often, if desired, you can stay anonymous. The ones below are a good place to start:

- Break the Cycle
    - » inspires young people 12-24 and supports them as they build healthy relationships and create a culture without abuse
    - » www.breakthecycle.org
- National Domestic Violence Hotline
    - » provides lifesaving tools and immediate support to enable victims to find safety and live lives free of abuse
    - » 800-799-SAFE (7233)
    - » text: LOVEIS to 22522
    - » www.thehotline.org
- National Teen Dating Abuse Helpline
    - » highly-trained advocates offer support, information and advocacy to young people who have questions or concerns about dating relationships
    - » 866-331-9474
    - » text: LOVEIS to 22522
    - » www.loveisrespect.org

- Victim Connect Resource Center
  - » confidential referrals for crime victims
  - » 855-4-VICTIM (855-484-2846)
  - » www.victimconnect.org

NOTE TO THE READER: If you are a minor and make a complaint about teen dating violence to certain people who work with children in their professional capacity, such as a teacher, they may be a "mandatory reporter." This means they are required to disclose suspected abuse or neglect of minors to law enforcement or child protective services.

Teen Dating Violence Quiz

Test your understanding of teen dating violence by taking this quiz. Hopefully, you'll get all of the answers correct because a single mistake could have real-world consequences if that answer contained the information you needed to stay safe.

Instructions: select the best answer from the available choices. Answers can be found in the back of the book.

1. Teen dating violence occurs only when teens are physically harmed by their partners.
    A. True
    B. False

2. Jesse is driving Drew home from school when they get into an argument. As has happened in the past, Jesse starts driving faster and faster and jerking the wheel, making the car go into another lane. Are Jesse's actions red flags of abuse?
    A. No. Jesse may have an anger problem but is not hitting or verbally abusing Drew.
    B. Maybe. It depends on whether Drew is frightened.
    C. Yes. Jesse is using intimidation to try to control Drew.
    D. More facts are needed to answer.

3. Simon and Jake start dating but don't tell their parents because Jake's parents don't know he is gay. Simon is angry at Jake, once again, and says he is going to tell Jake's parents about their relationship if Jake doesn't start doing what he tells him. Are Simon's actions red flags of abuse?

   A. No. Parents should know about their child's sexual orientation, so Simon is actually doing Jake and his parents a favor.
   B. Maybe. It depends on whether Simon was planning to "come out" to his own parents.
   C. Yes. Simon is using threats to try to control Jake.
   D. No. "Outing" someone is not against the law.

4. Over 80 percent of parents either believe teen dating violence is not a major issue or don't know whether it is an issue.

   A. True
   B. False

5. With rare exceptions, only boys commit teen dating violence.

   A. True
   B. False

6. Abusive intimate relationships are defined as a pattern of behavior where one partner seeks to gain power and control over the other.

   A. True
   B. False

7. Much of the time, there are no red flags of an abusive relationship that parents or observant friends might notice.

   A. True
   B. False

8. Miranda confesses to her friend Mei that her boyfriend Max has threatened to kill her if she breaks up with him. What can Mei do to try to help Miranda?

   A. Nothing until she gets more information.
   B. Question Miranda a bit to make sure she isn't exaggerating.
   C. Offer to intervene with Max so he never does that again.
   D. Listen to Miranda and suggest that she talk to a trusted adult or call a dating abuse hotline.

9. Teen dating violence and domestic violence are identical.
   A. True
   B. False

10. Digital abuse has yet to be recognized as a form of teen dating violence.
    A. True
    B. False

PART 3

Staying Safer Online

Digital Footprint and Digital Citizenship: People Change, the Internet Is Forever

KEY TAKEAWAYS

- Everyone who goes online leaves behind a digital footprint. You could call it your digital DNA— and it will be, to one extent or another, traceable to you for your lifetime.

- Employers and college admissions officers often check their applicants' digital footprints. It is not unusual for them to find something online about the candidate that causes them to "take a pass" on the individual.

- Your digital footprint is your "brand," and it can represent you in a positive or negative way.

- No one is perfect, and we all make digital mistakes from time to time. When we do, there are ways to clean them up.

- Digital citizenship is a critical way to maintain a strong digital footprint for the long haul.

Chapter Highlights

Setting the Stage

When I was growing up, we didn't carry around cameras; they were bulky and used expensive film that needed to be developed in a photo lab. As a result, there are no photos of me doing things I shouldn't have been doing. Similarly, if I wrote something down that was harsh, cruel, or otherwise inappropriate, it was seen only by a friend or two and the piece of paper on which it was handwritten was destroyed long ago. My world as a teen was analog and yours is digital—and the vast digital world rarely forgets.

About 95 percent of teenagers—regardless of gender, race, ethnicity, or socioeconomic background—have access to a smartphone and almost half say they are online "almost constantly." Carrying around a smartphone as you grow up is one of the reasons that young people coming of age today will be the first generation in history to create vast, digitized records of their entire lives. Pretty cool stuff. However, with the good comes the bad because no one can yet say what the full cultural, personal, or legal ramifications of this digital world will be. Like it or not, there will be some ramifications.

While the connectivity and freedom of the digital world make being a teenager today really exciting and unique, the permanence of one's digital content imposes a level of accountability, forethought, and risk management that, in my opinion, no teenager should have to face. It's a lot to comprehend: every time you go online you are shaping your digital legacy and, to some degree, the digital legacy of those whom you connect with digitally.

Despite all of my teenage mistakes, and there were many, the analog world I grew up in allowed me the benefit of do-overs. Unfortunately, do-overs are much harder to come by in today's digital world. This is true for *all* young people growing up in the digital age, not just the ones who may be in the midst of personal struggles, as I once was. I regularly witness and hear about teens who "have it together" and "are going places" but make digital blunders that negatively impact them, sometimes significantly and permanently.

> **Every time you go online you are shaping your digital legacy.**

Creating and maintaining a positive digital footprint and good digital citizenship takes ongoing vigilance as we go about our digital lives. We are in a truly unique period in human history. This chapter will help you focus on some of the essential ways to keep the integrity of your digital footprint intact for the long haul.

Everyone who goes online leaves a digital footprint—think about it as your digital DNA. It consists of the data you leave behind in your wake when you shop online, send emails, blog, post, like, and share. Importantly, it includes what other people share digitally about you. With every click your footprint grows. It can be buried but not completely erased. As such, the digital trail may form the basis of someone's judgment about you, fair or not, now or at some point in the future.

What You'll Learn in this Chapter

We'll first get an understanding of the significance and permanence of our digital footprint, since actions in the digital world can have real-life consequences. We'll then cover some ways we can effectively manage—or "curate"—our digital brand. This includes, if needed, ways to try to clean it up, although the effectiveness of this can be limited, depending on the circumstances.

Teenagers making mistakes is not news; they always have and always will. Even your parents and teachers likely had some missteps along the way. It's simply come to pass that our now digitally connected world makes it easy for a single indiscretion to reach a large audience with possibly short- and long-term ramifications.

So, please, never forget that if you have done something or ever do something that impacts your digital footprint in a way that concerns you, it's never too late to get back on track—and this chapter should help you. None of us is perfect.

Let's get to it.

Your Digital Footprint Is Your Digital DNA

As mentioned above, everyone who goes online leaves a digital footprint, and it consists of just about everything you do online: shopping, sending emails, favoriting, blogging, liking, sharing, following, and so forth. Even deleted photos, removed retweets, and unliked posts remain part of your

digital footprint, as they may continue to exist on an archiving server somewhere in the cloud, on a recipient's device, and/or in other digital domains. It's also a good assumption to expect that anything you do in the digital world may be found and shared by anyone, anywhere—because it very well might be.

Sue Thotz is a senior program manager for Common Sense Media, a large nonprofit organization that is a leading source of technology education for families and schools.

She says, "Even though we are often very short-term thinkers, we need to take the long- term view when considering our digital footprints. Older adults never considered that the things we were doing as young people, good or bad, would be discoverable and impact us in twenty, thirty, or forty years. That is no longer remotely true."

Since most teens are digitally active and their footprint can encompass most of their lives, it's critical to think about your "digital brand"—the manner in which you portray yourself in the digital world. This is extremely important because if you don't curate your digital brand thoughtfully, it can result in missed jobs or educational opportunities, embarrassing public sharing of personal information, damaged relationships, and more.

You may ask, "Why should I plan my digital persona any more than I plan my real-life persona?" There are *many* reasons! Here are several:

- Real-life interactions have the benefit of human perception—you can observe when someone misunderstands you and can do something in the moment to address that if you choose to. Online, you don't have the benefit of being face-to-face to better understand the context through which someone perceives your words, facial expressions, and actions.

> It's critical to think about your "digital brand"—the manner in which you portray yourself in the digital world.

- Digital content that was intended to stay private can spread quickly within our social circles and well beyond. The moment anything digital is posted or sent, we relinquish all control of where or when that content may end up.

- We create a lot of digital information about our interests and pursuits when we do things such as browse the web. Although we may think we are doing so anonymously, almost every action online can be traced back to us and is part of our digital footprint. This type of browsing behavior expands our *passive* footprint, which we'll talk more about later.

People Are Checking Your Digital Footprint

For years to come, "People are going to look at your digital footprint as part of their assessment of you," says Thotz. "For young people, we often point out that it'll likely be colleges and employers, but it's others, too, like a blind date, landlords, and prospective roommates." Someone will be making an assessment of the digital you, sometimes very quickly, and "you will not be there to provide any explanation or rationale for your online activities." We live in a highly competitive world, and decision-makers know how to explore people's online personas, to one degree or another, as part of their decision-making process.

Although some employers won't care to look into a job applicant's online presence, I myself do. I supervise over twenty prosecutors, legal secretaries, and paralegals, and whenever I'm interviewing for a vacant position, it's a highly competitive process. I want to hire someone who is suitable for the responsibilities that come with the job and am looking to find out more than what is on a job application.

I look online for anything about them that I can find relatively quickly, such as pictures, articles they've authored, work or personal recognitions received, leadership positions held, volunteer service, and/or a commitment to an activity. I expect most candidates to have some sort of online presence, and if I can't find it, I may be less likely to interview that person. Nearly 50 percent of employers feel similarly.

One of the places I go to gather information about employment candidates is their *public* social media accounts—about 70 percent of employers do likewise. (To answer a question I get all the time: colleges and employers are generally unable to access your private social media accounts. They can, however, sometimes get hold of your private images or posts when a friend or a follower shares them publicly.) I dig into not just what they've shared in years past but also what they've liked, whom they follow, with whom they're friends, *and even what their friends post.*

Most of what I find on social media about my job candidates is neutral—it doesn't influence my decision one way or another. There have been times when candidates have been helped (an old tweet that demonstrated a real concern for the well-being of others—a critical component of being a prosecutor) and others who have been hurt (a recent image of the person partying that I thought showed poor judgment to post publicly) by what I found on social media.

> It's not just employers who are checking out their candidates' digital footprints; over a third of college admissions officers are also checking.

Once again, I'm not alone: of the 70 percent of employers who do social media research, 57 percent found content that persuaded them not to hire candidates. Some of the most frequent reasons employers passed on a candidate include provocative or inappropriate photos or information, bad-mouthing a previous employer or employee, and poor communication skills.

It's not just employers who are checking out their candidates' digital footprints; over a third of college admissions officers are also checking. Brad Shear, an attorney who specializes in social media law, says, "Colleges are paying tech companies to scan the lives of applicants and advise whether they're good candidates for admission. They may contract with data brokers, utilize predictive analytics, and deploy other sophisticated techniques to conduct these types of searches."

Shear told me about one of his recent clients who was interviewing with an admissions officer for acceptance at a prestigious university. "My client expected to talk about his stellar grades, top test scores, amazing extracurricular activities, and volunteer work, but the interviewer was focused entirely on why my client was following a controversial figure on a social media platform."

The good news for those with a "clean" digital footprint (a term I use loosely seeing that people have widely different sensibilities) is that in at least one study, when college administrators checked the social media accounts of their applicants, it had a positive impact on the candidate 50 percent of the time. The bad news is that for 40 percent of the candidates, something was found that had a negative impact. (Nothing was found either way for the remaining 10 percent.)

A Positive Digital Footprint

We hear so many news stories about teenagers slipping up digitally in a way that negatively impacts their digital footprint. But we don't often hear about the many young people who are doing great things with their digital footprint and setting themselves up for personal and career success. Just one of those individuals is high schooler Devan Fink.

Devan, at the age of 11, started a baseball blog called *Cover Those Bases*. The blog has grown immensely and has opened doors into the professional baseball world that he never anticipated. He encourages teens to use social media to their benefit. "Social media as a whole often gets a bad rap. People think there aren't a lot of positives to it and that it really is detrimental to the development of teenagers. But for me, social media has been instrumental in my success. If you understand how to use social media in a positive way, you can really extract the value that it has."

Alan Katzman is a social media educator and strategist who founded a company called Social Assurity, LLC, that helps teens and young adults carefully curate their social media presence. He says that a high schooler's digital footprint "provides the student with a wonderful, positive opportunity to stand out and differentiate themselves. Social media is much more than just a communication tool between friends. It's a way for young people to tell their story to the world. When it's done right, potential opportunities explode because they've been able to use words, photos, and videos to tell a really compelling digital biography. They get to control the narrative and let the audience know who they are, what they stand for, and what they can bring to a college, a job, or wherever."

Katzman makes clear that our footprint doesn't have to be completely serious-minded and should "represent your personality and passions." However, it really does represent you—again, think of it as your digital brand—and, as such, it should be balanced with content that's also related to your education, career, and life goals.

As you can see, the stakes are high in our competitive world. In fact, there is even a thing called college admissions sabotage, which is when high school seniors (or others) notify college admissions officers about something from a classmate's social media past, including private posts or images, to hurt the applicant's chances of getting into the school the applicant wants.

That's just another reason it's so important to manage your digital footprint carefully, even if it means scaling back on what you share and

College Admissions Don't End with the Acceptance Letter

In just another example of private conversations gone public, a group of incoming Harvard freshmen from the Class of 2021 began a messaging group to share memes about pop culture. Eventually, the original hundred-person chat splintered off into a smaller, "private" social media chat in which the posts included memes and other images mocking sexual assault, deaths of children, and the Holocaust.

Harvard administrators found out about the private group, and ten students from the incoming class had their admissions revoked. In a written statement following the incident, the school reminded prospective students that "Harvard College reserves the right to post online. Occasionally (at least before applying to college or for a job), go back and remove posts from your feeds that aren't consistent with your objectives and goals. Removed posts may still be discoverable, but you've made them harder to find.

Active versus Passive Digital Footprints

Our "active" digital footprint comes from what we do online that connects content with our name or identity and may be discovered by people searching for us online. It is made up of the data we feed into online platforms or is fed by others using our names or identities.

The "passive" component of our digital footprint is the collection of things such as the searches we perform online and our browsing history—things that otherwise seem anonymous. Data is being collected about us even when we browse the web without logging in to identify ourselves or transact any actual business.

Also referred to as our "digital exhaust," this data may be collected without our knowledge. As a rule, sites will collect our IP (internet protocol) address every time we go online and that IP address establishes the connection to each of us personally.

Digital exhaust also includes things like clicking on a link to a search from a site that we are logged into, such as YouTube. The connection

withdraw an offer of admission under various conditions, including if an admitted student engages in behavior that brings into question his or her honesty, maturity, or moral character."

Some people may believe that these accomplished students shouldn't have had their admissions rescinded because they have the right to express themselves. People who think this are correct since those would-be Harvard students were able to post whatever they wanted—but that doesn't mean that there won't be consequences! Here it was a school; other times it may be a boss, friends, family, or perhaps the police. Any one of us can make a bad mistake, even those of us who are smart enough to get into Harvard.

between the service you are logged into and the site you are now browsing can include sharing the more specific personal information that is associated with your log-in.

In many cases, information about you from your digital footprint is being sold by websites and social media platforms to marketers so they can target us with more specific advertisements. For example, you conduct a search for a pair of shoes you want and for weeks afterward you get ads for those shoes as you are browsing on unrelated sites.

The more data a platform has about us, the more it can charge for laser-targeted ads. In many ways, we've become the products as much as the users of these platforms. An informal rule of thumb to go by is to assume that if a site or platform is free of charge, then you and your data are the products being sold.

The bottom line is that it's important to understand what our digital footprint looks like and to make it strong and positive. Whether active or passive, our digital footprint is often the first impression people making judgments and decisions have about us.

Getting Fired from Your Job before Even Starting

It was the night before Texas teen Bethany was set to start her first day working at a local pizzeria, and she was not looking forward to it. Bethany took to Twitter and tweeted "Ew I start this f***a** job tomorrow" (the letters omitted here were written out in the post), followed by numerous thumbs down emojis. An employee of the pizzeria saw her post and forwarded it to the business owner. Wasting little time, the owner fired Bethany on the spot by tweeting back at her, "No you don't start that FA job today! I just fired you! Good luck with your no money, no job life!" Working may not be fun for many, so Bethany was certainly not alone in how she felt. However, it's best to keep these feelings to yourself, or at least never put them in writing—particularly on social media!

Managing Your Digital Footprint

While our digital footprint is permanent, thankfully there are some things we can do to help ensure that it is the best reflection of who we are. You don't need to be afraid to have fun using your phone or other connected devices, but do consider doing some of the following things every so often:

- **Audit yourself.** Josh Ochs is the author of the *Light, Bright and Polite* book series for teens and young adults. His business, SmartSocial.com, teaches young people how to be safe on social media "so they can shine online." I talked with him about the importance of searching for yourself online to see what other people are seeing about you. He's a huge proponent of doing this: "Most colleges and employers are using Google to search the digital footprints of their candidates. The results are the new digital resume. Shouldn't you be seeing what they do?" Ochs suggests Google searches with keyword variations such as:

  » First Name + Last Name

  » Example: Jonathan Cristall

  » "First Name + Last Name" (in quotes)

  » Example: "Jonathan Cristall"

  » "First Name + Last Name" + City

  » Example: "Jonathan Cristall" Los Angeles

  » "First Name + Last Name" + School

  » Example: "Jonathan Cristall" Balboa High School

  » First Name + Middle Name + Last Name

  » Example: Jonathan Paul Cristall

  » Social Media Usernames

  » Example: @teachourteens

  » Image Results for "First Name + Last Name"

  » Example: Image results "Jonathan Cristall"

- **Set up a Google alert.** Get notified every time there's a post with your name. Again, consider multiple alerts for multiple versions of your name. (It's quick to set up; Google for a quick instructional.)

- **Chat with your friends.** Talk to your close friends about how you feel about their sharing your digital content. It makes little sense to be mindful about managing what you push out into the digital world if a friend's actions can quickly undo your efforts.

- **Post and share smartly.** We'll cover this in more detail shortly, but never post without first considering whether it's something you would want everyone in the world to witness. It can be hard to see now, but what you don't mind sharing now may change years from now. Only post things with the understanding that it will last forever—which is a mighty long time! **When in doubt, leave it out.** The same approach should apply to posts you accept onto your timeline, like, and people you follow.

Split-Second Decisions Can Have Long-Term Consequences

Ohio high school football star Jacob Smith was sitting in class when he impulsively decided to take a picture of his teacher, who was seated in front of him wearing a skirt. The photo did not show the teacher's face but was clearly inappropriate, showing her feet on the floor, legs uncrossed. Jacob thought it'd be funny to send the image to just a few friends via Snapchat. A screen recording was taken of the image and forwarded by a "friend" to the school administration. Jacob was removed from class, the police called, and then he was taken to the police station. He was kicked off the football team and expelled from school. Jacob had been a good student and hadn't had prior school disciplinary issues.

Word of the incident, along with many exaggerated and untrue accounts, spread throughout his community and well beyond. College football recruitment of him slowed. The emotional impact on Jacob (and likely the teacher) was huge. Friends shunned him, false rumors were spread, and his family was disappointed in him. His mistake, compounded by the power of social media, morphed into something much greater than he ever anticipated. Smartly, and by all appearances sincerely, Jacob owned up to his mistake, has learned from it, and apologized to those he hurt. He points out, though, "No matter where I go, I will still probably hear about it."

Alan Katzman has a good strategy here: "Remember that you are often catering to two audiences: (1) friends and (2) employers, colleges, and others." He urges young people to have two types of social media accounts: a private one for friends and a second public one for employers, colleges, and so on.

Katzman says, "Think about it like owning a television broadcast company. You have two channels: Nickelodeon and The History Channel. You aren't going to put SpongeBob on The History Channel and you aren't going to put a recounting of a World War II battle on Nickelodeon. In other words, one channel [your public account] should be for people who have never met you and might be making important decisions about you based on what they see. Both should be genuine and show who you are so tell them your story, but don't cross the channels."

Is There Anything I Can Do to Clean Up My Digital Footprint?

Yes, there are some things you can do! Please go to appendix 4 for some tips.

Brad Shear adds, "It's also a good idea not to use your email accounts all over the place. Have unique email addresses not tied to anything else but each of your channels."

- Follow the privacy guidelines in chapter 9. Those practical tips and tricks relate to the importance of setting up private social media accounts, not unnecessarily identifying yourself in usernames, periodically purging your friends and followers, reviewing privacy settings on your devices, protecting your log-ins, and much more.

- Practice proper digital citizenship. Being a good digital citizen, as we'll discuss below, is a very important way to help ensure that your good digital footprint remains intact.

Curating Your Digital Brand

Since you're going to be continuing to build your digital footprint, take a moment to think about what you want it to look like years from now so you can start to brand yourself now in a positive way. Most people curate their digital brand by focusing on the good things in their lives to post about and not sharing the negatives.

In fact, there is a great deal of research on the negative properties of social media. This happens, for example, when we compare our lives to what other people are posting about theirs—which is very often a more-perfect-than-reality version of themselves. This is just one of the ways social media can cause people of all ages, but particularly the young, to feel anxious and upset. Please remember that what people post on social media is a lot more fiction than reality and that real life happens behind the posts!

Someone may post a photo of the test they got an A on, recognition received for performing volunteer work, or walking across the stage at graduation. They likely don't post anything about the day they spent in detention or when they slipped down a flight of stairs rushing to get to their next class. This is actually smart to do because you want your digital brand to reflect your best self. The problem comes when we compare our own lives, with all the ups and downs, to others' lives as presented on social media. Everyone has a balance of good and bad in their lives, and none of us are without challenges, struggles, and embarrassments.

Defamation Happens

If you carelessly or maliciously say or write something about someone that is false and it harms their reputation, you may have defamed them. When you put defamatory statements in writing, it's called libel, and when it's spoken, the term used is slander. Although laws can vary by state, defamation is not a crime that will result in an arrest. It is a civil wrong called a tort, in which you, and possibly your parents, can be sued for monetary damages. The laws of defamation that are in place in the real world also apply to the digital one.

If you post on social media that Mr. H., your history teacher, molests children, unless you can establish that it's true you have probably libeled him. You're allowed to freely express your opinion about him without defaming them, though. You could post "In my opinion, Mr. H. is the worst teacher I've ever had" (though, remember, this is not a good way to build your online brand). Since this is merely your opinion, you're free to assert it without defaming him. However, you should expect that your opinion will make its way back to your teacher one way or another. You might get suspended or expelled if it violates a school policy or is disruptive to the school operation—even if you sent your opinion of Mr. H. from your personal computer at your home on a weekend. (See chapter 10.)

If you are active online, much of the value of that experience stems from the interaction your online presence has with the online presence of others, and your digital brand should reflect who you are in a genuine way. You may feel it's important to share your favorite TV shows, musicians, foods, travel adventures, hobbies, and many other details about yourself that come together to express who you are and what makes you special. It's totally natural to want to share those things, but it's also important to create balance.

What does that balance look like? As an example, if you are in high school and know that your goal is to become a marine biologist so you can work toward repopulating our oceans with many currently endangered species, then you should be thinking about ways to include your views on conservation and other related topics in your social media brand.

I'm not saying you need to repost and retweet every article that comes out from the *Journal of Marine Biology & Oceanography*. What I am saying is that if the University of Hawaii has one spot open in its marine biology program and the only thing differentiating you from other candidates is your daily post of another talking cat video, you've possibly missed a great opportunity to distinguish yourself.

> **Your digital brand should reflect who you are in a genuine way.**

Make sure you balance the fun, silly stuff with things that you want the admissions officers or prospective employers to see and know about you. Alternatively, if you don't want to do that, then at least don't post the talking cat videos or selfies every day. Occasional posts rather than frequent ones convey a level of maturity and balance. You may not be blogging daily about oceanic conservation in the Antarctic, but that's because you aren't posting every day.

Let's not forget that social media is not a one-way channel. You may be doing all the things you should to maintain a genuine, diverse, positive digital brand. However, since you are out there on the web, you must always face the possibility that someone could use your digital presence as a way to sabotage you, for example, snapping a picture of you while at a party and posting it with whatever comments the person likes.

Although you can't control what other people do with your digital data that they're able to access, you can do your best not to do anything that would create an opportunity for someone to get a photograph they could use against you (see chapter 11). If you're concerned about someone creating negative comments or posts on your sites or pages, then you can set up your privacy controls to have greater control over what other users can do on your pages. You can also tighten up many aspects of your digital privacy in your devices and accounts (see chapter 9).

Digital Citizenship

We all hear about and witness people who, from behind a screen, write or say things online that are awful, hurtful, and, at times, unlawful. Since they do not see how their words negatively impact the target, they are far more comfortable engaging in this conduct this way. There's a name for this: the online disinhibition effect. It refers to people who would *never* say nasty things to anyone in person but are comfortable doing so online because they're able to hide behind a screen.

Good digital citizenship means demonstrating and practicing safe, responsible, respectful, and legal use of technology.

The opposite of the online disinhibition effect is digital citizenship. Digital citizenship consists of three things: (1) having the social skills to take part in the online community in a mature way; (2) talking to someone trusted if something online is particularly troubling you; and (3) saying something if you see something. Let's explore in more detail these three aspects of good digital citizenship:

1. **Having the social skills to take part in the online community in a mature way.** A good digital citizen takes others' feelings into consideration at all times and acts ethically, positively, respectfully, and lawfully.

2. **Talking to someone trusted if something online is particularly troubling you.** Too many people, of all ages, are suffering emotionally because of things that happen online to them. When we don't talk to someone who can lend us a hand, we may find it hard to make the suffering go away. There are people who care and want to help. (Please see the "Find Your Person, Whoever That May Be" section in the Introduction.)

3. **Saying something if you see something.** If you witness troubling things happening to others and it's safe for you to help, you should. This could mean saying something at the time to the person engaging in the wrongful acts, reporting the acts to a trusted adult, reporting to the digital platform where the acts occur, or simply saying something kind to the target either at the time or after the fact.

Being mindful of the importance of good digital citizenship is not only a great way to ensure that our brand is what we want it to be for the long haul, it's also just plain common decency because we should treat others the way we want to be treated—in the real world and the virtual one.

Dr. Enrique Dans, a senior advisor for Innovation and Digital Transformation at IE University in Spain, puts a fine point on this: "The digital landscape is an inescapable part of our life, and acting properly and responsibly in such a landscape defines who we are, our principles and our priorities. We must understand and embrace digital citizenship in the same way we understand citizenship in the physical world."

Here are some rules of thumb of good digital citizenship. If you stick to these, you and your brand will be in great shape now and in the future.

- Choose your words wisely and don't bad-mouth others online—teachers, peers, employers, or institutions. Even if you feel justified doing so, it's still a bad look for you.

- Think twice before sharing anything while you're angry or upset. When we're angry or hurt, we may share mean and hurtful things that we will later regret. Take a few minutes, hours, or perhaps even

Online Misconduct

Sometimes people's online activity becomes so poor that it crosses the line into unethical—or even criminal—behavior. The following are some examples of things people should never do:

Doxxing. This is when someone publishes online another person's private contact information, such as their address, phone number, and place of work. Doxxing might feel like satisfying vengeance when someone has done you wrong, but it can be traumatizing and physically dangerous to the target.

Creating deepfakes. These are doctored videos that make a person appear to say or do something that the person never did. These videos, often pornographic in nature, are used in a number of disturbing ways, including as image-based sexual abuse or revenge porn (see chapter 11). In the twenty-first century, you can no longer believe everything you see.

Public shaming. Public shaming is a form of internet vigilantism in which someone appoints themselves as the person in charge of doling out "justice." Often the target has done something inappropriate themselves or may have said something highly offensive or ignorant.

days to cool off before sharing. Also, it's not just what you say but how you say something, so don't use caps lock when sharing as it's generally perceived as YELLING.

- Don't post details about relationship "drama" or private information about your friends, parents, current or former romantic partners, and others. **Keep private things private whether it involves you or someone else.**

- Don't share provocative photos, which can include nudes and those in which you're depicted drinking, smoking, vaping, or appearing to be under the influence. Learn more about this in chapter 11. Also, if you're going to take group photos, offer to use *your* phone so that you have control over the image.

- Don't share things that might make you appear intolerant. When information is traveling fast, people can make snap judgments. Some examples could be expressing racist views, judging the sexuality or

Shamers will publicly humiliate their targets. An offshoot of public shaming is "canceling someone," which occurs when a group of people, perhaps friends, boycott someone by unfollowing them on social media, no longer talking with them, and so on for something they did that offends or is perceived as "wrong." Sometimes the "canceling" that occurs among peers is a harsh response to an innocent mistake and disproportionately harmful to the subjected person.

Trolling. Trolling is a form of online harassment where a "troll" starts quarrels intentionally by posting inflammatory material or by insisting on a debate while ignoring or misinterpreting everything the other person says. Trolls enjoy using the anonymity of the web to get other people angry and worked up. If you encounter a troll, do not engage. As the saying goes, don't feed the trolls.

Swatting. This is the false reporting of a serious crime, such as a bomb or murder, to trigger police or other emergency services to respond rapidly to another person's address. In at least one such situation, the intended target of this dangerous prank was mistakenly shot and killed in his home by the responding police.

religious beliefs of others, and obviously much more. Remember, your audience today may not be your audience tomorrow.

Sue Thotz and Alan Katzman went out of their way to emphasize to me that anything in one's digital footprint that displays intolerance toward others is "radioactive." Katzman says, "Whether you're going to a college or into an office, they want to assemble a group of people who can get along, treat each other with mutual respect, and build safe, diverse communities. Images holding a beer may be radioactive to many, but intolerance is a whole other level."

To underscore his point, Katzman tells me that he was on a conference call with the dean of admissions for a large public university. The dean told the group on the call that the school would be looking at the social media accounts of its applicants and that anything that displayed intolerance was probably going to be a "deal killer." Someone asked about coming across a photo of a kid holding a beer, to which the dean replied, "If a condition of admission to our school was that you don't drink until you're 21, we'd have no one on campus." Of course, other college admissions officers will feel differently about underage drinking, but the point is a good one: **intolerance is almost never tolerated.**

- Double-check what you write for punctuation or grammatical errors. Good writing is important to both prospective employers and college admissions officers.

- Never share anything online that you wouldn't say to the recipient in person with a room full of friends, family, and teachers listening.

- Verify, verify, verify! It's never good to share information that turns out to be false. In short, get the facts before you react. Remember, even Wikipedia is an open forum to which anyone can add content. Equally, when you see information online, remember that it may be untrue. **Don't believe something just because it's online.**

- Only share what you own or what you have permission to share. Give credit when you share someone else's content.

- Remember: what can get you into trouble in the physical world can often also get you into trouble in the digital one.

These are but a few examples of what it means to be a good digital citizen. It's certainly not an exhaustive list. However, I think you get the idea: being a good digital citizen, for teens and adults alike, not only shows plain decency but, selfishly, also is in our own best interests in protecting our very valuable digital brands.

What Three Things in This Chapter Matter Most to You?

We all take away different lessons from reading the information presented in this chapter. What resonates with one person may not be meaningful to another and vice versa. I certainly hope that you've learned a heck of a lot more than three things in this chapter, but if three things were all you learned, I still consider it a win. Even a single piece of information could be invaluable if it was just what you or someone you're with needs in a critical moment.

With the information from this chapter fresh in your mind, please take a few moments to write below the three things that you consider the most important.

1. _____

_____

2. _____

_____

3. _____

_____

What Would You Do if It Happened to You?

You're in your junior year of high school and you start thinking about applying to colleges. Is it a worthwhile exercise to take some time and look at what you've digitally shared, liked, and so forth on social media?

Some Thoughts about "What Would You Do if It Happened to You?"

When considering the answer to this question, some will instantly recall questionable social media posts/shares/likes. If some of the things you've done in the past aren't a great look for you, you should go back and try to clean them up. If you don't recall anything questionable, it may still be worth doing a quick review to ensure that your recollection is accurate.

There are numerous ways to do this. You can track down those shares yourself and remove them. You can utilize software that will highlight certain categories of posts for your review. Another alternative is to pay a service that will do this on your behalf. Regardless, someone may still have a copy or it could be archived somewhere. Yet you've made it more difficult for others to find it if you remove it. (Remember, there's more about cleaning up your footprint in appendix 4.)

Whether or not you've shared things that you might possibly regret, this is a great time to start pushing things into your publicly shared social media accounts that make you look good. This looks different to different people but should be authentic to *yourself* and consistent with the values and priorities of the employer or schools in which you're interested. Remember, social media can make you a less attractive candidate for a school or a job or a *more* attractive candidate. While you're doing this, be sure to reread any of your online bios to make sure they're consistent with your immediate goals.

Final Thoughts

If I were going to sum up in a sentence what I hope you got out of this chapter, it would be a saying that you heard once earlier in this book, at the end of chapter 1: "With great power comes great responsibility."

Having access to the digital world almost everywhere you go puts a lot of power and countless opportunities at your fingertips. When utilized responsibly, this can be of great benefit to you and perhaps others you interact with. Unfortunately, too many people—of all ages—act irresponsibly. The trick is to understand that we must remain vigilant in our digital lives at all times.

When I was a teenager, we didn't worry about our reputations because that was something that adults worried about. For people coming of age today, this is no longer true because your digital footprint is a part of your reputation and it's something you need to start thinking about at a young age. Fair or not, **what you do digitally today can impact your reputation as an adult.**

Perhaps the easiest way to make sure that our digital footprint remains a positive reflection of us is to always act as a good digital citizen. This is a no-brainer for most people because they care about treating others the way they want to be treated and conduct themselves accordingly. However, even if some people don't care about others, it is still in the best interests of their digital brand to conduct themselves as if they do.

Finally, and perhaps most importantly, if you've already made a digital misstep or ever do, you aren't alone! No one is immune from having a lapse of judgment—adults included (I know I have). It is never too late to get yourself back on track.

Sue Thotz frequently sees young people make serious digital mistakes but "never one that there is no recovering from." She goes on to say, "There is no mistake to our digital footprint or involving digital citizenship that is greater than the love people have for you. Yes, the stakes are high and we want you to know a good pathway to success, but we *all* make digital mistakes. You are not perfect and that's okay!"

Where Can I Get More Information?

This chapter contains the essentials of digital footprint and citizenship. For those who want to know more and dig deeper into this topic, a Google search is a good place to start and will deliver numerous resources, some with valuable information. Here are some you can start with:

- Common Sense Media
    - » a leading source of technology education for families and schools
    - » www.commonsense.org
- ConnectSafely
    - » dedicated to educating users of connected technology about safety, privacy and security
    - » www.connectsafely.org
- Electronic Frontier Foundation
    - » defending digital privacy, free speech, and innovation
    - » www.eff.org
- Internet Safety 101
    - » a resource and teaching series that paints a comprehensive picture of the dangers children encounter online
    - » www.internetsafety101.org
- NetSmartz
    - » online safety program operated by the National Center for Missing and Exploited Children (NCMEC)
    - » www.netsmartz.org

Digital Footprint and Digital Citizenship Quiz

Test your understanding of the importance of your digital footprint and digital citizenship by taking this quiz. Hopefully, you'll get all of the answers correct because a single mistake could have real-world consequences if that answer contained the information you needed to stay safe.

Instructions: select the best answer from the available choices. Answers can be found in the back of the book.

1. Your digital footprint is entirely what you share on social media.
    A. True
    B. False

2. Your digital footprint can be completely erased if you go into all of your social media posts and delete them.
    A. True
    B. False

3. Employers cannot lawfully exclude candidates from employment based simply on their social media posts.
    A. True
    B. True, but only in some states.
    C. False

4. Admissions officers at federally funded colleges are prohibited from refusing admission to applicants who are minors based on what they find in the applicants' digital footprints.
    A. True
    B. True, but only in some states.
    C. False

5. Jeff posts on social media that his high school history teacher, Mr. H., is a child molester. He knows it's untrue and has hurt his teacher's reputation. Can he be held accountable for his actions by his school or Mr. H.?
    A. Yes, but only if the posting was made during school hours.
    B. Yes, but only if the posting was made on a school-owned digital device.
    C. Yes, because it was not true and harmed his reputation.
    D. No, because the laws of libel and slander do not apply to the internet.

6. If you want your digital brand to remain intact, it's a good idea to practice good digital citizenship.
   A. True
   B. True, if your state has a digital brand statute.
   C. False
   D. False, because digital citizenship has almost nothing to do with your digital brand.

7. One important component of good digital citizenship is to mind your own business if you witness someone being seriously mistreated online.
   A. True
   B. False

8. If you make a mistake online, you can just delete it and it'll be gone for good.
   A. True
   B. False. Deleted items may still show up in your digital footprint.

9. To one extent or another, there are ways to clean up your digital footprint.
   A. True
   B. False
   C. True, if you are under 18.
   D. False. You cannot clean up your digital footprint.

10. If something particularly troubling happens to you online and you're not sure what to do, it is a good idea to:
    A. Toughen up because what happens online is the virtual world, not the real one.
    B. Ignore your feelings and they'll eventually go away.
    C. Talk to a trusted adult.
    D. Retaliate

CHAPTER 9

Digital Data Privacy: More Important Than Privacy at Home?

KEY TAKEAWAYS

- In many ways, losing the privacy of the information in our electronic devices can be more troublesome than losing privacy in our homes.

- Privacy in our digital devices is paramount to many but not always paramount enough to take basic steps to help protect it.

- Private social media accounts are great to have but are never as secure or private as we think.

- Doing things to help protect our digital privacy doesn't take much time but can pay huge dividends—for the long haul.

- Digital privacy helps maintain a strong, positive digital footprint.

Chapter Highlights

Setting the Stage

You can learn more about most people by searching their phone than by searching their home. To explain my point, I ask teens and adults who come to my digital workshops a question: what would they rather have searched by a stranger, their phone or their home? About 90 percent say they'd sooner have their home searched, explaining that the contents of their phones are "off limits."

The quest for privacy (the "right to be let alone") did not start in the digital age, of course. Protecting one's privacy has long been considered a fundamental human right. So much so that its principles have been rooted in legal concepts and laws for generations (as you may have recognized in other chapters).

Although "privacy" can mean different things to different people, we all want the ability to withhold ourselves and our information from others, at least some of the time. It's like closing the front door to our homes.

Digital privacy, a relatively new and evolving concept, is the maintaining of our ability to use digital technologies without compromising our (1) information privacy, (2) communication privacy, and (3) individual privacy.

Dr. Enrique Dans, introduced in the last chapter, sums up the importance of digital privacy this way: "Privacy is power. When we lose it, we give that power to someone else and become powerless." Losing that power can be significant when our devices contain loads of information about our activities and us—which is now commonplace because of the widespread use of these devices to help manage and enhance so many aspects of our lives.

An unparalleled collection of information could be discovered about us from complete, unfettered third-party access to our phones and other digital devices. Information can be found in our:

- calendar: whom we've been spending time with, whom we're planning on spending time with, the places we are going and have gone to
- emails and text messages: whom we've digitally conversed with and about what topics
- contacts: the names and perhaps private information about people we know and associate with
- social media apps: everything we do on social media and some of what our friends do too
- internet browser: what sites we've visited and what we've been doing on those sites
- camera roll: the pictures we've taken and shared, the images that have been shared with us, the places we've traveled, and who's been there with us
- phone log: who has been calling us and whom we've been calling

I think you get the idea. We all keep loads of personal digital information on our devices and much of it, even when we have nothing to hide, we don't want to share with everyone, particularly strangers.

On the other hand, a search of our homes will reveal:

- what we keep in the fridge
- how many televisions we have
- whether we make our beds in the morning
- the clothes in our closet
- art that's hanging on our walls
- what we keep in our night table drawers

Of course, there are more private things in our homes, such as personal financial statements, but much of the time disclosure of the contents in our smartphones and other devices would be more intrusive.

Having *complete* digital privacy may not be possible if you spend any time "connected" because our data is constantly collected and sold and our locations are tracked—much of the time without our knowledge (one good source of information about this is the *New York Times* Privacy Project. Also, some states are starting to pass digital data privacy laws that give us rights to how our data is collected and used). However, the seventeen digital privacy protection steps outlined below are like putting strong locks and an advanced alarm system in your home: they aren't impossible to sur-mount, but they make it more difficult to break in. For most of us, when it comes to ensuring the integrity of our data, that'll do just fine.

What You'll Learn in this Chapter

In this chapter we'll cover seventeen ways that you can help keep your private digital information from slipping from your grasp. Implementing even a few of the best practices in this chapter can help protect you from mistakes made by your hand or the hand of another. They can also help you stay out of the grasp of cyberbullies, hackers, sextortionists, identity thieves, stalkers, sexual predators, and all sorts of other ne'er-do-wells.

I like how social media lawyer Brad Shear, introduced in the last chap-ter, summed up his thoughts about my seventeen-step plan. Shear, who works with National Football League (NFL) prospects on social media issues before they get drafted, equates my list with what he tells his clients: "You're probably not going to crash your car, but if you do, seat belts and airbags keep you safer. The things in this chapter are the equivalent ways of not driving into a ditch."

Let's get to it.

> **NOTE TO THE READER:** Since the methods to deploy many of the steps described in the next section vary by the type of device and software version and evolve over time, I have not included that information herein, but it is very easy to find. A quick Google search for articles and videos on any of the steps will provide short articles and videos (my preference) to install them on your device or accounts.

A Seventeen-Step Program to Help Safeguard Your Digital Data

Here are the seventeen steps, in no particular order:

Step 1: Have Private Social Media Accounts (But Don't Become Complacent!)

An important starting point for maintaining the integrity of your digital privacy is to have a private social media account. While the utility of this first step can depend on if and how you use social media, many people will benefit by having at least one private social media account. It provides, to one degree or another, a barrier of sorts to help better ensure that your private "stuff" stays that way. (However, you probably *do* want one public social media account to "brand" yourself. See chapter 8 for details.)

With the good of having private accounts comes the bad: complacency. I see and hear about way too many young people whose private digitized content, like an image or post, is shared with people whom they didn't intend for it to be shared with. Don't get me wrong, it's great that so many young people are using private accounts to help protect their data, but not so great when they have a false sense of security that what they share will *always* stay private.

This sort of mishap happened to Alexandra, 18 years old, who had just been named the "Sea Goddess" of the Maine Lobster Festival, a huge honor for her, her family, and her local community. Hours after she was crowned the winner, two photos she had posted to her *private* Instagram account—one of her holding a joint (a marijuana cigarette), the other of her holding a Juul (an electronic cigarette used for vaping nicotine or cannabis)—were forwarded anonymously to the pageant organizers.

Alexandra was immediately stripped of her crown, which many thought was terribly unfair. In an interview afterward, she revealed that only her "exclusive friends" had access to the private account that contained the pictures and that well before the pageant she had deleted those posts. Clearly, one of Alexandra's "exclusive friends," or someone they had shared the images with, sent them to the pageant organizers. There are countless stories just like Alexandra's.

It may be hard to imagine now, but today's friends or trusted intimate partners may not be your friends or partners tomorrow. They could even turn out to be enemies. Even worse: a frenemy—whom you may be more likely to lower your guard around.

If any of these people have access to private digital information that isn't a "good look" for you, they can easily share it with others whom you did not intend to see it. Or someone could just hold on to the information and way down the road, long after you've forgotten about it, expose it.

Even true friends, either as a harmless joke or out of sheer carelessness, can inadvertently destroy your digital privacy by passing along content from your private account. This even happened to me as an adult when I put something out digitally that I probably shouldn't have and sent it to a close friend for his eyes only. He was careless and others saw it. I was embarrassed, and it put a strain on our friendship.

The takeaway here is to have at least one private social media account and to **always ask yourself before you post or write anything digitally—private or public—if it "got out," now or in the future, would it be a bad look for me?** If the answer is yes or maybe, then strongly consider not creating that content digitally.

Always keep in mind that rather than sharing something sensitive or inappropriate digitally, you can always go "old school." Take it offline and wait until you see the person with whom you want to share it.

Step 2: Password Protecting Devices and Strong Passwords Are a Must

One of the most basic safety precautions we can implement is to lock the home screen of our smartphones and other digital devices with a password or biometrically, for example, by facial recognition or a thumbprint. According to one recent study, nearly 30 percent of smartphone users do not use either. If you are within this 30 percent, there aren't many easier or faster ways to help secure your device than to add a password or biometric identification.

Whether the password is to access your device or an online account, some best practices will help ensure that the integrity of that password stays intact. Here are some ways to make sure that your passwords do what they're supposed to do:

- Never share your password with any of your friends. If it's already been shared, change it. One of the last things you want is someone having access to any of your accounts where they can see private information and cause complete mayhem by, for example, changing your password so you're blocked from accessing your own account and then posting things without permission.

- Have complex *and* unique passwords for each website that you frequent and change them periodically. They can be a mixture of upper- and lowercase letters, symbols, and numbers. Passwords should ideally be at least fifteen characters long. By using different passwords for *each* of your online accounts, you can limit the damage that can be done if a password falls into the hands of someone it shouldn't. If so, only one account is compromised, instead of all of them.

- Given the number of passwords most need, use a password management app to store all of your log-in and password information. These apps only necessitate remembering one password to access the app. As Dr. Enrique Dans points out, "A good password manager is a great friend."

- Don't post your password in a place where anyone can see it. I know this sounds obvious, but many keep their password written on a Post-it note on their desk or computer.

- Do your best to avoid typing passwords into devices that are shared, for example, those at the school library, or that you don't own, control, or trust. If you do, be sure to manually log out when a session is complete.

Step 3: Enable 2FA (When Available)

You can make your online accounts more difficult to hack or be accessed by an unauthorized user—even someone who has your password—by enabling a simple security enhancement called two-factor authentication, also known as 2FA or multifactor authentication.

By default, almost all online accounts require a username and a password. 2FA adds an extra layer of protection by requiring two different ways to prove your identity—something you have with you (one of your devices) and something you know (your log on credentials). A simple way to understand this is to think of an ATM card. To withdraw money, you need two things: the card (something you have) and your PIN (something you know).

Many of the world's most popular social media sites have made 2FA readily available from their security settings. Moreover, with or without 2FA enabled, many sites now ask verification questions. Never use answers to these questions that other people might know.

Bad Cyber Actors Can't Always Shield Their Identities

Many people who do things online that they shouldn't only feel secure doing so because they're using a private social media account or have set up social media/email/text accounts/apps using an alias. These tactics can be a barrier of sorts to discovering someone's identity but not as much of a barrier as many people think.

Former police detective Bruce Anderson is a specialist in cyber intelligence, internet forensics, and cyber investigations and the cofounder of Cyber Investigation Services, a licensed private investigative agency. He told me that for most people, a determined cyber investigator will be able to track down your identity. "You've got to be pretty doggone good to not get caught."

Anderson and his firm have investigated pretty much every type of cybercrime: "There isn't much we haven't handled: cyberstalking, cyberbullying, sextortion, financial crimes, and more." I asked him about tracking people down via their IP address (a unique numerical address assigned to all connected devices that identifies things such as

Step 4: Check Your Privacy Settings

At least once a year, take a few moments to personalize your privacy settings on *all* of your social media sites and digital devices. Making certain that these settings are fine-tuned helps to ensure the integrity of your digital privacy. Platforms change their privacy options over time, so once they're set up, you need to go back periodically to make sure they're still doing what you want them to.

The more you stay on top of your security settings, the greater confidence you can have about what you share.

Step 5: Software Updates

Keep your devices, including your internet browser, up to date with the latest patches and software versions. Not only does updating bring new features to your devices, but it ensures that you're running the most secure software version.

Private investigator Bruce Anderson tells me, "There's nothing that cannot be hacked by someone who knows what they're doing; software updates are an important step to make it more difficult." (Speaking of

the Internet Service Provider (ISP) and the region, city, and zip code where the device went online). Anderson responded more broadly to make his point: "No one is as anonymous as they think they are. We're able to track people down by their digital footprint. Everyone leaves their prints behind. Can you get away with a crime online? Sure. But it's gotten real, real hard."

People who want to discover the person hiding behind the curtain of a private account can try to do so by hiring a private investigator, like Anderson. In other situations, when activity from a private account triggers a police investigation (for example, intense cyberbullying), the police can obtain a search warrant that requires a digital platform to disclose all user information from that account. Or, if there's a civil lawsuit among private parties related to activity from a private account, subpoenas can be issued (court orders compelling a third party to turn over evidence under their control) that require a digital platform to disclose user information from the account.

hacks, he also suggests not to "put private images in the cloud where a good hacker can get 'em. Young folks in particular need to remember that it's not just high-profile targets that have to be diligent about their cybersecurity.")

Each time a software update happens, go back into your device or app and confirm your privacy settings to ensure that they haven't reverted to the default settings. Also make sure to have strong, updated virus protection on your computers.

Step 6: Prune Friends and Followers

At least every year, reassess the followers and "friends" on social media platforms that you've authorized to access your pages. If you aren't friends

or at least friendly with some of these people in the real world, it might be best to prune them from your digital one. On some platforms you can simply restrict when and what you share with certain people of your choosing.

You wouldn't share your posts with a stranger on the street, so why let someone who amounts to a stranger have that same information online? While you're at it, you can also cut down on the number of companies that may have access to your personal information by deleting apps and their respective accounts that you don't use. You can also manage which apps are able to access aspects of your phone by going into your device's settings.

Watch Out for Phishing

Phishing is the fraudulent attempt by cybercriminals to steal your sensitive information—such as usernames, passwords, credit card details, photos, and pretty much anything else on your digital devices—by disguising themselves as a trustworthy entity in an electronic communication such as an email or text (when made via text, it's called "smishing," or SMS phishing).

These emails or texts will look official and have an urgent yet professional tone. They will include a link that, when clicked, directs users to a fake website that looks legitimate. For example, you could receive an email that appears to be from Instagram advising that someone has attempted to access your account and a new password must be created to secure it. The link would take you to what looks like the Instagram log-in page. Only this page would not be the real log-in page, just an almost identical lookalike aimed at tricking you into typing your log-in email and password so that they can be stolen.

A few red flags of phishing include offers that are too good to be true, messages that have a sense of urgency and that compel you to act fast, attachments you weren't expecting (don't open them!), and hyperlinks that you are directed to click. Don't click on these links. Instead open a new browser tab and go to the websites through a trusted search engine; or you can hover your cursor over the hyperlinks and make sure they are what you expect them to be.

Step 7: Think Twice Before Sharing Your Cell Phone Number

Since it's unusual to change cell phone numbers, they've increasingly become gateways to our identities. Whether it's to sign up for programs that offer store discounts or to sign into apps and websites, the use of one's cell phone number is common. Phone numbers are no longer just a bunch of digits. In many instances, your phone number is a stronger identifier of you than your name—maybe even more so than your Social Security number, since its privacy is regulated—yet we've been conditioned to share our phone number without hesitation.

When your number is used to conduct advanced and not-so-advanced searches, lots of information about you can be discovered. It can be used to gather information about you that would assist a hacker, scammer, stalker, or anyone else who doesn't have your best interests at heart.

While it's probably not practical to completely stop giving out your cell phone number entirely, think twice before doing so. You can use an app like Google Voice to create a second phone number to give out to people and brands you don't entirely trust.

Step 8: Cover Your Webcam

It is becoming increasingly easier for digital ne'er-do-wells to hack into computers. In some circumstances, they spy on us by gaining access to our webcam and microphone, and by tracking our clicks and keystrokes with the use of malware (malicious software) surreptitiously installed on our devices.

In the event that you are hacked in this way, having a webcam cover and a microphone cover on your computer can reduce the potential harm. These only costs a few bucks to buy, but if you want to save the money, you can use black electrical tape over your camera and microphone. Some people also put covers on the camera lens of their smartphones. These are also inexpensive, but they are used less frequently because our phones, unlike an open laptop or a desktop computer at home, don't often provide the types of images a hacker wants.

Step 9: Limit How You Identify Yourself

Depending on the app or site and how you choose to use it, consider a username, bio details, and even email addresses that do not disclose too much personal information about you, such as your name, birthday, gender, age, or indications about where you live or the school you attend.

> ## Be Like Mark Zuckerberg (in One Way)
>
> Mark Zuckerberg, the billionaire founder of Facebook, posted an image of himself to Facebook that inadvertently captured his open laptop in the background. A keen observer noticed that both his webcam and his microphone were covered in black tape. There were a number of news stories about this image in which journalists were asked whether Zuckerberg was paranoid or just cautious. The answer was uniformly the latter. Such measures have long been regarded as a basic, inexpensive security safeguard. Lysa Myers, a security researcher at the data security firm ESET, says, "Covering the camera is a very common security measure. If you were to walk around a security conference, you would have an easier time counting devices that don't have something over the camera."
>
> Hacks are a growing problem for consumers, not just people who are high-value targets such as billionaires or celebrities. Stephen Cobb, a senior security researcher at ESET, notes that the threat is to everyone because there are "people scanning the internet for accessible webcams for a range of motives, from voyeurism to extortion." Do yourself a favor—if you don't have a cover on your webcam or microphone, put this book down for a few minutes and order them online or make them.

The more information you put in your social media profile and user IDs (and even your posts), the easier it is for people with bad intentions to use that information to their advantage and to your detriment. If you have a public social media account to maximize your digital brand (as discussed in the previous chapter), you'll need to strike some sort of balance because you do want people to be able to find you. Still, think twice about how much more personal information, other than your name, you add to that profile and username.

Step 10: Turn Off Live Photos

The Live Photos setting on iPhones adds video and audio for about 1.5 seconds before and after a photo is taken. So your "pictures" are actually short videos. Some people have gotten themselves into unfortunate situations by inadvertently sharing these images when something private or embarrassing was said or done before or after the image was captured. Live Photos can be turned off in your phone's photo settings or disabled for photos you want to share that were captured using Live Photo.

Step 11: Lock Screen Message Previews

When you receive a message or a voicemail, your phone will typically display not only the identity of the person but also part of the message's content. When you're sitting with others nearby, such as in a classroom, shoulder-surfers, like the girl pictured here, can get a glimpse at information you may not want them to see. These preview settings can be altered in your device.

Step 12: Restrict Who Can Contact You via AirDrop

AirDrop on iPhone and its equivalent AirDroid on Android devices allow unknown people to contact you and send images from nearby devices. One problematic aspect of this is cyberflashing—in which explicit images are sent without the recipient's consent. What is also troubling is that if you've named your phone, your AirDrop will show that name to the person AirDropping you. To avoid this, turn off AirDrop in your settings or restrict its use to contacts only.

Step 13: Use Internet Security Software

At the very minimum, use antivirus-type security solutions on your computer. These can be helpful when it comes to preventing someone unauthorized from accessing your devices and cloud-based storage and breaching your privacy. For more robust protection, internet security solutions are even better. Reputable security products, details of which can be found online, feature stronger protection against phishing, hackers, and numerous other cyber threats that could result in a data breach.

Step 14: Use Secure Websites

Not all websites are created equal. Secure sites, which encrypt your data, will be identified in your browser as HTTPS, not HTTP, and display a little lock symbol, as depicted here, to the left of the URL. Using secure websites is particularly important when you engage in financial transactions online.

Step 15: Talk with Your Friends

Have you ever had a fun night hanging out with friends, being silly, and doing things that, while not wrong or illegal, you don't want others to see? Maybe you shoved a whole piece of cake into your mouth. Maybe you tried on a ridiculous costume. Then, at the end of the day, maybe you opened your favorite social media app and found that a friend had described what you all were doing or maybe even posted photos that you believe to be unflattering.

Most friends have no ill intentions but may have different sensibilities about what is appropriate to share digitally. You may share something with a friend expecting that it will remain private. Unfortunately, the friend may not understand your expectation. It's therefore a good idea to talk to them about how you feel about their sharing content and photos about you. You may have adjusted your privacy settings so strangers can't see your posts, but your friends may not have.

A good friend will understand your concerns about making sure your "brand" is what you want it to be. At the same time, ask your friends how they feel about what you share online about them. That will demonstrate that you care about their boundaries too.

Step 16: Limit Use of Public Wi-Fi

Public Wi-Fi that does not necessitate the use of a password for access can be found in popular public places such as coffee shops, malls, restaurants, airports, and hotels. The security of these networks can be weak or nonexistent, and they can be a goldmine for cybercriminals who want to steal your log-in credentials or hack into your computer. Anything sent over this type of unsecured network can potentially be seen by others on the network, because the traffic isn't encrypted by the Wi-Fi connection itself.

If you need to access a secure Wi-Fi network for your laptop but one isn't available, use your phone as a hot spot, which creates a secure network to log into. As an alternative, if you are going to be on public Wi-Fi, consider using a robust internet security solution on your device or a virtual private network (VPN). More information about these can be found online. By the way, be sure to password-protect your home Wi-Fi too.

Step 17: Use Geotagging and Location-Sharing Thoughtfully

On many smartphones and tablets, when you take and share a photo, the precise geographic location of that photo can be retrieved by anyone who wants that information and is a bit tech savvy. The geographic data in the image, called metadata, consists of coordinates such as latitude and longitude but may also include bearing, altitude, distance, and place names. This can be potentially dangerous, particularly for targets of stalking, because it tells a perpetrator where they are. Photo-geotagging options can be modified in your device settings, and some picture-sharing sites automatically strip location data out of any photos you post.

Even if GPS coordinates are removed from photos you share, it will be of little effect if you post pics in which you identify yourself as currently being present at a certain location. For example, posting a selfie saying "Hello from Hotel Kona in Hawaii" tells a burglar that you aren't home. Since it's common to want to share our precise locations with friends and family, you can wait until after you've departed the location to share it.

Also, many apps constantly share your precise location using GPS, Bluetooth, and Wi-Fi. You can go into your device and disable location tracking for all apps or restrict it for certain apps. For example, in apps, change the geo-location setting from "Always" to only "While Using the App."

Similarly, mobile devices have a unique mobile advertising ID that tracks our online activity and is sent to and used by developers and marketers. You can disable this feature in your device's privacy settings.

What Three Things in This Chapter Matter Most to You?

We all take away different lessons from reading the information presented in this chapter. What resonates with one person may not be meaningful to another and vice versa. I certainly hope that you've learned a heck of a lot more than three things in this chapter, but if three things were all you learned, I still consider it a win. Even a single piece of information could be invaluable if it was just what you or someone you're with needs in a critical moment.

With the information from this chapter fresh in your mind, please take a few moments to write below the three things that you consider the most important.

1. _____

_____

2. _____

_____

3. _____

_____

What Would You Do if It Happened to You?

After your senior-year final exams, you and some of your friends decide to have a celebratory slumber party. While at the party, you decide to give yourself a facial treatment to help clear up some acne.

Your friends come into the bathroom, see you in a green facial mask, and start to laugh. You admittedly look kind of funny and laugh too. One of your friends is very active on social media and posts regular status updates. You suspect that this friend is going to push out a post about your facial treatment. You're a bit embarrassed about drawing attention to your acne and also sensitive to other friends' feelings who weren't invited to the party. What would you do?

Some Thoughts about "What Would You Do if It Happened to You?"

It can be difficult to speak to someone about what you don't want them posting about you. They may say you're being too sensitive or to "chill." If their account is private, they may tell you that you're overreacting since only friends will see it. You should be true to yourself, though, and still talk to them. If you don't, you may always be uneasy spending time with them.

If you tell this friend that you don't want anything posted on social media about your facial treatment or your attending the party, your request should be respected. It doesn't mean your friend has to agree with your feelings, but that's beside the point. You want to be around people who understand your boundaries and respect your wishes. If they don't, then they probably aren't acting like friends, and if you choose to hang out with them, you should expect that anything you do is fair game to post about.

Final Thoughts

When it comes to digital privacy, I strongly urge you to never digitize and send something that, if exposed, *might* make you look bad. Not only do such acts put your digital privacy at risk of greater exposure, they can also compromise a positive digital footprint.

Follow at least some of these seventeen tips and tricks to help "lock down" your devices. When we become diligent in these best practices early on in life, they become habit and will often continue well into the future—a smart move that gives you greater confidence about what you're doing.

Where Can I Get More Information?

This chapter contains the essentials of digital data privacy. For those who want to know more and dig deeper into this topic, a Google search is a good place to start and will deliver numerous resources, some with valuable information. You can also refer to the five sources listed at the end of chapter 8.

Digital Data Privacy Quiz

Test your understanding of the importance of digital privacy by taking this quiz. Hopefully, you'll get all of the answers correct because a single mistake could have real-world consequences if that answer contained the information you needed to stay safe.

Instructions: select the best answer from the available choices. Answers can be found in the back of the book.

1. To guarantee 100 percent digital privacy, your social media accounts should be private.
   A. True
   B. False

2. Malicious software (malware) can be surreptitiously installed on computers that can turn on webcams and microphones, and track our clicks and keystrokes.
   A. True
   B. False
   C. True, but in all likelihood, only while traveling abroad.

3. If law enforcement obtains a search warrant for a private social media account, in most instances, a social media site administrator can simply ignore it and not turn over the information sought.
   A. True
   B. False

4. Every device that goes online has a unique, public IP (internet protocol) address that can provide information such as the region, city, and zip code where the device went online.
   A. True
   B. False

5. Safiya wants to send her friend Darius an email that says something private about a student in her ninth-grade biology class. What is the best way for her to ensure that her email will not be read by anyone besides Darius?

    A. Don't put it in writing and wait until she sees Darius and tell him in person.

    B. If she trusts him, get a commitment first (preferably in writing) from Darius that he won't share it.

    C. Don't put it in an email and send it by text.

    D. Don't put it in an email and instead send it via social media.

6. If friends know any of your digital passwords, it's probably okay so long as:

    A. They agree not to share or use the password without your consent.

    B. It's not okay and you should change your password and keep it private from friends.

    C. You trust them.

    D. All of your social media accounts are private accounts.

7. Software updates for your digital devices used to be an important way to protect your privacy but have become useless.

    A. True

    B. False

8. For your personal safety and the integrity of your digital privacy, at least every year you should go through your friends and followers on social media and remove the people whom you don't know in the real world.

    A. True

    B. False

9. When you aren't using the webcam on your computer, you should keep a webcam cover on.

    A. True
    B. False, so long as you always remember to keep your laptop closed when not in use.
    C. False, so long as you have the latest software updates on your device.
    D. Both B and C.

10. When selecting a social media user ID, be sure it includes your date of birth, gender, and name of your school.

    A. True
    B. False

CHAPTER 10

Cyberbullying:
Bullying on Steroids

KEY TAKEAWAYS

- As many as one in four teens experience cyberbullying.
- Cyberbullying is more likely to be inflicted by a friend than a stranger.
- Cyberbullying can negatively impact not only the targets but also witnesses.
- Even when perpetrated from a personal digital device, from home on a weekend, cyberbullying can lead to serious school and even legal consequences for the bully.
- There are numerous ways to stay safer from cyberbullies and to help a target of cyberbullying.

Chapter Highlights

Setting the Stage

Bullying is nothing new and has been an unfortunate part of growing up for countless generations. However, in the past, the bullies were identifiable and their bullying would often end at the close of the school day. Now, with connected devices so deeply integrated into our everyday lives, bullying has taken a more insidious turn in the form of cyberbullying—which can feel inescapable.

> Cyberbullying is the willful and repeated harm inflicted on someone through the use of electronic devices. As discussed in greater detail below, there is also a real or perceived power differential between the people involved.

One of the most harmful aspects of cyberbullying is that if posted online, the digital taunts and insults can be shared with countless people, both inside and outside the target's social circle. This means that the target of the abuse can be hurt repeatedly.

Cyberbullying is like bullying on steroids and is a total game changer.

When I run my digital safety workshops, I get to speak to many young people—some who have had digital acts committed against them that amount to cyberbullying (although they almost never use that term). They're often feeling hurt and confused and unsure how, or whether, to deal with the "drama." It's heart-breaking for me to see young people feeling this way.

These conversations often happen after the workshop and are therefore necessarily brief. With limited time and facts at my disposal, I find myself usually asking the same question: have you told any adults you trust about it? Most of the time the answer is "No" or "Not yet" or "They don't get it."

I then give my advice: *it is not your fault that this is happening*—no one deserves to be treated cruelly—and there is help to be had. The right trusted adult—who

isn't necessarily a parent—may very well be capable of providing meaningful support and solutions. Moreover, even if a caring adult doesn't get it or know exactly what to do, they'll know you're hurting and will want to help.

Since I'm at many of the same schools over multiple dates each school year, I sometimes get to have follow-up discussions with these young people. Although my perception is in no way scientific, I have noticed a distinct trend when we have these conversations: the ones who have spoken to someone about the cyberbullying seem to be in much better emotional shape and, more times than not, got the help they wanted or needed.

What You'll Learn in this Chapter

In this chapter, I'll elaborate on the advice mentioned above and provide some important information to help address cyberbullying. We'll cover what cyberbullying is, the different forms it can take, the impact on targets, and the potential consequences for the cyber aggressor/bully. We'll then transition into discussing some tips and techniques to stay safer from cyberbullying, getting help if you are a target of cyberbullying, and helping others if they are targeted.

Let's get to it.

What Is Cyberbullying?

Although many young people know it as "roasting," "beef," "drama," or getting "dissed," cyberbullying, generally, occurs when three elements are present: (1) willful and repeated harm, (2) harm inflicted through the use of electronic devices, and (3) a real or perceived power differential between the people involved, although it can be difficult to define "power" in the digital context.

It is worth noting that this definition is a bit academic since it helps illustrate the material in this chapter, but school and school district policies and state laws will define acts of cyberbullying in their own ways. For example, some school policies classify cyberbullying as "severe and pervasive" instead of "repeated harm."

With respect to the first element of the above definition, "willful and repeated harm," cyberbullies want to hurt, humiliate, or embarrass their target. Although a single incident may be mean or cruel—for example, a text message telling someone they're "worthless"—it is not likely cyberbullying, at least not technically, unless the aggressive behavior is repeated over time. However, if a single digital act is shared in a place where it can be seen repeatedly, the harm to the target continues every time someone sees it, likes it, or adds a comment. In this way, one act can inflict repeated harm.

> **Cyberbullies want to hurt, humiliate, or embarrass their target.**

The second element from the definition, "harm inflicted through the use of electronic devices," refers to bullying that happens on digital platforms or spaces, including gaming platforms, text messages, emails, group chats, social media, and many others.

The third element, "a real or perceived power differential between the people involved," is a bit more difficult to understand. As quick background, in traditional cases of bullying, bullies target someone who has less power than they do because it provides them with a greater ability to accomplish their objectives. The power could be superior size, strength, age, social status, and certainly many other things. As mentioned above, power differential is less clear in the digital world.

Interestingly, one of the leading nationwide researchers on cyberbullying, Dr. Justin Patchin, a professor of criminal justice at the University of

Wisconsin-Eau Claire and the cofounder of the Cyberbullying Research Center, doesn't include a power differential in his definition, though many researchers and academics do. Dr. Patchin believes that the power differential is implied by the bullying itself: "If the willful harm is happening repeatedly and the target doesn't want it to happen, that's evidence that they can't do anything about it." (Patchin also thinks that the definition I use "is perfectly fine.")

Not All Digital Nastiness Is Cyberbullying, but Can Still Be Harmful

It's important to understand that not all malicious acts that take place digitally constitute cyberbullying. For instance, a fight or disagreement between two people online, or someone being spontaneously rude or inconsiderate, may not be cyberbullying.

Dr. David Finkelhor, the director of the Crimes against Children Research Center, introduced in chapter 3, wants young people to know that just because something may not be technically cyberbullying or violate a school policy, it might still be cruel and harmful to the targets. He says, "There's a lot of peer victimization that is very serious but doesn't qualify as bullying because there isn't a power differential and repetition. Yet these acts can still have elements of injury."

The takeaway here is that if someone experiences emotional pain based on the digital acts of another, whether it falls cleanly into the definition of cyberbullying or not, it warrants being addressed in the same ways that cyberbullying should be.

Types of Cyberbullying

Cyberbullying can take a number of different forms. Below are some examples of acts that may amount to cyberbullying. Moreover, some may be crimes in their own right. Remember please that words matter and have the ability to cause significant harm, particularly when digitized.

- sending or posting mean, hurtful, embarrassing, and/or discriminatory remarks
- digitally sharing someone's secrets or spreading lies, rumors, or other information to embarrass, humiliate, or damage someone's reputation or relationships

- creating false online identities or fake images or videos imperson-ating the target
- logging into someone's online account and impersonating them
- creating hate pages
- making digital threats or cyberstalking someone
- alienating the target through social exclusion, for example, tagging someone in a group photo who isn't in the picture so they will see that they were excluded
- intentionally posting private or "bad" photos or videos of the target

While the above are some important examples, many readers already know how cyberbullying looks and sounds because about 60 percent of young people have witnessed it.

How Widespread Is It?

About 95 percent of teens own or have access to a smartphone. This near-constant connection to the digital world means that young people today are more susceptible to becoming victims and perpetrators of cyber-bullying. Sadly, some teens believe that cyberbullying is simply a part of growing up. It shouldn't be.

Are There Red Flags That Indicate That Someone Is Being Cyberbullied?

The presence of red flags does not necessarily mean someone is being cyberbullied, but they are often present and can be an important tool to evaluate whether someone might be a target. Here are some of the red flags:

- losing interest in their digital devices or appearing anxious when using them
- missing school and getting newly suffering grades
- becoming withdrawn and isolated
- not talking about their digital activities
- dropping out of activities that they once enjoyed
- experiencing mood, behavior, and personality changes
- engaging in self-harm ideation and self-harm

Although studies can vary, one in four teens experiences cyberbullying and about one in six teens has done it to others. LGBTQ youth experience nearly three times as much cyberbullying online as non-LGBTQ youth. The most common medium for cyberbullying is through a cell phone, and *young people are seven times more likely to experience cyberbullying from friends than from strangers.*

Many targets of cyberbullying know the identity of their tormentor and are usually also bullied at school. Dr. Patchin adds that his own research shows that "it's very rare for a student to be bullied online and not also in school."

Who Are the Cyberbullies and Their Targets?

There are many reasons people cyberbully. Some may be targets of bullying themselves who are taking out their frustration on others or targeting those who bully them. It may be that they see their acts as being funny, or as a way to stay popular or feel powerful. Some bully because it helps them cope with their own low self-esteem. Others are ignorant of the harmfulness of their actions.

One of the reasons that cyberbullying occurs with such frequency and is damaging to the target is that it's easier for people to post, like, or favorite something hurtful about someone from behind a computer screen than to say it to them in person. As mentioned earlier in the book, this is called the online disinhibition effect, because the person does not see how their words affect the target.

Cyberbullies often target those whom they perceive as "different" in physical appearance or with actual or perceived differences in:

- intelligence
- race/ethnicity
- learning abilities
- sexual orientation and not adhering to gender stereotypes

How Does Cyberbullying Impact Targets?

Being cyberbullied can be extremely painful and negatively impact the health and well-being of its targets. One teen, Patricia, who was a target of

cyberbullies, described it to me as a "shadow" that was always hanging over her. She said, "It made everything feel dark and took the joy out of things that I used to love doing."

Patricia is far from alone in how she was impacted by cyberbullying. It can cause or contribute to anxiety, depression, confusion, sadness, anger, frustration, isolation, thoughts of or actual self-harm, eating disorders, school delinquency, drug abuse, and much more.

One teen told the Cyberbullying Research Center that "it makes me hurt both physically and mentally. It scares me and takes away all my confidence. It makes me feel sick and worthless."

Potential Consequences for Those Who Cyberbully

There are at least three ways someone can get into serious trouble for cyberbullying: at school, with the police, and/or in a civil court of law—and in some circumstances all three (of course, one can get in trouble with their parents too). Let's find out more about each.

1. At Your School

Schools and school districts often will have a code of conduct that includes harassment and bullying prevention policies. Many policies will also cover or specifically define what actions fall under the category of cyberbullying. Moreover, schools may have an "acceptable-use" policy that prohibits cyberbullying on electronic devices used at or issued by the school.

Violating your school's policy can result in suspension, expulsion, prohibition from extracurricular school activities, and more. *It won't matter*

Overt and Covert Cyberbullying

I asked therapist Danielle Brooks, who we met in the Introduction, how often young people come to see her about cyberbullying and she responded without hesitation, "All the time."

Brooks breaks down cyberbullying into "covert" and "overt" behaviors. "Overt cyberbullying is saying or doing something directly to somebody. Covert cyberbullying is more nuanced. Examples include someone who always comments on your five friends' pictures but not yours, or someone who says something positive about other people's posts in your circle of friends, but on yours they're neutral."

Brooks goes on to share, "Covert cyberbullying can be so much more harmful because bystanders can be less likely to intervene. When overt cyberbullying happens, you could look like a person with a bad moral compass or a bad friend if you don't do something. When it's covert, it's less likely to be noticed by bystanders and can be so palpable and destructive to the target."

whether you didn't read and understand the policy because ignorance of it is not an excuse.

Some young people (and adults) don't think that their public school can discipline them for cyberbullying if it takes place off-campus because of their right to freedom of speech under the First Amendment to the US Constitution. In many instances, they're completely wrong because even cyberbullying that's perpetrated from home, after school hours, and from one's own devices is unlikely to be constitutionally protected speech and can be cause for school discipline.

To be clear, students who attend public schools do have some First Amendment rights because these schools accept government funding and are therefore governmental actors for purposes of the First Amendment. However, public school students will *not* be protected by their First Amendment rights if the speech (which includes the spoken and the written word):

- creates actual or foreseeable substantial disruption of the learning environment (it's worth noting that 64 percent of students who experience cyberbullying said it really affected their ability to learn and feel safe at school)

- infringes on civil rights, meaning political and social freedom and equality
- is intended to degrade or disparage someone or a group based on race, gender, religion, sexual orientation, ethnicity, or other classifications
- utilizes school-owned technology to harass

In contrast to public schools, most private schools do not accept government funds and their students do not, therefore, have First Amendment rights. As a result, students' off-campus activity or speech, written or verbal, which violates the school's code of conduct, can subject them to school discipline.

2. With the Police

Most states have made cyberbullying a criminal offense that can result in cyberbullies being arrested. Even if your state hasn't criminalized cyberbullying, all states have various criminal laws that may apply to cyberbullying behaviors. While laws vary by jurisdiction, some offenses include in-person stalking or cyberstalking, in-person harassment or cyberharassment, identity fraud, online impersonation causing harm, hate crimes, and other types of threatening behavior.

Therefore, violating a cyberbullying law or one of its offshoots can bring the police to your front door or classroom. Needless to say, if the

A School's Reach into Your Private Life

Jordan, an eighth-grade public school student from Ohio, wrote only a few words on social media, on a weekend, from his own phone, at his home, that got him suspended from school for ten days. It started when another student posted online about whether he should drink bleach and kill himself, and Jordan posted "Do it." The student wrote back, "You want me to KMS?" (meaning "kill myself") and "Thanks." Jordan responded, "Ur welcome."

The school found out about it and Jordan was pulled out of class by a police officer, escorted to the principal's office, and questioned. His police come knocking, the situation has become quite serious and can come with corresponding consequences.

Cyberbullies often don't think they'll be discovered if they use anonymous email addresses and the like, but when a determined cyber investigator or police officer wants to track someone down online, they often can. Dr. Justin Patchin points out, "It is very difficult for cyberbullies to completely cover their tracks. With enough resources and knowledge, it's uncommon for the aggressor to stay completely anonymous. That's the reality of cyberbullying compared to traditional bullying: there's always evidence of cyberbullying."

3. In a Civil Court of Law

There are two primary court systems in the United States: criminal and civil. Criminal court and its related laws are imposed to protect society as a whole. The police enforce criminal laws by making arrests and then handing the case over to a prosecutor, who decides whether or not the person should be charged with a crime in a court of law. Civil court is different. It's where people go to resolve a private dispute, which is most often about money.

For example, if someone hit you with their car, you could sue the person in civil court and seek "damages" (financial compensation) for your medical expenses, time missed from work, and "pain and suffering."

When it comes to cyberbullying, the aggressor—and possibly their parents—can be sued in civil court to financially compensate the victim for the pain and suffering that they endured because of the cyberbullying.

---

phone was confiscated, and school officials obtained his password and searched his phone.

Jordan's father was frustrated and confused. He asked in a television interview, "Where do they get the power to reach into your life after school hours, off school property, not even talking about school issues, for something, a question that was asked and answered with two words?"

The answer to this question is not complicated—**when students do things, even out of school, that a school administrator concludes substantially disrupts the school environment, they can be subjected to school discipline.**

A court order, called an injunction, in which the judge orders the aggressor to stop the cyberbullying, may also be obtained. Violation of that court order could land the aggressor in jail.

Will My School Help Me If I'm a Target?

Since schools are at the center of kids' lives, the negative impacts of cyberbullying (and the face-to-face bullying that may accompany it) are often felt at school. Schools have a legal responsibility to ensure that the school environment is a safe place to learn.

However, schools are often confronted with somewhat complex questions about whether to deal with cyberbullying or not, and if so, how to address it—particularly when the cyberbullying occurs off campus. Complexities or not, some schools will do a much better job handling these situations than others. As such, bringing in a parent or other trusted adult to help you interface with the school is an important step to take.

Be Mindful of What You Write

In one high-profile case, Aya, a 15-year-old girl from Florida, was arrested for cyberbullying and charged by prosecutors after she sent hundreds of threatening messages to three other teenage girls. The case was well documented in her community. One of her text messages to the targets said, "If this isn't bullying, then I don't know what is." Aya had been friends with the other girls until they had a falling out. The court system and her school sorted out her punishment, but the real consequence may be that for many years she'll be known in her community, and perhaps beyond, for being a teen cyberbully.

Before seeking assistance from your school—assuming the situation doesn't necessitate immediate action—you should assemble all the evidence at your disposal. Also, be sure to familiarize yourself with the laws in your state and the school or school district policies on bullying and cyberbullying, which may include the overall governing of educational programs, codes of conduct, acceptable use policies for school-issued electronics, and, depending on the facts, policies/regulations/laws on sexual harassment, stalking, cyberharassment, and cyberstalking.

For some tips about approaching administrators at your school for assistance, see appendix 5.

Going to the Police?

If you're being cyberbullied and are concerned for your personal safety, or if the activity falls into the realm of a possible hate crime—targeting your race, gender or gender identity, sexual orientation, and so on—you should strongly consider making a police report with your local police station. If you're in imminent danger, call 911. After making a report to the police, you should also inform your school that you have done so.

For some important ways to most effectively make a police report, see appendix 3.

Staying Safer from Cyberbullying

While there's no way to guarantee that cyberbullying won't happen to you, there are ways to keep yourself safer. Never forget that if you are cyberbullied, or bullied in person, *it is not your fault.*

- **Talk to someone about it.** If ignored, cyberbullying is likely to only get more serious. Yet many targets don't tell the adults in their lives about being bullied. The reasons for this can vary, but fear of losing access to their devices is common. (Incidentally, many experts think taking away devices can be counterproductive. Dr. Elizabeth Englander, a professor and the director of the Massachusetts Aggression Reduction Center at Bridgewater State University, focuses on preventing high-risk digital behaviors in youth. She says, "I'd prefer to see parents working with kids. I don't like to see situations where kids who disclose something difficult to their parents feel like they're being punished for doing so.")

  Other reasons include fear of retaliation from the bully, believing the adult won't help or might make the bullying worse, or not recognizing it as cyberbullying. Despite these fears, speaking to someone who you believe will react rationally and logically can help stop the bullying. Please see the "Find Your Person, Whoever That May Be" section in the Introduction for information about getting support.

  When it comes to cyberbullying targets who are underclassmen, Dr. Patchin suggests approaching student leaders and upperclassmen

A Great Big Brother

Some teens have taken their personal experiences of cyberbullying a step further and are at the center of efforts to reduce and eliminate it. Arizona teen Matthew Kaplan found out from his younger brother that he was being relentlessly cyberbullied via texts and on social media. Matthew took action and created an anti-bullying workshop that he presented to his younger brother's class.

The impact on Matthew's brother's classmates was tremendous, and during the program the bullies apologized to his brother. Matthew went on to turn that single workshop into a nonprofit, The Be ONE Project (thebeoneproject.org) to help stop bullying. Matthew is proud of his work and wants people to know that "everyone should be able to go to a school where they feel . . . valued and accepted by their classmates. And I want to make sure they can."

they know "who can probably identify adults in the school administration who can be trusted, discreet, and willing to help. If ignored, cyberbullying is very likely to only get more serious."

- **Be a good digital citizen.** Be polite and respectful to other people online. Take a moment to reflect on what you're doing electronically and make sure it isn't intended to negatively impact others. For more information about what makes a good digital citizen, see chapter 8.

- **You can ask them to stop.** If it feels safe and the target is so inclined, "Calmly and clearly asking the aggressor to stop may or may not work, but it probably won't make matters any worse," says Dr. Patchin. He recommends against engaging with the aggressor if the "please stop" evolves into the target retaliating against the aggressor, as described in the next point.

- **Don't retaliate.** Your natural instinct may be to lash out against the person who is cyberbullying you, but doing so can make it less clear who the real victim is. As Dr. Patchin points out, "Even if one person started and escalated it, it's going to look like it was a two-way street—which can be perceived as a fight, not bullying."

- **Spend less time online.** Spending more time online does not cause cyberbullying, but children involved in cyberbullying report higher rates of internet use. If you're being bullied, it's not a bad idea to try to avoid the "places" where bullying happens. Dr. Englander says "there may be no way to completely avoid cyberbullying, but you can certainly reduce its incidence and impact by spending less time online."

- **Keep things private.** As detailed in chapter 9, there are many steps you can take to reduce the chances of your private information getting into the hands of people that you don't want it to, including cyberbullies.

- **Preserve evidence.** Preserve or copy all relevant evidence and keep it secure. More information about evidence preservation can be found in appendix 3 and in other parts of this book.

- **Report it.** Report the bullying to the content provider or site administrator, whether or not you know the identity of the cyberbully. All reputable electronic platforms will prohibit cyberbullying as part of their terms of use and will describe how it should be reported. The aggressor's account may be suspended and the damaging material removed from the site. Some platforms are more

Lucie's Story

Lucie, a tenth grader, was upset with some students from her school and made a social media post that she later described as "immature, angry, and rude." It was widely shared and Lucie soon began being bullied both in person and online.

Lucie apologized to the people that her original post was directed to, but it didn't do any good and the attacks continued and escalated, with even strangers from other schools now participating. Lucie was hurt that many of her friends weren't supportive of her and only tried to comfort her privately. "No one had the courage to actually defend me on social media."

Lucie, feeling confused and sad, decided to talk to her parents. They reached out to her school advisor, who told them that all students had signed a code of conduct that included cyberbullying. The school contacted the mother of the cyberbullying ringleader, but her daughter helpful than others, and if your complaint isn't being handled properly, escalate your concern to a supervisor.

Block access. Use available technology tools to prevent the cyberbully from contacting you or posting on your feed or timeline. Reputable electronic platforms, like many of the popular social media and gaming sites, will allow you to block other users. A cyberbully who can't reach you will find it difficult to cyberbully you.

However, it is worth noting that blocking the aggressor can sometimes escalate the situation once the person discovers that they've been blocked. It can also make what is being posted about them invisible to targets when many want to know what is being said.

To address the shortcomings of simply blocking someone, some sites or apps are trying new features to help reduce or stop cyberbullying without having to block someone. For example, Instagram recently added a feature called Restrict, which allows users to secretly stop bullies from commenting on their posts.

The effectiveness of this sort of cyberbullying countermeasure remains to be seen but is worth knowing about. A Google search can provide you with a rundown of the latest available tools on each platform and how to use them.

defended her actions by showing the school a screenshot of Lucie's mean post that had started this chain of events. This certainly didn't excuse the cyberbullying, but it made the water a bit murkier for the school in its investigation.

Lucie's experience made her realize "how important it is to be careful about what you put online." She hopes that her story will be a reminder to people that "the Internet is definitely not the right place to let your emotions and angry feelings toward a person or situation out."

Lucie and the girl who was the ringleader of the cyberbullying eventually made their peace and a pact to only spread kindness online. Lucie wants anyone who's being cyberbullied to know that they aren't alone. She says, "Don't be afraid to ask for help and to share your story, look at your own actions, and do not say negative things on the internet and get caught in the moment. It can and will get better, I promise."

Phone numbers can also be blocked from calling or texting you on your smartphone—check your device settings or contact your cell provider.

- **Get a lawyer.** It can be worthwhile to get a lawyer involved when the situation is serious. Although doing so won't be necessary in many situations and not financially feasible in others, an attorney can help protect you and get your school more involved. If the cyberbully is anonymous, an attorney may be able to do things that uncover the bully's identity.

Once Again . . . the Importance of Bystander Intervention

We discussed bystander intervention in chapters 4 and 5. It's worth mentioning again for those who did not read those chapters and because intervening in the context of cyberbullying can be different.

Bullies like an audience and cyberbullying often happens in front of others. I'm perfectly aware that few readers would ever cyberbully someone. Sadly, though, because cyberbullying has become such a common occurrence, merely not being a cyberbully is not enough. All of us can play a role to stop it.

When we're around other people and see something that looks wrong, we may not take action because we convince ourselves that someone else will. This is called the bystander effect, a phenomenon in which the more people who are present, the less likely it is that someone will help a target or victim.

When you see something that just isn't right, trust your instincts and don't ignore the situation, especially if others aren't doing something to help. If you are the courageous person to speak up, it'll make it much easier for others to join you. Remember, courage inspires courage.

Keep in mind that cyberbullies have no power without followers and inactive, nonintervening electronic bystanders. This gives bystanders, who often outnumber the cyberbullies, incredible power to do something to help a target.

Those who watch but do nothing can make the target feel like everyone has turned against them, particularly if their friends are also silent. These people unintentionally can cause additional hurt by passively empowering the cyberbully and providing an audience for the bully's aggressive acts. The bully regards the bystanders' inaction as *support* of the cyberbullying.

Oftentimes it takes only one or two people to shut down cyberbullying and can be just what the target needs in that moment. In fact, bystanders intervening in a bullying situation can stop it within ten seconds 57 percent of the time.

Depending on your comfort level, there's *always* something you can do to help, and standing up to injustice can be a rewarding and powerful experience. Doing so not only helps the target but also everyone involved because studies demonstrate that students who *witness* bullying may also suffer psychological distress.

If it's physically safe, here are some of the ways to help:

- At a bare minimum, don't participate whatsoever in the cyberbullying. Digitally "laughing" via an LOL, LMAO, or anything equivalent is participating.

- Tell the aggressor to stop, that their actions are not cool or funny, or anything else that's similar and fits your comfort level. This can be particularly effective if you know and have a positive relationship with the bully.

- There's safety in numbers, so ask other bystanders, particularly those with whom you are friends, to also say something and/or to stop sharing, watching, following, or responding to what the cyberbully posts or sends. This is called "no-platforming" and can be very effective.

- On behalf of the target, anonymously report the cyberbullying to the content provider, site, app, or game. Since cyberbullies are likely violating the site's terms of use, their account may get suspended as a result.

- Save digital evidence of the cyberbullying and provide it if requested.

- Tell a trusted adult—anonymously if you prefer. You aren't being a "snitch"; rather, you're trying to help someone who's hurting and facing a potentially serious problem.

Helping Someone Who's Been Targeted . . . Even After the Fact

If you aren't able to intervene in real time, you can still support the target in a number of other ways, even after incidents of cyberbullying. Don't underestimate how much a quick, kind, or thoughtful word can help the target feel better and stronger.

Dr. Englander emphasizes to me that there are countless things that "bystanders can do to help support targets of bullying. Research has consistently shown that helping the target of bullying, even after the fact, is more effective and helpful than confronting or attacking somebody who's being aggressive."

Here are just a few ways to help:

- Post or say something supportive to the target. For example, saying that the person deserves to be treated with respect, what the bully said is ridiculous and not true, and other similar sentiments can help the person feel less alone.

- Encourage the target to talk to an adult they trust.

- Take screenshots of the cyberbullying such as text messages, social media posts, or comments so that the targeted person will have evidence when they seek help.

- Offer to help the target find more formal support, such as a school counselor, and, if appropriate, offer to accompany the person to report the cyberbullying to school officials.

- Show support, however you can. You may not know exactly what to do to help, and that's okay. Being someone that the target can talk to can be invaluable. Saying something like "I'm here to help you. We'll get through this together" can be incredibly impactful on the target.

What Three Things in This Chapter Matter Most to You?

We all take away different lessons from reading the information presented in this chapter. What resonates with one person may not be meaningful to another and vice versa. I certainly hope that you've learned a heck of a lot more than three things in this chapter, but if three things were all you learned, I still consider it a win. Even a single piece of information could be invaluable if it was just what you or someone you're with needs in a critical moment.

With the information from this chapter fresh in your mind, please take a few moments to write below the three things that you consider the most important.

1. _____

_____

2. _____

_____

3. _____

_____

What Would You Do if It Happened to You?

You notice that your friend Brent has posted several comments on social media about a girl at your school, Noelle, whom you don't know very well. Brent started out by posting about Noelle's clothes, and how they look like a homeless person dressed her. Eventually, Noelle starts responding to Brent, asking him to stop. Brent then starts calling Noelle a baby for not being able to take a little teasing.

Do you think you should intervene? Why or why not?

Some Thoughts about "What Would You Do if It Happened to You?"
Would you talk to your friend Brent? It can be really scary to confront a friend, but there are many ways you can intervene. Maybe he doesn't realize how his words sound to others.

By talking to Brent about it, or even mentioning it in passing, you're showing that you care about him and that you believe he's capable of being kinder to others. Would you talk to the target? Even if you don't know someone well, reaching out with encouraging words can make a world of difference to someone who is hurting and feeling alone.

Final Thoughts

I hope that this chapter has helped you better understand the many different digital acts that can amount to cyberbullying. You should now also be aware of some things you can do to keep yourself safer from being targeted. Whether or not you follow those guidelines, keep in mind that if you are cyberbullied, it is not your fault, anyone can be targeted, and there are people who care about you and want to help.

If you see something that you believe to be cyberbullying or simply a cruel digital act, try to intervene at the time and help as best you can. Of course, it'd be great if you also helped targets of in-person bullying too. If you were being bullied in person or digitally, you'd want others to lend you a hand, so please lend a hand to others.

Where Can I Get More Information?

This chapter contains the essentials of cyberbullying. For those who want to know more and dig deeper into this topic, a Google search is a good place to start and will deliver numerous resources, some with valuable information. Here are a few you can start with:

- Cybersmile Foundation
    - » professional help and support services for cyberbullying
    - » www.cybersmile.org

- Cyberbullying Research Center
  - » comprehensive information about all aspects of cyberbullying
  - » www.cyberbullying.org
- PACER's National Bullying Prevention Center
  - » anti-bullying resources
  - » www.pacer.org/bullying
- Stop Bullying
  - » official website of the United States government related to bullying and cyberbullying
  - » www.stopbullying.gov

Cyberbullying Quiz

Test your understanding of cyberbullying by taking this quiz. Hopefully, you'll get all of the answers correct because a single mistake could have real-world consequences if that answer contained the information you needed to stay safe.

Instructions: select the best answer from the available choices. Answers can be found in the back of the book.

1. Cyberbullying can be defined as the willful and repeated harm of another inflicted through the use of electronic devices.
   A. True
   B. False

2. Cyberbullying can include:
   A. Creating false online identities impersonating the target.
   B. Intentionally posting bad photos or videos of the target.
   C. Sharing someone's secrets or spreading lies about them.
   D. All of the above.

3. Youth are more likely to experience cyberbullying from friends than from strangers.
   A. True
   B. False

4. The most common medium for cyberbullying is the smartphone.
    A. True
    B. False
    C. True, for those under age 14.

5. Cyberbullies often target people whom they perceive as similar to them.
    A. True
    B. False

6. On the weekend from his house and on his personal cell phone, Reyhan cyberbullies Lennon, a student in his math class. Can Reyhan be disciplined by his school?
    A. No, because under these specific circumstances, he has First Amendment rights to free speech.
    B. In many instances, yes.

7. The only way the police will come to the assistance of a cyberbullying target is if there is a death threat.
    A. True
    B. False

8. If you are cyberbullied, digitally retaliating against the aggressor may be warranted and potentially an important way to demonstrate that you tried to get the bullying to stop.
    A. True
    B. False

9. Often, the most critical step for cyberbullying targets to take is to:
    A. Talk to a trusted adult.
    B. Report the cyberbullying to the site administrator, but only if you know the identity of the aggressor.
    C. Delete the communications so you're less likely to be blamed.
    D. Ask friends on the digital platform to create an anonymous account to try to track down the aggressor.

10. Most cyberbullies don't want an audience to the cyberbullying so they are less likely to get in trouble.
    A. True
    B. False

CHAPTER 11

Smartphone Cameras: Tales of Sexting, Porn, and Falling Off Bridges

KEY TAKEAWAYS

- Underage sexting can lead to an arrest, social stigma, bullying, and, most often, regret.

- Revenge porn is the potential aftermath of sharing nude image of ourselves.

- Selfies are a great form of personal expression, but there are circumstances in which a selfie can lead to great embarrassment, lost opportunities, arrest, cyberbullying, and even physical injury or death.

- When you're with a friend, frenemy, an acquaintance, or anyone else and a camera comes out at an inopportune time, be prepared to swiftly ask the person to put the camera away—which can take great courage to do.

- Heavy consumption of online porn can lead to unforeseen emotional and physical consequences, including changes in the developing teen brain.

Chapter Highlights

Setting the Stage

I get asked from time to time what I think the biggest difference is between coming of age today and coming of age in the past. The answer I give: carrying around digital cameras. Sure, one could argue it's social media or smartphones in general, since those are definitely part of the equation. Yet I believe the most significant part of that equation can be when our actual likeness—*not just our names or user IDs*—is permanently represented in an image that causes us (or others) great discomfort.

As you're probably fully aware, digital images and video recordings can exist forever—or at least way longer than any of us will. With a click of a button an image can spread like wildfire, and snap judgments can be made about the people depicted. The images can remain archived online, be stored in the cloud or on someone's hard drive or phone, and be accessed with a few clicks and resurface suddenly. Images we regret taking immediately or sometime later can lead to a whole host of negative outcomes, such as messing up one's digital footprint, becoming a victim of revenge porn, sextortion, or cyberbullying, and even getting arrested.

That said, the most frequent consequence of being depicted in such an image is not being arrested or the like but emotional turmoil. This turmoil may not be directly caused by the image itself but by the social stigma that the person feels from others. We all know that some people can be judgmental and cruel about such things. Although bullying and shaming are not the fault of the person targeted, that fact doesn't always lessen the emotional impact.

What You'll Learn in this Chapter

My goal in this chapter is twofold: (1) to help the reader to think twice before taking or sharing an image or video of themselves or another person that may be later regretted by either; and (2) to remind us all to be more understanding and ease up on our judgments of people whose private images are made public.

We'll cover the ways you can best prevent generating visual evidence against your own best interests, starting with underage sexting. We'll then shift briefly to the horrible scourge of revenge porn. It'll then be on to the potential physical and emotional dangers of our cameras and a bit about the harmful effects of online porn.

Let's get to it.

What Is Sexting (aka Nudes, Noods, Noodz, Nudz) and How Common Is It?

> Sexting, or "nudes," is the use of digital technology to send or receive images or videos in which the person depicted is nude, partially nude, engaging in sex acts, or wearing revealing clothing.

People of all ages have been known to exchange nudes, but the consequences, as we'll soon see, can be the most detrimental for minors. Although statistics vary when it comes to the frequency of sexting, a recent systematic review of underage sexting found the following:

- One in four received a nude.
- One in seven reported sending a nude.
- One in eight had been forwarded a nude without consent from the original sender and/or recipient.

- Other emerging research has found that adolescents who sext are more likely to experience anxiety, depression, and substance abuse and to engage in potentially problematic sexual behaviors such as failing to use contraception and having multiple sexual partners. To be clear, though, the results of these studies have found a link between sexting and these conditions and behaviors but not that one causes the other.

The Potential Legal, Social, and Emotional Consequences of Underage Sexting

Jamie is a high school sophomore, age 16. She's in an intimate relationship with Paul, also a sophomore, age 16. For weeks Paul has pressured Jamie for a nude, threatening to break up with her if she doesn't send one. He promises to delete it upon receipt and not show anyone else. Jamie finally agrees and takes a topless photo of herself, saves it on her smartphone, and sends it to Paul. Despite his promise to the contrary, Paul saves the photo to his camera roll and then forwards it to his friend, Ingrid, age 17. She also saves the image and then sends it to many people at their high school.

The sharing of the image continues, and within minutes the image has been seen by many students at their school and beyond.

Have Jamie, Paul, or Ingrid committed serious crimes related to child pornography—in addition to possibly other crimes—that could result in their being arrested and prosecuted, spending some time in jail, and having to register as a sex offender? Yes, all of them have because **creating, possessing, *or* distributing nude or partially nude images of anyone under the age of 18—*even if the image is of yourself*—can be a serious crime related to child pornography**. (Although the definition of child pornography offenses and their offshoots varies by jurisdiction, it can be generally defined as a form of child sexual exploitation and abuse involving any visual depiction of sexually explicit conduct involving a minor.)

Technically, who among them has committed the greatest number of criminal acts related to child pornography? Many people would say it's Paul, but it's not. It's actually Jamie, who *created* child pornography when she took the topless image of herself, *possessed* child pornography when she saved the photo, and *distributed* child pornography when she sent the image to Paul. Paul and Ingrid similarly possessed and distributed child pornography but did not create it.

You may think that likening sexting between minors to child pornography is absurd. I agree. Those types of laws were meant to protect children from sexual predators, not to prosecute children. Yet most states have child pornography laws that are antiquated and don't distinguish between consensual sexting between young people (*not* the situation with Jamie above, in which she was coerced) and adults who prey on children.

Old Enough to Have Sex but Not Send Nudes

Vihaan and Sonja, 16-year-old high schoolers from North Carolina, were boyfriend and girlfriend when they exchanged nudes. Later, during a police investigation at their high school, officers were searching students' phones. Vihaan was not a target of the investigation, but his phone was still searched. The officers found the nudes, and Vihaan and Sonja were arrested and charged with multiple felonies related to child pornography. They also suffered serious school discipline. The most outrageous part of all this is that the age for sexual consent in North Carolina is 16, so it was lawful for them to have sex but *unlawful* to sext!

Although it is unusual, there are many accounts of children being arrested, prosecuted, and having to register as sex offenders under child pornography laws related to sexting. As far as I'm concerned this is a misapplication of the law. It doesn't mean that the participants shouldn't face consequences in some situations, but prosecution under child pornography laws seems awfully severe. The law simply hasn't kept up with technology (or with terminology, since many academics, law enforcement officers, and others believe the term child pornography should, in some instances, be substituted with the more accurate term child sexual abuse material).

If the police had gotten involved in our hypothetical situation here, they likely would have focused on who they believe is the most deserving of their time and energies—probably Paul and to a lesser extent, Ingrid. Paul is the worst actor because he coerced Jamie for the image and lied to her when he promised to delete it after receipt. He also lied when he promised not to share the image with anyone. Ingrid's acts of sharing the image made matters worse, and she might also face serious consequences. While Jamie did violate the law, she may be viewed as engaging in an act that is not uncommon and ultimately as being victimized by others.

Dr. David Finkelhor, the director of the Crimes against Children Research Center, introduced in chapter 3, acknowledges, "In general, the sense we get from our research on underage sexting is that the prosecutors were understanding of the [victimized] teens and not likely to prosecute." However, when deciding whether anyone involved should be arrested or prosecuted, "Police and prosecutors often take into account who disseminated [the image(s)], how widespread the dissemination was, whether there was malicious intent, the age of the perpetrators, the number of victims, and other delinquent or criminal behavior that may be occurring."

Laws Are Starting to Change . . . Slowly

To rectify the use of harsh child pornography laws that may be used to prosecute young people for underage sexting, some states have passed laws that can reduce the penalties and other consequences for minors who consensually sext images.

The sexting of images involving minors is usually still a crime in these states—the involved parties are just less likely to face the more serious child pornography-related criminal charges. An internet search about the laws in your state for minors who possess or share nudes should give you the details of any applicable laws.

Also, regardless of your age or the laws in your state, **if a minor sends you a nude, you should delete it. Don't save it, forward it, or show it to a friend.**

If a school gets involved in an underage sexting situation involving its students—which typically occurs when a school administrator searches student phones during a school investigation—the administrators will almost certainly notify the police. No matter what the police choose to do or not do, the school may still impose school-related discipline. This can amount to disqualification from school programs, suspension, or expulsion.

Despite the potential for serious consequences when police, prosecutors, or school administrators get involved in a youth sexting situation, I believe, as do the academic researchers with whom I spoke, that *the far more likely consequence for underage sexting is regret and social stigma.*

Dr. Kami Kosenko, introduced in chapter 4, says, "The greatest risk that young people face when exchanging nudes in a relationship in which there is an equally balanced power dynamic isn't being arrested for an offense related to child pornography. Rather it's the forwarding of the images to unexpected recipients, which we know can lead to bullying, cyberbullying, revenge porn, social isolation, and sextortion incidents of the person depicted in the image."

Unsolicited Sending of Nudes

You would never have sexual contact with anyone without first obtaining consent, nor would you just walk up to someone and flash them. So please don't cyberflash anyone by sending an unsolicited nude of yourself or anyone else. Doing so may be a crime and also amount to sexual harassment. Not to mention it's likely to make the recipient feel violated and uncomfortable and may result in psychological distress.

Sending nudes that have not been asked for is like flashing someone in person, which I expect no reader of this book would do.

Dr. Geoffrey Luurs is an assistant professor at Murray State University who has studied and researched sexting extensively. He wants young people to remember that "sexted photos have a way of traveling. The 'just for yous' become 'I showed my friends this,' and that can be damaging emotionally and socially. We have enough colloquial data to say that nude photos can lead to social problems for young people when they expand beyond their intended target. There are also many instances of these images making their way into the hands of sexual predators, which can result in sexual exploitation crimes being perpetrated against the person depicted."

People whose nudes have been shared without permission may feel humiliated, depressed, and anxious. They may not want to go to school or talk to anyone who may have seen or even heard about the image, and that

can isolate them from needed support. People may unfairly blame the person for taking the photo when it was someone else's deception that inflicted the damage. The person can also be "slut shamed," which describes a situation in which peers viciously ridicule someone, most frequently a girl, for being perceived as sexually promiscuous.

Even in an ongoing intimate relationship, before you share a nude, please reflect on the fact that few middle or high school relationships will stand the test of time. When relationships end, there can be a lot of anger and resentment. We just never know how people will handle breakups, and some may break their promises to us by doing awful things we never expected. Or, even with no ill-intention on the part of your partner, someone could discover the nude on their device.

Trusting the Person You Send a Nude To

You may be considering sending a nude to someone you trust. You may have good reasons for trusting them, but what if the person is careless with their device and loses it with your image on it? Or one of the recipient's friends starts snooping through their photos and comes across it? Or they are hacked? How about a parent checking the recipient's phone and finding the image? There are countless scenarios in which, either intentionally or accidentally, unintended recipients can see you in one of your most private moments.

Ways to Say No to Requests for Nudes

First and most importantly, it's never cool to pressure or intimidate someone to send you a nude, and in some instances it can actually be a crime. On the flip side, it's always okay to say no to requests for a nude. Here are just some of the ways to say no:

- Tell the truth—you're just not interested in participating and never will be. Tell the person to stop asking. If the person making the request cares about you, the requests should stop.

- Tell the person that your parents monitor your devices, they have your passwords, and any picture you take gets pushed to cloud-based storage that your parents access. It doesn't matter whether this is true—it's a potentially easy way to say no that won't feel like rejection.

- Use humor to diffuse the situation. Say "My camera isn't working so I drew you a pic instead" and send them clip art of a stick figure.

- Offer an alternative: "Let's save some time: we could spend the next hour with you asking and me saying no, or we could meet in person and have some fun."

- Cut to the chase: "A picture is worth a thousand words. You're worth one: NO."

Dr. Luurs adds, "Saying no to a sexting request can be difficult for many reasons. Some young people feel pressured to sext as part of courting, others to maintain a relationship where they are being pressured into sex-related activities, others have sex-related topics just dropped in their lap. The easiest answer is to just say no, and be firm with it. There are various other ways to say no a bit less directly, such as 'I'm not ready,' 'You're funny, no way,' or 'Gross! Never.'"

Dr. Kosenko wraps up this topic by pointing out that "sexting can be a part of courting rituals nowadays and it may come off as prudish for adults to say that underage sexting is something that youth blanketly should never do. It's more important for them to stop and think about the potential consequences before they do it." She also agrees with every other expert on this topic whom I spoke with: **never send a nude that shows your face or anything else in the image that may identify you.**

So You've Sent a Nude

If you've already sent a nude and are concerned that the person in possession of the image has bad intentions, please understand that you are not to blame because someone has or might violate your trust.

Selfies Gone Bad

Selfies can be a great symbol of self-expression. I get it. Yet we've all seen cringe-worthy selfies that have been posted and shared online—some of which have gone viral. It could be an image taken in front of a mirror

What Is Revenge Porn?

Revenge porn is the distribution of sexually graphic images of individuals without their consent. (Reader note: "Image-based sexual abuse" is actually a more accurate way to describe this behavior because it is not always motivated by "revenge" and the images are abuse, not porn, which implies consensually produced materials.) The lead-up to an incident of revenge porn is when someone in an intimate relationship knowingly provides a nude to his or her partner. (As mentioned earlier in this book, I use the word "knowingly," not "willingly," because a target may be forced or coerced into providing an image.) Then a breakup occurs and the recipient of the image is angry and digitally that inadvertently captures something embarrassing in the background; a picture taken showing people who reasonably expected privacy, such as in a gym or a public bathroom (which may also be a crime); or an image of someone beaming at a funeral, in front of a house that's burning down, or at any other place that is a "bad look" for a selfie.

It's bad enough to take a selfie like one of these that's out of line with your short- and long-term goals, but it's another thing entirely to get yourself injured or killed while taking one (and possibly putting the well-being of those around you at risk). Crude terms like "killfies" or "selfiecide" have started being used to describe this growing problem, particularly for young people. The precise statistics on deaths by selfie are difficult to determine because it is not yet classified as an official cause of death. Some of the most frequent locales for selfie injuries and deaths are train tracks, cliffs, bridges, bodies of water, in moving vehicles, and posing with guns or wild animals.

Selfie-related injuries (and deaths) happen so often that numerous tourist destinations have installed "no selfie zone" signage to help remind tourists to be careful. Others have done things such as publish guides to taking safe photos (for example, the US National Park Service) or created a pledge visitors can make that includes practicing safe selfies (Yellowstone National Park). Kathy Kupper, a spokesperson for the US National Park Service, explains one of the reasons why selfie deaths and injuries are increasing: "When people are on vacation, they may not be looking for hazards the same way they do in their everyday lives."

---

distributes the images or videos of their ex-partner with the intent to hurt, embarrass, or cause distress to that person. The angry aggressor may also do this for their own arousal and amusement.

One in ten former partners has threatened to expose nude or partially nude images of an ex online, and 60 percent have followed through on the threat. Understandably, revenge porn can be incredibly traumatizing for victims, half of whom report that they were also harassed or cyberstalked by third parties who viewed the material.

In many instances, the sharing of this type of material is a serious crime subjecting the perpetrator to arrest and prosecution.

While studies are preliminary, most selfie-related deaths appear to involve young people—under the age of 25. This may be because young people take more selfies than older adults, may seek greater recognition on picture-based social media, and are scientifically shown to be governed more by impulsivity, as discussed in the Introduction. This can be a dangerous combination of circumstances if you aren't thoughtful about what you're doing and where you're doing it.

Before you snap that next selfie, pause a moment to make sure that it's safe to take and that it will prove to be a good look for you, or at least not a bad one. In other words, stay situationally aware.

When a Camera Comes Out at an Inopportune Time

There will likely be a point during your teen or young adult years when you'll be doing something in private that you don't want captured on camera. Not necessarily illegal, just something that isn't for public consumption.

Right then and there, a friend, a frenemy, an acquaintance, or an intimate partner will pull out a camera and start snapping pictures or shooting video to commemorate the occasion. You'll have only a moment's notice to react if you don't want the image taken.

Here are five of your choices:

1. Allow the image to be taken and hope for the best.

2. Allow the image to be taken and ask the person not to post it on social media or share it with anyone.

3. Ask the person to put away their camera.

4. Remove yourself from the situation—at least until the camera is put away.

5. If the picture has already been taken, you can ask the person to delete it.

1. Allow the image to be taken and hope for the best. Hope is not a strategy, and I strongly suggest not choosing this first option. Even if the person is someone you trust who promises not to share the picture, friends can make mistakes and be totally clueless about what images aren't cool to share on social media or elsewhere.

What Bridges and Train Tracks Have in Common

Triston, an 18-year-old from Texas, was driving with friends over a bridge when they decided to stop and take some selfies. Trying to get an ideal selfie, he accidentally fell over the edge of the bridge and onto the ground fifty feet below. Triston was rushed to the emergency room and treated for, among other things, a punctured lung, a pelvic fracture, multiple lacerations, and a broken rib. The treating physicians were astonished that he survived the fall and described it as "miraculous" and "inexplicable." Not wanting others to make a similar mistake, Triston shared his own story and described his injuries this way: "I broke my face a whole bunch."

Triston was *really* lucky. Three teenage girls, two of them sisters, from Utah were not. They stopped at a set of train tracks to capture a selfie, looking buoyant and excited in the photo. Tragically, other loud trains in the area stopped them from hearing a train approaching from behind. They were struck and killed.

You're probably thinking that you would never have a lapse of judgment that resulted in your getting seriously injured or killed while taking a selfie. You're probably right, but no one is immune from making a bad decision, even an impulsive one, that can lead to injury or death.

Moreover, your crush, intimate partner, or friend today may not be one tomorrow and could even end up angry with you for a perceived slight. There's no way to know where the image of you might end up, now or in the future. Remember, it doesn't have to be something illegal; it could just be showing you smiling and holding a red Solo cup (a type of cup often used for drinking alcohol at parties) at a get-together that some may wrongly assume contains alcohol. Such a misperception may not be that big of a deal, but it may be something that you just don't want floating around.

2. Allow the image to be taken and ask the person not to post it on social media or share it with anyone. This is better than option one but not by a lot. If you trust the person, and they agree to your request, that may be good enough for many in such a situation, though. In my opinion, it shouldn't be, but, of course, that'll be your decision if this happens.

Other times, people may push back on you and ask what you're worried about or why you don't trust them. You can offer whatever explanation you like to get them to understand your concern. Absent the use of

It's Not Just Illegal Acts That You Don't Want Captured

In this image of a young man drinking beer upside down from a keg (called a keg stand), let's assume that he's lawfully allowed to drink alcohol. So what he's doing is not against the law, but it's still a bad look for him. He might not care if his parents or other people in his social circle see the image. However, if a prospective employer or school admissions officer see it, it could be harmful because, to some, he looks immature and not serious minded. In a highly competitive world, fair or not, that may be just enough to sink his ship.

physical force, which I don't recommend, there's no way to stop someone from posting a picture to social media or to force the person to delete it. **This is why anytime a phone is out and pointed your way, go into high alert and assume every photo or video will be shared.** I always do the same.

3. Ask the person to put away their camera. In the moment, this may be uncomfortable to do, but it's a wise move. Someone who cares about you will understand. Anyone who gives you a hard time about putting the camera away isn't acting in your best interests and probably shouldn't be trusted with the image. If you're uncomfortable about the presence of the camera, it's likely that others are too; you were just the person brave enough to say something about it. Hopefully, others will follow suit.

4. Remove yourself from the situation—at least until the camera is put away. If you don't want an image of you taken or shared, quickly remove yourself from the scene. You can go to the bathroom, make a phone call, get some fresh air, or come up with any other reason to step away. A downside of this approach is that if you haven't made clear that you're uncomfortable about the presence of the camera, when you return someone may take out the camera again. Of course, in some situations the camera comes out and pictures are taken so quickly that you're unable to remove yourself.

Nazi Salutes Are Always a Terrible Look

A large group of senior male high school students from Wisconsin got together to take pre-prom photographs. In one image, almost all of the tuxedo-clad students give what resembles a one-armed Nazi "Sieg Heil" salute, many smiling and laughing while they did so. Jordan Blue, a student who didn't make the gesture, looks visibly agitated in the picture. "When I saw what was happening, I was so upset."

Blue goes on to say, "I couldn't leave the photo, as it was taken within five seconds." The photo made international headlines and received widespread condemnation. It's been reported that the image has resulted in the loss of college scholarships for some of the students depicted in the photo. With no time to take evasive action, Blue did what he could to disassociate himself from the acts of the others. At times, that may be the best one can do.

5. If the picture has already been taken, you can ask the person to delete it. It's always okay to ask people to delete photos and social media–related posts of the image if you're uncomfortable about it. Some will gladly grant your request to delete the image and/or not post it; others will tell you to "get lost." It can be hard to ask someone to delete a photo or not to post it to social media. However, stand your ground, be respectful, stay physically safe, and ask again if your request is refused.

Guilt by Association

In the image below, some young teens are hanging out and most of them are smoking weed and drinking beer—illegal for all of them. The teen sitting in the middle is not partaking. Still, once this picture is taken, if it's seen by others outside this group, they may conclude that this teen was partaking with the others, even though there is no visual evidence of it. This is called "guilt by association," meaning that we may be considered to have done something wrong based on the behaviors of the company we keep.

The teen in the middle isn't smoking weed or drinking with her friends, but many who see this picture will assume she was. It's called guilt by association.

Online Porn: Potentially Far More Harmful Than Many Realize

Although it veers me a bit out of my lane, I cannot write an entire book about life safety skills for teens and not cover, albeit briefly, online porn—which is commonly accessed by people from their phones. Dr. Cara Natterson is a pediatrician and a *New York Times* best-selling author whose books focus on parenting and puberty. One of her books, *Decoding Boys*, makes clear (as does other research) that *compulsive viewing of porn can be very harmful to young people*. Dr. Natterson tells me that with so many young people owning or having access to smartphones at a young age, "Early exposure to online porn begins as young as 10 or 11 years old, sometimes even younger."

When porn is viewed compulsively during adolescence as the brain is developing, Dr. Natterson points out, "It causes a positive feedback loop that rewires the brain, making it more likely for both boys and girls to get addicted to porn." Addiction of any sort can have a negative impact on our lives, and porn is no exception. It can result in, among other things:

- isolation in order to watch porn
- the normalizing of sexual violence, frequently depicted in porn
- objectification; that is, reducing someone to the status of a mere object, which is particularly true of women in porn
- early onset of erectile dysfunction, which can happen when real sexual interactions are no longer arousing because the brain has been conditioned to be stimulated by porn, not a sexual interaction with someone else
- a misunderstanding of sexual consent and a belief that sex is a one-sided choice

Learning about sex through porn is like learning how to drive by watching *The Fast and the Furious* movies—a terrible idea.

If you think you may be addicted to porn, please talk to a trusted adult and/or seek the help of an addiction counselor.

What Three Things in This Chapter Matter Most to You?

We all take away different lessons from reading the information presented in this chapter. What resonates with one person may not be meaningful to another and vice versa. I certainly hope that you've learned a heck of a lot more than three things in this chapter, but if three things were all you learned, I still consider it a win. Even a single piece of information could be invaluable if it was just what you or someone you're with needs in a critical moment.

With the information from this chapter fresh in your mind, please take a few moments to write below the three things that you consider the most important.

1. _____

_____

2. _____

_____

3. _____

_____

What Would You Do if It Happened to You?

There's a guy at school, Byron, who has been flirting with you. One night while you're texting back and forth, he asks you to send nudes. You try to change the subject, but he keeps asking, telling you that other people do it all the time, it's no big deal, and he promises that no one else will ever see it. You have a crush on Byron and want him to like you.

What would you say to Byron? Would you send the photo?

Some Thoughts about "What Would You Do if It Happened to You?"

Would you send the photo? It's hard to say no to people, especially when you like them and are hoping for a relationship. Luckily, there are ways you can say no without it seeming like you aren't interested in that person. You could tell Byron that your parents monitor your phone, or you could suggest that the two of you hang out in person and get to know each other better. If he still keeps pressuring you, consider whether you really want to date someone who doesn't respect your boundaries.

If you're inclined to send the photo, do your best not to make an impulsive decision. Think about the possible long-term consequences of sharing the image. If you do end up sending it to Byron, it should be because you've thought about the potential consequences, not because he pressured or coerced you into doing so. Additionally, you certainly don't want to capture your face in the image or anything else that might identify you.

Final Thoughts

When it comes to many of the topics in this book such as sexual assault, teen dating violence, and street safety, it's instantly obvious by their wording alone how they can cause harm. The topic of digital cameras can seem less so. However, as we've seen, the use of digital cameras can cause various types of harm.

Although it is not typical for teens to be arrested and prosecuted for underage sexting, some are. Unfair social stigma is far more frequent. It is also statistically unlikely that any of us will die from taking a selfie. However, some do, and even if it's not a death, injuries can happen, some of them quite serious.

When it comes to revenge porn, like other ills, no one thinks that they'll become a victim, and most won't. Yet revenge porn has become a huge problem in our society, the extent of which we are only starting to comprehend and probe because it's a relatively new crime. While victims are *never* to blame for the wrongful or illegal acts of another, we do know that we are less likely to become victims of revenge porn if we refrain from taking nude images of ourselves—particularly ones in which we are identifiable.

I hope this chapter has given you food for thought and consideration. When we stay mindful about the potential harms that the use of digital cameras can cause us or others, we're able to remain safer in so many ways—physically, emotionally, and legally.

Where Can I Get More Information?

This chapter contains the essentials of smartphone camera safety and decisions. For those who want to know more and dig deeper into this topic, a Google search is a good place to start and will deliver numerous resources, some with valuable information.

There are agencies and service organizations whose mission is to provide meaningful support for anyone in need of information and resources related to revenge porn. You can contact them about a specific concern you have for yourself, a friend, a loved one, or even a stranger. Often, if desired, you can stay anonymous. Here are a few you can start with:

- Cyber Civil Rights Initiative
    » provides victims of revenge porn with support and referral services
    » 844-878-2274
    » www.cybercivilrights.org
- Cyber Civil Rights Legal Project
    » helps victims of revenge porn with free legal services
    » www.cyberrightsproject.com
- My Consent
    » resources and legal information for victims of digital harassment, particularly revenge porn
    » www.withoutmyconsent.org

Smartphone Cameras Quiz

Test your understanding of smartphone camera safety by taking this quiz. Hopefully, you'll get all of the answers correct because a single mistake could have real-world consequences if that answer contained the information you needed to stay safe.

Instructions: select the best answer from the available choices. Answers can be found in the back of the book.

1. In most states, possessing a nude image of anyone under 18 can result in being charged with possessing child pornography or other similar crimes.
    A. True
    B. False, because the child pornography laws apply to sexual predators over 18.
    C. True, but only if the sender sends the images across state lines.
    D. False, so long as the sender and the recipient are legally allowed, under state law, to engage in sexual activity.

2. One in ten ex-partners have threatened that they would expose nude or partially nude photos of their ex online, and 60 percent of those who threatened followed through on their threats.
    A. True
    B. False

3. The potential aftermath of sending a nude includes revenge porn and sextortion.
    A. True
    B. False

4. Deaths and injuries while taking selfies are most common for those over the age of 25.
    A. True
    B. False

5. Kai and Imani, boyfriend and girlfriend who are 16 years old, live in a state in which 16 is the age of consent for sex. During a school investigation, the police discover nudes the pair have taken of themselves and shared with one another on their phones. Can Kai and Imani be charged with child pornography-related crimes?
    A. No, so long as they were in a consensual, sexual relationship.
    B. No, since they've reached the age of sexual consent.
    C. Yes, but only if the images were sent over the internet.
    D. Yes, unless there's a law in their state to the contrary, since they're minors.

6. Abe, Jake, and some of their friends, all 17 years old, are hanging out at one of their homes drinking beer. Jake wants to take a picture of the group drinking, send it to some girls they know, and invite them to come over. He promises to delete the photo after sending it and will ask the recipients to do the same. Abe trusts all of them completely. Should Abe allow the picture to be taken?

   A. Yes, since he completely trusts Jake.
   B. Yes, because drinking a beer is widely accepted in society and it's unlikely that the photo would be seen by anyone that he doesn't already know.
   C. No, unless the recipients promise in writing to delete it.
   D. No, because even if he trusts everyone involved, friends can make mistakes and others may still see it.

7. It may be a crime to take a picture of someone in a place where it's reasonable to expect privacy.

   A. True
   B. False

8. Sending an unsolicited nude may be a crime.

   A. True
   B. False

9. If someone under 18 sends you a nude, so long as you didn't request it, you can't get in trouble for saving it.

   A. True
   B. False

10. Compulsive viewing by young people of online porn can lead to:

    A. Nothing that impacts anyone other than oneself.
    B. Erectile dysfunction.
    C. The normalization of sexual violence.
    D. Both B and C above.

Best Wishes for Your Future

Dear Reader,

Well, you made it to the end of the book! Whether you read it from cover to cover or jumped around studying individual chapters as needed, thank you for taking the time to read and to consider the "how-to's" and "how-not-to's" herein. You may even find yourself coming back to the book sometime in the future to catch things you might have missed or to remind yourself of an important lesson.

I hope that someday the information in this book will be taught to all young people as part of the standard curriculum at every school. In the meantime, you are a step ahead and taking away a tool kit of life skills that will help you, or perhaps someone you care about, stay safer and make more informed choices both now and for many years to come.

This may be the end of the line for us together, but you are off and running and are just beginning your own exciting life journey. I wish you the best of luck, happiness, and great success!

Warmly,

Jonathan Cristall

P.S. I love hearing how this material has helped you or the people you care about. Please share your stories and stay personally connected with me via my website at WTDTT.com.

Appendix 1:
Where Can I Get Help or
More Information?

A preliminary list of resources is provided below. Much like the chapters in this book, there are plenty of overlapping points between each category. For example, RAINN.org is listed under sexual assault, but it can also provide meaningful assistance related to other types of sexual violence.

Some service organizations are available twenty-four hours a day, seven days a week, and 365 days a year. Many of them allow individuals who reach out to remain anonymous, if that is their preference. Some resource providers can even connect you to local services in your area.

Please don't be discouraged if any given resource does not provide you with the exact help you want or the information you seek—there are many more resources than those listed below.

Categories (listed alphabetically):

1. Active shooters/gun violence
2. Cyberbullying
3. Digital safety
4. Miscellaneous
5. Police interactions
6. Revenge porn (image-based sexual abuse)
7. Sextortion
8. Sexual assault
9. Sexual harassment
10. Stalking
11. Teen dating violence

1. Active shooters/gun violence

- Say Something
    - » a youth violence prevention program providing anonymous reporting of safety concerns to help identify at-risk individuals and intervene if necessary
    - » 844-572-9669
    - » www.saysomething.net
- Stop the Bleeding Coalition
    - » training and resources so citizens can be the "first responders" in an emergency in which there's uncontrolled bleeding
    - » www.stopthebleedcoalition.org

2. Cyberbullying

- Cybersmile Foundation
    - » professional help and support services for cyberbullying
    - » www.cybersmile.org
- Cyberbullying Research Center
    - » comprehensive information about all aspects of cyberbullying
    - » www.cyberbullying.org
- PACER's National Bullying Prevention Center
    - » anti-bullying resources
    - » www.pacer.org/bullying
- Stop Bullying
    - » official website of the United States government related to bullying and cyberbullying
    - » www.stopbullying.gov

3. Digital safety

- Common Sense Media
    - » a leading source of technology education for families and schools
    - » www.commonsense.org

- ConnectSafely
  - » dedicated to educating users of connected technology about safety, privacy and security
  - » www.connectsafely.org
- Electronic Frontier Foundation
  - » defending digital privacy, free speech, and innovation
  - » www.eff.org
- Internet Safety 101
  - » a resource and teaching series that paints a comprehensive picture of the dangers children encounter online
  - » www.internetsafety101.org
- NetSmartz
  - » online safety program operated by the National Center for Missing and Exploited Children (NCMEC)
  - » www.netsmartz.org

4. Miscellaneous

- Futures Without Violence
  - » a nonprofit working to end violence against women and children
  - » www.futureswithoutviolence.org
- Lambda Legal
  - » national legal organization whose mission is to achieve full recognition of the civil rights of lesbians, gay men, bisexuals, transgender people, and those living with HIV
  - » www.lambalegal.org
- LGBT National Youth Talk-line
  - » provides telephone, online, private one-to-one chat, and email peer support, as well as factual information and local resources for cities and towns across the United States
  - » 800-246-PRIDE (7743)
  - » email: help@lgbthotline.org
  - » www.glbthotline.org

- National Center for Victims of Crime
  - » leading resource and advocacy organization for crime victims
  - » www.victimsofcrime.org
- National Child Abuse Hotline
  - » prevention and treatment of child abuse
  - » 800-422-4453
  - » text: CHILDHELP to 847411
  - » www.childhelp.org
- National Suicide Prevention Lifeline
  - » national network of local crisis centers that provides free and confidential emotional support to people in suicidal crisis or emotional distress
  - » 800-273-TALK (8255)
  - » As this book is on its way to publication, the Lifeline may soon be adding an easier-to-remember national crisis hotline phone number: 988.
  - » text: HOME to 741741
  - » www.suicidepreventionlifeline.org
- Project Safe Childhood (US Department of Justice)
  - » a nationwide initiative to combat the growing epidemic of child sexual exploitation and abuse
  - » www.justice.gov/psc
- Safe Place
  - » supportive services for young people in need of immediate help and safety
  - » National Runaway Safe-line: 1-800-RUNAWAY (786-2929)
  - » text: HELP to 69866
  - » www.nationalsafeplace.org

- Substance Abuse and Mental Health Services Administration (SAMHSA)
    - » substance use and mental disorder information, services, and research
    - » 800-662-HELP (4357)
    - » www.samhsa.gov
- TEEN LINE
    - » helps troubled teenagers address their problems teen-to-teen
    - » 800-852-8336
    - » text: TEEN to 839863
    - » www.teenlineonline.org
- The Trevor Project
- crisis and suicide prevention helpline for LGBTQ youth
- 866-488-7386
- www.thetrevorproject.org
- Victim Connect Resource Center
    - » confidential referrals for crime victims
    - » 855-484-2846
    - » www.victimconnect.org

5. Police interactions

- American Civil Liberties Union (ACLU)
    - » a non-profit organization that defends the fundamental rights outlined in the United States Constitution and the Bill of Rights
    - » 212-549-2500
    - » www.aclu.org
- Flex Your Rights
    - » educates the public about how basic Bill of Rights protections apply during encounters with law enforcement
    - » www.flexyourrights.org

6. Revenge porn (image-based sexual abuse)

- Cyber Civil Rights Initiative
  - » provides victims with support and referral services
  - » 844-878-2274
  - » www.cybercivilrights.org
- Cyber Civil Rights Legal Project
  - » helps victims with free legal services
  - » www.cyberrightsproject.com
- My Consent
  - » resources and legal information for victims of digital harassment, particularly revenge porn
  - » www.withoutmyconsent.org

7. Sextortion

- Child Rescue Coalition
  - » Works to stop the spread of sexual abuse material via decentralized file sharing networks and offers educational tips for parents
  - » childrescuecoalition.org
- Federal Bureau of Investigation (FBI)
  - » lead federal agency for investigating cyber crime, which includes its Violent Crime Against Children Program
  - » 800-CALL-FBI
  - » www.fbi.gov and www.IC3.gov to report (the FBI's Internet Crime Complaint Center)
- National Center for Missing and Exploited Children (NCMEC)
  - » resources pertaining to child victims of sexual exploitation
  - » 800-843-5678 for resources and reporting
  - » www.missingkids.com for resources and reporting
- THORN
  - » works to stop the spread of sexual abuse material
  - » text: THORN to 741741
  - » www.stopsextortion.com

8. Sexual assault

- National Helpline for Men Who Were Sexually Abused or Assaulted
    - » helps men who have unwanted or abusive sexual experiences live healthier, happier lives
    - » www.1in6.org/helpline
- National Human Trafficking Hotline
    - » connects victims and survivors of sex and labor trafficking with services and support
    - » 888-373-7888
    - » text: HELP to 233733
    - » www.humantraffickinghotline.org
- National Sexual Assault Hotline
    - » connects callers with a trained staff member from a sexual assault service provider in your area
    - » 800-656-HOPE (4673)
- National Sexual Violence Resource Center
    - » leading nonprofit in providing information and tools to prevent and respond to sexual violence
    - » www.nsvrc.org
- Rape, Abuse & Incest National Network (RAINN)
    - » the nation's largest anti-sexual violence organization
    - » www.rainn.org

9. Sexual harassment

- Hollaback!
    - » a people-powered movement to end harassment
    - » www.ihollaback.org
- Know Your IX
    - » educates on Title IX and offers resources to empower students who look to stop sexual violence
    - » www.knowyourix.org

- Stop Sexual Assault in Schools
  - » educates students, families, and schools about the right to an equal education free from sexual harassment
  - » www.stopsexualassaultinschools.org
- Stop Street Harassment
  - » dedicated to ending gender harassment
  - » www.stopstreetharassment.org
- US Department of Education Office for Civil Rights (OCR)
  - » enforcers of Title IX of the Education Amendments Act of 1972
  - » www.ed.gov/ocr
- US Equal Employment Opportunity Commission
  - » enforcers of Title VII of the federal Civil Rights Act of 1964
  - » www.eeoc.gov

10. Stalking

- Victim Connect Resource Center
  - » confidential referrals for crime victims
  - » 855-4-VICTIM (855-484-2846)
  - » www.victimconnect.org
- Please also see the resource providers for teen dating violence and sexual assault

11. Teen dating violence

- Break the Cycle
  - » inspires young people 12-24 and supports them as they build healthy relationships and create a culture without abuse
  - » www.breakthecycle.org

- National Domestic Violence Hotline
    - » provides lifesaving tools and immediate support to enable victims to find safety and live lives free of abuse
    - » 800-799-SAFE (7233)
    - » text: LOVEIS to 22522
    - » www.thehotline.org
- National Teen Dating Abuse Helpline
    - » highly-trained advocates offer support, information and advocacy to young people who have questions or concerns about dating relationships
    - » 866-331-9474
    - » text: LOVEIS to 22522
    - » www.loveisrespect.org

Appendix 2:
Reporting Sexual Harassment to School Administrators

The following are some suggestions for helping ensure that your school treats you fairly and takes your complaint seriously. Most of these—for instance, keeping a chronology of the harassment, gathering evidence, and sending confirmatory letters—are *completely* optional and not a prerequisite to making a report of sexual harassment or having that report properly investigated.

Also, having a trusted adult by your side as you navigate the steps below can be helpful. When facts warrant and if it's a possibility for you, experienced attorneys can also be of great service.

1. **Obtain a copy of the sexual discrimination and harassment policy or code of conduct for your school and/or school district** (having such a policy or code is a legal requirement at all Title IX schools). The policy can often be found online or in the student handbook and should include or define what acts are considered to be harassment, where those acts must have occurred (for example, on campus and at school events), how and to whom to report the acts, and what actions the school may initiate when it learns of them.

   If your school isn't bound by Title IX, it is still likely to have a written sexual harassment policy and may be required to have an anti-harassment policy by state law (though religious schools are not required to). Also, since sexual harassment is essentially sexualized bullying, a school policy on bullying or other aggressive behaviors may also apply to actions that amount to sexual harassment.

If your school doesn't have a sexual harassment policy, you can ask or demand that it implements one. With or without a written policy in place, though, schools must take reasonable steps to ensure that the school environment is a safe place to learn.

2. **Prepare a detailed written statement describing what occurred to the best of your ability.** Doing so will help you organize your thoughts and remember important parts of the events. Detail in your statement, again, to the best of your ability, how the acts of harassment violated school policy.

Before writing the statement, consider making a chronological log (a timeline) of past and ongoing instances of harassment, such as what happened, when it happened, where it happened, how it made you feel, what you did, what the person did, and who the witnesses were.

Use your log to assist in the drafting of your statement. You want to do this carefully because if and when you share your statement, it may be looked at with skepticism if you substantively change parts later.

Gather as much of the evidence of the harassment as reasonably possible, including text messages, social media posts, photos/videos, etc. Attach copies of the evidence to your written statement.

3. **Report the harassment to your school.** The procedure varies by school or school district, but that can often be found online. At schools bound by Title IX, the policy will dictate how the report must be made and where or to whom to make it—very likely the Title IX office or Title IX coordinator (coordinators are mandated at all Title IX schools). Depending on these procedures, your written statement may be able to serve as the report or complaint.

Follow the procedures so you lodge your report with someone who is empowered and required to institute corrective measures at the school—doing so attributes "actual knowledge" to the school—which is necessary for the reporting party.

If your school isn't bound by Title IX or is bound but doesn't have a Title IX coordinator as required, report your complaint to someone as high in the administration as possible and to the Department of Education's Office for Civil Rights.

After you make the complaint, some type of intake meeting should be set up quickly for you and a school investigator or Title IX coordinator. Hopefully, you'll go to this meeting with a trusted adult at your side. Since relaying what happened in person can be emotionally difficult, having your written statement with you can help. Also, when you put your statement in writing, you aren't relying on someone else's note-taking skills. If the school hasn't yet received your written statement and/or supporting evidence, provide it to them at the meeting.

After the intake meeting, draft and send a letter confirming what the school representative said it would do (or wouldn't do) and what your expectations are. If you previously provided your written statement and/or accompanying evidence, be sure to mention that in your letter. Include another copy of your statement for ease of reference and to better establish that it was provided to them.

The letter should be emailed, sent certified mail (return receipt requested), or via UPS or FedEx. This proves that you sent it and that it was received (which may not necessarily be the case with email).

On an ongoing basis, add to your log any further incidents of harassment and the names, dates, actions taken, and, perhaps, actions not taken in response to your complaint.

Although it may not be within the financial means for many people, having a lawyer or a victim advocate (who may be available free of charge) attend the meeting and/or write or send the letter can be helpful. However, if your school fails to take reasonable steps to help end the harassment (or if you've been accused of harassment and believe that your due process rights—the procedures and rules that ensure the fair treatment of individuals who are involved in disputes—were violated), you should strongly consider consulting with a lawyer to advocate on your behalf.

In some circumstances, the target of the harassment may be able to sue the school and/or school district in a civil court of law for monetary compensation for pain and suffering, as well as medical and other expenses that were caused by the harassment. The harasser can also be sued for these same injuries. Some lawyers will represent the victim without charging any legal fees because they'll seek recoupment of them from the school and/or the person engaging in the wrongful activity (this is called taking a case on a contingency). You can also seek referrals for low-cost or pro bono lawyers (who perform public interest legal work without charge), who might file the lawsuit on your behalf without any cost to you.

Since Title IX is enforced by the US Department of Education's Office for Civil Rights (OCR), if you've been unsuccessful with the school's administrative process (or if there is no Title IX coordinator, as required by law), report the harassment directly to the OCR office responsible for your state. You can call 800-421-3481 or check OCR's website at www.ed.gov/ocr. Be advised that there are time limits within which you must file your claim.

If you have questions about completing the OCR forms, help can be found at stopsexualassaultinschools.org.

Appendix 3:
Tips for Making Police Reports

Whenever you're concerned for your personal safety or for someone whom you care about, don't delay getting the police involved. In an emergency, call 911. In less exigent situations, you can go to a police station and speak to a police officer on duty and, if you choose, report a crime.

When time allows, it can be worthwhile to plan ahead for your visit to the station. In some circumstances, doing things from the list below can increase the likelihood that the police will be able to conduct a successful investigation of a reported crime, though none is a prerequisite to making a police report. Still, you want to "make your case" as best as possible and here are some ways:

- **Plan to bring a trusted adult.** A trusted adult not only provides you with important emotional support but also can give you more credibility with some police officers. A trusted adult might also be able to help you with the other things listed below. Please note that while minors can make police reports without being with a parent or guardian, in some circumstances, such as when child sexual abuse is involved, the police will notify the parent or guardian.

- **Bring proof that a crime was committed.** Every jurisdiction is different when it comes to the range of crimes that get reported to the police and, therefore, the ones they have the most experience investigating. For example, some police officers may be unfamiliar with crimes that take place in the digital world or various laws that may apply to an unusual situation in the physical one.

    When the crime is something that you (and, hopefully, your trusted adult) don't believe the police are likely to routinely see, if possible, try to do a bit of research in advance to have at least a baseline understanding of it. Depending on how obscure or uncommon the law may be, consider bringing a printout of the actual text. If you are unsure which laws your state has that might apply to your given situation—for example, cyberbullying—a Google search should give you some answers.

- **Obtain and preserve evidence.** Police need evidence to substantiate allegations. While they may be able to obtain evidence on their own, you can help get an investigation going if you provide copies of all (as much as reasonably possible) physical and digital evidence that is in your possession or easily accessible to you. Digital evidence can include correspondence such as email and text messages, photos, videos, screen recordings, screenshots, instant messaging logs, web pages (which can be saved as PDFs), and social media profiles and posts. For acts that may amount to digital crimes, make it a habit to screenshot everything as soon as you see it, since social media posts and other digital evidence can be removed, or messages might automatically disappear from some apps and websites.

  Include the evidence that relays the whole story, not just that which is favorable to you. If any of the evidence might incriminate you in a serious crime, it's usually best to first speak with a trusted adult or a lawyer before handing it over.

- **Be well organized.** The better organized you are, the easier you make it on the police. When a series of events are involved, it can be helpful to a detective assigned to your case if you prepare a written timeline of the events (or as many as you can recall), in chronological order, listing the date and approximate time of each incident, a description of what happened, and any evidence in your possession (including names and contact information for witnesses) that substantiate your allegations. Your timeline doesn't have to be perfect, but do your best under the circumstances to make it as thorough as possible.

  If evidence is in the hands of someone else such as a website or email service provider, you should also identify that in your timeline. A police officer can send an evidence preservation request to the provider to help prevent the destruction of that evidence, which may occur in their normal course of business. You can also send the request yourself. There are samples online.

- **Stick to the facts.** Keep things as straightforward as possible by sticking to the facts. While you want to tell the complete story, you also want it to be concise.

- **Be resilient.** Many officers you speak with will be helpful and courteous and treat your matter with the seriousness that it deserves. Others may not and, in some situations, might blame the victim (one more reason it's ideal to have a trusted adult at your side). Always try to keep your cool, and, if you aren't being treated the way you should be, consider asking to speak to that officer's commanding officer.

- **Get a copy of the report.** After making your crime report to the officer on duty, ask for a copy of it and ask whether the officer knows which detective the matter will be assigned for investigation. Take a picture of the report just in case you lose it.

- **Follow up.** If you haven't been contacted by a police detective assigned to investigate your report after a reasonable time has passed, follow up by going to or calling the station and asking who the assigned detective is. Police stations are often busy places, and how soon they take action depends on the seriousness of the alleged wrongdoing. You may need to follow up as often as you believe is warranted under the circumstances.

- **Act promptly.** If you wait too long to make a police report, the statute of limitations (the maximum time after an event within which claims must be initiated) may preclude the police from making an arrest for certain types of crimes.

Appendix 4:
Is There Anything I Can Do to
Clean Up My Digital Footprint?

The short answer is yes. Your unflattering digital data may not disappear, but you can make it more difficult to find.

Rich Matta is the chief executive officer of ReputationDefender, a business that focuses on online reputation management. Matta and his team work with many young people to repopulate Google searches under their name "so that something negative appears on page 5 of a Google search instead of page 1. Over 90 percent of people never click past page 1 of a Google search so owning that real estate can be really valuable."

Matta further explains that ReputationDefender (and other similar services such as BrandYourself.com) helps its clients "over time, to create factually accurate content about themselves online that will rise to the top of the Google rankings. This not only suppresses the negative information, but you've also taken the opportunity to present search results that reflect who you are in the best possible light."

While ReputationDefender is a pay-for-service, its techniques—or at least some of them—can be done for free by the individual. It's not always easy to do, but for some tips you can go to the self-help section of ReputationDefender.com or search online for other resources.

The idea is to bury the bad by creating loads of new, positive content about yourself. In his book, *The Virtual Handshake: Opening Doors and Closing Deals Online*, Scott Allen says, "It's not that you can make the stuff disappear. It's that you make so much more good stuff that you can't find the bad stuff."

Here are just a few of the things you, or a pay-for-service, can do:

- Check if your state has an online eraser law. Although the effectiveness of such laws remain to be seen, these laws gives minors a limited right to remove information that they posted online as registered users of sites, networks, or apps. As of publication, there isn't a corresponding federal law, but there likely will be in the foreseeable future.

- Consider whether it's time to update your bios, profile pictures, and banner images/information in your profiles. If they're from years ago, they may not reflect who you are now or who you are trying to become. Also, social media educator Josh Ochs, introduced in chapter 8, suggests using the same photo for each of your public accounts since "doing so makes it easier for people to connect the dots between all of your professional, fun, relevant forms of social media."

- As the saying goes, a picture is worth a thousand words. Make sure that all of yours say something good about you.

- Remove old tweets, Instagram posts, and other similar shares, whether private or public, that aren't consistent with your brand.

- Review the hashtags and likes that you have used or posted and that others have used on your posts. On some platforms, you can go back and remove the ones that are not a good look for you.

- There are apps and websites, some of them free, that'll run a report on your feeds and will flag posts that may be of concern, including those that contain profanity, mention drugs or alcohol, make inappropriate comments, and more. You can also add your own custom keyword searches such as the name of your school, a teacher, a former intimate partner, and so on. Once you get your report, you can then decide what to edit or remove.

Appendix 5:
Reporting Cyberbullying to a
School Administrator

The following are some suggestions for helping ensure that your school treats you fairly and takes your complaint seriously. Most of these things, such as keeping a chronology of the cyberbullying and the sending of confirmatory letters, are *completely* optional and not a prerequisite to making a report to your school or having that report properly investigated.

As mentioned in other parts in the book, having a trusted adult by your side as you navigate the steps below can be incredibly helpful and may be mandatory if you are a minor. When the facts warrant and if it's a possibility, experienced attorneys can also be of great service.

1. **Obtain a copy of the bullying and/or cyberbullying policy for your school or school district.** The policy can often be found online and/or in the student handbook and should include or define what acts are considered to be bullying.

    In the unlikely event that your school doesn't have an anti-bullying policy, you can ask or demand that it implements one. With or without a written policy in place, schools must take reasonable steps to ensure that the school environment is a safe place to learn.

2. **Prepare a detailed written statement to the best of your ability describing what occurred.** Doing so will help you organize your thoughts and not forget important parts of the story.

    Before you write the statement, it's a good idea to make a chronological log (a timeline) of past and ongoing instances of cyberbullying and in-person bullying, such as what happened, when it happened, where it happened, what you did, what the person did, and who the witnesses were. Assemble all of the corresponding evidence—or as much as you're able to obtain.

Use your log to assist in the drafting of your statement. You want to do this carefully because once you put the events in writing, it may be looked at with skepticism if you substantively change parts later.

Remember to gather *all* evidence of the cyberbullying, including text messages, social media posts, photos or videos, and the names of witnesses. Attach a copy of the documentary evidence to your written statement.

3. **Request a meeting with a school administrator to report the bullying, and bring your written statement.** It's important to meet with someone at your school who is empowered to institute corrective measures at the school—often the principal or assistant principal. Since relaying what happened in person can be emotionally difficult, having your written statement with you can help. If the school hasn't yet received your written statement and/or supporting evidence, provide it at the meeting.

   If your school is bound by Title IX of the Education Amendments Act of 1971 and the cyberbullying/bullying targets someone's gender, then the bullying could also amount to gender discrimination, which is prohibited under federal law. If so, see the information about Title IX in chapter 5 and appendix 2.

   After the meeting, draft and send a follow-up letter to the school representative you met with confirming what the school said it would or wouldn't do and what your expectations are. This is a key step because it is important to document that you've put your school on notice. When doing so, be sure to acknowledge the written statement and accompanying evidence that you provided earlier and include another copy of your written statement for ease of reference to better establish that it was provided to the school official.

   The letter should be emailed, sent certified mail (return receipt requested), or via UPS or FedEx. This proves that you sent it and that it was received, which may not necessarily be the case with email.

   If you have the financial means to do so and the bullying is severe, it can be ideal to have a lawyer attend the meeting and/or write and send the letter on your behalf. In many instances, getting an attorney involved at this stage may only be necessary if the school has already demonstrated an inability or unwillingness to act.

Similar to what was mentioned in appendix 2, if the cyberbullying continues and is not being properly addressed by the school, working with an attorney to encourage your school to take action can be effective. The lawyer can send letters, make calls, and use other tools to put pressure on school administrators to act. In severe cases, a lawyer can file a lawsuit on behalf of you and your parents in an attempt to compel the school or school district to act. Sometimes, attorneys will do so without charging any legal fees because they'll seek recoupment of them from the school and/or the person engaging in the unlawful activity (this is called taking a case on a contingency). You can also seek referrals for low-cost or pro bono lawyers (who perform public interest legal work without charge) who might file the lawsuit on your behalf without any cost to you.

Before the situation escalates to a lawsuit, if the school is not meeting its responsibilities, bring your complaint or concerns to other people in positions of authority at the school and/or in the school district, also known as going up the chain of command. It's likely that the school district will have a formal complaint process for reporting bullying.

Professor Elizabeth Englander, introduced in chapter 10, says, "Ultimately, though, the extent to which schools will be able to provide assistance may depend on if the aggressor(s) goes to the same school as the target. If they do not or it's unclear, the school should still work with the target to make the school a safer place for them to learn. Communication with schools is key. Even if schools lack the jurisdiction to take direct action, they can always help support a student and they can always keep an eye on the situation in school to see if the social problems are happening there as well."

If your school doesn't intervene in the situation or provide the appropriate level of support, you may need to be persistent. Professor Justin Patchin, introduced in chapter 10, urges targets and their support system to "make a stink. Don't let them off the hook. If you aren't getting the right response from the assistant principal, go to the principal. If the principal isn't stepping up, then go to the school board, the school superintendent, and so on. Just don't give up. Demand that the school take action or create a policy that can be more easily enforced."

Appendix 6 (for Parents): Talking to Your Children and Having Them Talk to You

Ways to Convey the Book Material to Your Children

Below are my top ten ways to help relate the topics in this book to your children (or other young person for whom you care). Since no one knows your child better than you, choose what you believe will work best. Everyone's situation is different, and often complex.

1. Start on any chapter that interests you. Read it in its entirety, or just those pages or sections that are most important to you.

   Any of the topics can arise with our children over a period of days, months, or years, so this book is intended to be an ongoing resource as new needs arise. In fact, it's probably best, and perhaps a necessity, that parents discuss the topics in this book with their kids over a period of weeks, months or even years.

2. I teach the book's concepts, as best I can, to my three sons in three different ways. One of my sons will read chunks of chapters, one will read only a page or two, or let me read it with him, and one refuses to read. Every child is different; you'll need to adapt to yours.

3. When trying to talk to my sons individually about the content of this book, I get in just two to three minutes of discussion, depending on the son, before I get shut down. Accordingly, I am always brief but to the point. For me, it's a necessity and less is often more.

4. What works today may not work tomorrow. Be flexible and adapt to the unique circumstances we all face.

5. I am not above "incentivizing" my sons, or taking a privilege away, to help facilitate the learning of what I believe are the most important parts of this book.

6. *Any* of the skills or advice you can convey, by hook or by crook, may serve them well. As you read through the book, what resonates with you is different from what resonates with others—we all take something different from each topic. Stay focused on what *you* think is most important. Even one thing they're able to learn can be exactly the information they need in that moment that helps them or someone they care about.

7. Each chapter in this book provides a quiz you can give your teen or take yourself. If their score is less than 100 percent, have them learn the distinct portion(s) they missed. (To assist in this regard, the Answer Key in the print versions of this book has the page numbers where the correct information in the chapter is found.) Alternatively, regardless of how they do on a quiz, use it as a conversation starter.

    Disclaimer: the quizzes are not intended to be difficult and are not a comprehensive review of the chapter materials.

8. I've found that lecturing doesn't work well, particularly when we're angry or annoyed. Asking open-ended questions by weaving in the book's material and concepts is often a better strategy and lets your child lead the conversation—which many like to do. A real-life example from a news story can be a great way to start, and plenty of examples are spread throughout the chapters. A good time to talk with your kids is when their guard is down or at least lowered such as during a car ride, dinner, or going out for a treat. While these conversations can be awkward, an awkward conversation is better than no conversation.

9. Many times, it's easier for our kids to talk to an adult who is not their parent. They also tend to give more credibility to information passed on from an adult who is not their parent. So find a "safe adult" to act as your surrogate. Offer to return the favor for their child.

10. Finally, have monthly, quarterly, or periodic family meetings—we do all three depending on how busy we are. I use a written agenda that's distributed to the "attendees." Each person gets to air any of their

gripes for one or two minutes. My wife Lisa and I then give kudos to each of our boys for something they've done well since the last meeting. We all then set a personal goal for the next month.

Finally, we get to "Dad's Safety Minute." During this part of the meeting, I cover in two minutes or less something from this book. You might be surprised how much I can cover in two minutes. Since my sons won't sit for long, each meeting lasts between ten and fifteen minutes.

Getting Your Children Talking to You in a Time of Need

The list above offers some good ways to start a talk with your kids, but *how can you get them to start a talk with you?* As parents and guardians, we'd like our children to first come to us when they're struggling or suffering.

Danielle Brooks, whom we met in the Introduction, is a clinical therapist who specializes in the treatment of families, children, and teens. She tells me that most of the young people she treats are "suffering but don't tell their parents the degree they are in pain. They are skeptical about trusting that adults can really understand and help them. But it is important to note that most teens either show their pain through acting-out behaviors or do a test-the-waters-minimal-feeling disclosure."

The common reason, explains Brooks, is "Many young people feel that adults don't understand their struggles, are judgmental, and just give them consequences." She continues by pointing out what should be obvious: "Why would they tell us [the parents] anything if we're just going to respond by giving them consequences?"

Brooks urges parents to communicate the message to their kids that "they're going to make mistakes all the time and it's because they're at the stage of development when it's about living and learning." She also suggests "not to lead with consequences and assure them that you'll always do your best to help them. If you aren't sure how, the two of you will navigate it together and find someone who will. We may not know what to do initially, and that's okay." Remember, none of us had to navigate many of the things our kids may have to—cyberbullying, social media pressures, maintaining your digital footprint, and so on.

Lisa and I do what Brooks advises: encourage our children to approach us in a time of need. I call it the "Forever Warranty." If they are in a time of need, they can come to either of us and we will help in the moment without asking any questions other than how we can help.

Brooks echoes this: "We need to let our children know that if they ever need us, we'll be there no matter what." Brooks deepened her explanation: "If our kids are afraid we will use what they tell us against them, then why would they tell us? It's critical to establish a clear message to our children that if they come to us first versus us finding out from someone else, we won't punish and we will focus on helping." In summation, Brooks states her Golden Teen Parenting Rule: "When you need me, call me. No matter what the circumstances. I will help you and your freedom won't be taken away and I won't then micromanage your life. Just call me. I will help. No questions asked."

Continuing with this theme, I would like to share a moment I had with Los Angeles County deputy district attorney Michael DeRose, introduced in chapter 6. He's a veteran sex crimes prosecutor, and of all the interviews I conducted for this book, his stood out.

I was asking DeRose about the emotional toil it must take on him to prosecute sexual violence cases with minors as victims. His response surprised me: "Probably the most difficult part is watching parents blame their child for their victimization." He often sees parents "get really upset with their kids."

DeRose reflects on one of his cases in particular: "The victim was a really good kid, a good student. She had never been in trouble. And the perpetrator put her through hell. It really pained me to see how angry her parents were with her for engaging in risky sexual behaviors with the defendant that ultimately led to her victimization. I know that they had her best interests at heart, or at least thought they did, but that type of reaction did not serve her well."

He adds: "We've all made mistakes as kids. It's just that some mistakes weren't available to our generation. If your child ever becomes a victim . . . react with empathy and support—be on and by their side. When they trust you, the more likely they will be to report their victimization early on so you can save them from further trauma."

Chapter Quizzes Answer Key

NOTE TO THE READER: the page numbers referenced below correspond to those in the print version of this book only.

Chapter 1: Your Rights with the Police (quiz begins on page 24)

Question 1:   A (page 13)
Question 2:   B (page 9)
Question 3:   B (page 15)
Question 4:   A (page 6)
Question 5:   A (page 4)
Question 6:   B (page 17)
Question 7:   B (page 14)
Question 8:   B (page 6)
Question 9:   A (page 6)
Question 10: A (page 6)

Chapter 2: Safer Police Interactions
(quiz begins on page 45)

Question 1:   A (page 29)
Question 2:   B (page 40)
Question 3:   D (page 35)
Question 4:   B (page 35)
Question 5:   B (page 33)
Question 6:   B (page 31)
Question 7:   A (page 30)
Question 8:   A (page 34)
Question 9:   B (page 36)
Question 10: A (page 40)

Chapter 3: Street Safety (quiz begins on page 75)

Question 1:   C (page 49)
Question 2:   A (page 53)
Question 3:   D (page 52)
Question 4:   C (page 58)
Question 5:   C (page 58)
Question 6:   D (pages 52/62)
Question 7:   B (page 65)
Question 8:   B (page 68)
Question 9:   B (page 69)
Question 10: C (page 71)

Chapter 4: Sexual Assault and Consent (quiz begins on page 108)

Question 1:   B (page 89)
Question 2:   D (page 90)
Question 3:   D (page 96)
Question 4:   C (page 86)
Question 5:   B (page 86)
Question 6:   B (page 88)
Question 7:   C (page 94)
Question 8:   A (page 85)
Question 9:   C (page 86)
Question 10: D (page 96)

Chapter 5: Sexual Harassment
(quiz begins on page 133)

Question 1:   B (page 115)
Question 2:   B (page 118)
Question 3:   A (page 119)
Question 4:   D (page 114)
Question 5:   B (page 115)
Question 6:   A (page 117)
Question 7:   D (page 114)
Question 8:   A (page 117)
Question 9:   C (page 121)
Question 10: B (page 116)

Chapter 6: Sextortion
(quiz begins on page 155)

Question 1:   B (page 137)
Question 2:   A (page 136)
Question 3:   A (page 138)
Question 4:   C (page 138)
Question 5:   A (page 146)
Question 6:   A (page 139)
Question 7:   C (page 151)
Question 8:   B (page 150)
Question 9:   A (page 147)
Question 10: B (page 138)

Chapter 7: Teen Dating
Violence **(quiz begins on page 182)**

Question 1:   B (page 164)
Question 2:   C (page 165)
Question 3:   C (page 166)
Question 4:   A (page 159)
Question 5:   B (page 169)
Question 6:   A (page 159)
Question 7:   B (page 173)

Question 8:   D (page 174)
Question 9:   B (page 162)
Question 10: B (page 166)

Chapter 8: Digital Footprint
and Digital Citizenship
(quiz begins on page 210)

Question 1:   B (page 190)
Question 2:   B (page 190)
Question 3:   C (page 191)
Question 4:   C (page 193)
Question 5:   C (page 201)
Question 6:   A (page 203)
Question 7:   B (page 203)
Question 8:   B (page 190)
Question 9:   A (page 199)
Question 10: C (page 203)

Chapter 9: Digital Data Privacy
(quiz begins on page 231)

Question 1:   B (page 217)
Question 2:   A (page 224)
Question 3:   B (page 221)
Question 4:   A (page 220)
Question 5:   A (page 218)
Question 6:   B (page 219)
Question 7:   B (page 221)
Question 8:   A (page 222)
Question 9:   A (page 224)
Question 10: B (page 224)

Chapter 10: Cyberbullying
(quiz begins on page 257)

Question 1:	A (page 236)
Question 2:	D (page 239)
Question 3:	A (page 241)
Question 4:	A (page 241)
Question 5:	B (page 241)
Question 6:	B (page 243)
Question 7:	B (page 247)
Question 8:	B (page 249)
Question 9:	A (page 248)
Question 10:	B (page 252)

Chapter 11: Smartphone Cameras
(quiz begins on page 278)

Question 1:	A (pages 262/4)
Question 2:	A (page 269)
Question 3:	A (page 265)
Question 4:	B (page 270)
Question 5:	D (page 263)
Question 6:	D (page 270)
Question 7:	A (page 269)
Question 8:	A (page 265)
Question 9:	B (page 262)
Question 10:	D (page 275)

Recommended Reading

De Becker, Gavin. *The Gift of Fear and Other Survival Signals That Protect Us from Violence*. New York: Dell, 1999.

Domitrz, Michael J. *Can I Kiss You?: A Thought-Provoking Look at Relationships, Intimacy, and Sexual Assault*. Milwaukee: Awareness, 2016.

Finkelhor, David. *Childhood Victimization: Violence, Crime, and Abuse in the Lives of Young People*. New York: Oxford University Press, 2008.

Fontes, Lisa Aronson. *Invisible Chains: Overcoming Coercive Control in Your Intimate Relationship*. New York: Guilford Press, 2015.

Friedrichs, Ellen. *Good Sexual Citizenship: How to Create a (Sexually) Safer World*. Jersey City, NJ: Cleis Press, 2019.

Harding, Kate. *Asking for It: The Alarming Rise of Rape Culture—and What We Can Do About It*. Boston: Da Capo Press, 2015.

Hanson, Jason. *Spy Secrets That Can Save Your Life*. New York: Tarcher-Perigee, 2015.

Heitner, Devorah. *Screenwise: Helping Kids Thrive (and Survive) in Their Digital World*. Brookline, MA: Bibliomotion, 2016.

Hinduja, Sameer, and Justin W. Patchin. *Bullying Beyond the Schoolyard: Preventing and Responding to Cyberbullying*. Thousand Oaks, CA: Corwin, 2014.

Jacobs, Tom. *What Are My Rights?: Q&A About Teens and the Law*. Minneapolis: Free Spirit Publishing, 4th Ed. 2019.

Levy, Barrie, and Patricia Giggans. *What Parents Need to Know About Dating Violence*. Seattle: Seal Press, 1995.

Natterson, Cara. *Decoding Boys: New Science Behind the Subtle Art of Raising Sons*. New York: Ballantine Books, 2020.

Ochs, Josh. *Light, Bright and Polite 3: Teens/Young Adults.* MediaLeaders, 2017.

Patchin, Justin W., and Sameer Hinduja. *Words Wound: Delete Cyberbullying and Make Kindness Go Viral.* Minneapolis: Free Spirit Publishing, 2013.

Pfaff, John. *Locked In: The True Causes of Mass Incarceration and How to Achieve Real Reform.* New York: Basic Books, 2017.

Pipher, Mary. *Reviving Ophelia: Saving the Selves of Adolescent Girls.* New York: Ballantine Books, 1995.

Pollack, William. *Real Boys: Rescuing Our Sons from the Myths of Boyhood.* New York: Random House, 1998.

Sales, Nancy Jo. *American Girls: Social Media and the Secret Lives of Teenagers.* New York: Vintage Books, 2017.

Scheff, Sue. *Shame Nation: The Global Epidemic of Online Hate.* Naperville, IL: Sourcebooks, 2017.

Smith, Joanne N., Mandy Van Deven, and Meghan Huppuch. *Hey, Shorty!: A Guide to Combating Sexual Harassment and Violence in Schools and on the Streets.* New York: Feminist Press, 2011.

Snortland, Ellen. *Beauty Bites Beast: Awakening the Warrior Within Women and Girls.* Pasadena, CA: Trilogy Books, 1996.

Snyder, Rachel Louise. *No Visible Bruises: What We Don't Know About Domestic Violence Can Kill Us.* London: Bloomsbury Publishing, 2019.

Strong, Sanford. *Strong on Defense: Survival Rules to Protect You and Your Family from Crime.* New York: Pocket Books, 1996.

Weinberger, Jesse. *The Boogeyman Exists: And He's in Your Child's Back Pocket.* Scotts Valley, CA: CreateSpace Independent Publishing Platform, 2017.

Willard, Nancy E. *Cyber-Safe Kids, Cyber-Savvy Teens: Helping Young People Learn to Use the Internet Safely and Responsibly.* San Francisco: Jossey-Bass, 2007.

Endnotes

Chapters 1 and 2

Agorist, Matt. "Police in the US Kill Citizens at Over 70 Times the Rate of Other First-World Nations." Global Research. Last modified January 8, 2015. Accessed November 22, 2019. https://www.globalresearch.ca/police-in-the-us-kill-citizens-at-over-70-times-the-rate-of-other-first-world-nations/5438391.

Brame, Robert, et al. "Cumulative Prevalence of Arrest from Ages 8 to 23 in a National Sample." *Pediatrics* 129, no. 1 (January 2012): 21–27. https://doi.org/10.1542/peds.2010-3710.

Collier, Lorna. "Incarceration Nation." *Monitor on Psychology* 45, no. 9 (October 2014): 56. https://www.apa.org/monitor/2014/10/incarceration.

Fields, Gary, and John R. Emshwiller. "As Arrest Records Rise, Americans Find Consequences Can Last a Lifetime." *Wall Street Journal*. Last modified August 18, 2014. Accessed November 12, 2019. https://www.wsj.com/articles/as-arrest-records-rise-americans-find-consequences-can-last-a-lifetime-1408415402.

Friedman, Matthew. "Just Facts: As Many Americans Have Criminal Records as College Diplomas." Brennan Center for Justice. Last modified November 17, 2015. Accessed November 22, 2019. https://www.brennancenter.org/our-work/analysis-opinion/just-facts-many-americans-have-criminal-records-college-diplomas.

Gross, Samuel R., Maurice Possley, and Klara Stephens. *Race and Wrongful Convictions in the United States*. National Registry of Exonerations. Irvine: University of California, Irvine. March 7, 2017. http://www.law.umich.edu/special/exoneration/Documents/Race_and_Wrongful_Convictions.pdf.

Hirschfield, Paul. "Why Do American Cops Kill So Many Compared to European Cops?" The Conversation. Last modified November 25, 2005. Accessed December 2, 2019. http://theconversation.com/why-do-american-cops-kill-so-many-compared-to-european-cops-49696.

Lartey, Jamiles. "By the Numbers: US Police Kill More in Days Than Other Countries Do in Years." *Guardian*. Last modified June 9, 2015. Accessed November 22, 2019. https://www.theguardian.com/us-news/2015/jun/09/the-counted-police-killings-us-vs-other-countries.

Lee, Michelle. "Does the United States Really Have 5 Percent of the World's Population and One Quarter of the World's Prisoners?" *Washington Post*. Last modified April 30, 2015. Accessed November 22, 2019. https://www.washingtonpost.com/news/fact-checker/wp/2015/04/30/does-the-united-states-really-have-five-percent-of-worlds-population-and-one-quarter-of-the-worlds-prisoners/. Liptak, Adam. "U.S. Prison Population Dwarfs That of Other Nations." *New York Times*. Last modified April 23, 2008. Accessed November 13, 2019. https://www.nytimes.com/2008/04/23/world/americas/23iht-23prison.12253738.html.

National Center for Transgender Equality. "Failing to Protect and Serve: Police Department Policies Towards Transgender People." Last modified May 4, 2019. Accessed November 23, 2019. https://transequality.org/issues/resources/failing-to-protect-and-serve-police-department-policies-to-wards-transgender-people.

Sentencing Project. "Report to the United Nations on Racial Disparities in the U.S. Criminal Justice System." 2018. Last modified April 19, 2018. Accessed November 22, 2019. https://www.sentencing-project.org/publications/un-report-on-racial-disparities/.

Warren, Jenifer. *One in 100: Behind Bars in America 2008*. Washington, DC: PEW Center on the States, PEW Charitable Trusts, February 2008. https://www.pewtrusts.org//media/legacy/uploaded-files/wwwpewtrustsorg/reports/sentencing_and_corrections/onein100pdf.

Chapter 3

Active Shooter Incidents in the United States in 2016 and 2017. The Advanced Law Enforcement Rapid Response Training (ALERRT) Center at Texas State University and the Federal Bureau of Investigation, US Department of Justice, Washington DC. April 2018. https://www.fbi.gov/file-repository/active-shooter-incidents-us-2016-2017.pdf/view.

Aveni, Thomas J. "Officer-Involved Shootings: What We Didn't Know Has Hurt Us." Police Policy Studies Council. Last modified August 2003. Accessed November 22, 2019. http://www.theppsc.org/Staff_Views/Aveni/OIS.pdf.

Battered Women's Support Services (BWSS). "Facts on Violence Against Women and Children." Last modified 2019. Accessed November 22, 2019. https://www.bwss.org/resources/informa-tion-on-abuse/numbers-are-people-too/.

Bennett, Sarah, David P. Farrington, and L. Rowell Huesmann. "Explaining Gender Differences in Crime and Violence: The Importance of Social Cognitive Skills." *Aggression and Violent Behavior* 10, no. 3 (March–April 2005): 263–88. https://doi.org/10.1016/j.avb.2004.07.001.

Bergen, Peter. "America's Unyielding Plague of Gun Violence." Cable News Network (CNN). Last modified February 15, 2018. Accessed November 22, 2019. https://www.cnn.com/2017/10/02/opin-ions/america-lethal-nation-opinion-bergen/index.html.

Blad, Evie. "Do Schools' 'Active-Shooter' Drills Prepare or Frighten?" *Education Week* 37, no. 5 (September 2017): 1–12. https://www.edweek.org/ew/articles/2017/09/20/do-schools-active-shoot-er-drills-prepare-or-frighten.html.

Blair, Pete J., and Katherine W. Schweit. "A Study of Active Shooter Incidents in the United States." Texas State University and Federal Bureau of Investigation, US Department of Justice, Washington DC. 2014. https://www.fbi.gov/file-repository/active-shooter-study-2000-2013-1.pdf.

Brady United. "The Truth About Suicide and Guns." Brady Center to Prevent Gun Violence. Last modified 2018. Accessed November 22, 2019. https://www.bradyunited.org/reports/suicide-preven-tion-report-2018.

Centers for Disease Control and Prevention (CDC). Web-based Injury Statistics Query and Re-porting System (WISQARS). National Center for Injury Prevention and Control. Accessed July 22, 2019. https://www.cdc.gov/injury/wisqars/index.html.

Children's Defense Fund. *School Shootings Spark Everyday Worries*. Last modified September 2018. Accessed November 22, 2019. https://www.childrensdefense.org/wp-content/uploads/2018/09/You-Gov-SafeSchools-Final-Sep-18-2018.pdf.

Cunningham, Rebecca M., Maureen A. Walton, and Patrick M. Carter. "The Major Causes of Death in Children and Adolescents in the United States." *New England Journal of Medicine* 379, no. 25 (December 2018): 2468–75. https://doi.org/10.1056/nejmsr1804754.

Diliberti, M., M. Jackson, and J. Kemp. *Crime, Violence, Discipline, and Safety in U.S. Public Schools: Findings from the School Survey on Crime and Safety: 2015–16.* US Department of Education, National Center for Education Statistics, NCES 2017-122. https://nces.ed.gov/pubs2017/2017122.pdf.

Everytown for Gun Safety. "Mass Shootings in America: 2009 to 2019." Last modified November 21, 2019. Accessed December 1, 2019. https://everytownresearch.org/reports/mass-shootings-analysis/.

Fulton, April. "In Texas and Beyond, Mass Shootings Have Roots in Domestic Violence." National Public Radio. Last modified November 7, 2017. Accessed December 2, 2019. https://www.npr.org/sections/health-shots/2017/11/07/562387350/in-texas-and-beyond-mass-shootings-have-roots-in-domestic-violence.

Grinshteyn, Erin, and David Hemenway. "Violent Death Rates: The US Compared with Other High-Income OECD Countries, 2010." *American Journal of Medicine* 129, no. 3 (March 2016): 266–73. https://doi.org/10.1016/j.amjmed.2015.10.025.

Hedegaard, Holly, Sally C. Curtin, and Margaret Warner. "Suicide Mortality in the United States, 1999–2017." *NCHS Data Brief* no. 330 (November 2018): 1–7. https://www.cdc.gov/nchs/products/databriefs/db330.htm.

Hensley, Nicole. "Kissing Couple Oblivious to Armed Robbery at Montana Bar." *New York Daily News.* Last modified April 9, 2018. Accessed November 15, 2019. https://www.nydailynews.com/news/national/kissing-couple-oblivious-armed-robbery-montana-bar-article-1.2598765.

Hjelmgaard, Kim. "Americans Really Like Their Guns. They Own 42% of 650 Million Civilian Firearms Worldwide." *USA Today.* Last modified November 7, 2017. Accessed December 2, 2019. https://www.usatoday.com/story/news/world/2017/10/03/americans-really-like-their-guns-they-own-42-650-million-civilian-firearms-worldwide/726321001/.

Howard, Jacqueline. "Gun Deaths in US Reach Highest Level in Nearly 40 Years, CDC Data Reveal." Cable News Network (CNN). Last modified December 14, 2018. Accessed December 3, 2019. https://www.cnn.com/2018/12/13/health/gun-deaths-highest-40-years-cdc/index.html.

International Association of Chiefs of Police. *Model Policy.* Last modified April 2018. Accessed November 22, 2019. https://www.theiacp.org/sites/default/files/2018-08/ActiveShooterPolicy2018.pdf.

Karp, Aaron. "Estimating Global Civilian-Held Firearms Numbers." Small Arms Survey. Last modified June 2018. Accessed December 1, 2019. http://www.smallarmssurvey.org/fileadmin/docs/T-Briefing-Papers/SAS-BP-Civilian-Firearms-Numbers.pdf.

Kruzel, John. "Do More Than 7 in 10 Police Bullets Miss Their Mark?" PolitiFact. Last modified May 25, 2018. Accessed December 1, 2019. https://www.politifact.com/truth-o-meter/statements/2018/may/25/shannon-watts/do-more-7-10-police-bullets-miss-their-mark-gun-co/.

Macias, Amanda. "FBI Director Shares Advice He Gives to His Children about Living in Today's Dangerous World." Business Insider. Last modified September 15, 2016. Accessed December 1, 2019. https://www.businessinsider.com/fbi-director-shares-advice-kids-2016-9.

MacInnis, Laura. "U.S. Most Armed Country with 90 Guns per 100 People." Reuters. Last modified August 28, 2007. Accessed November 15, 2019. https://www.reuters.com/article/us-world-firearms/u-s-most-armed-country-with-90-guns-per-100-people-idUSL2834893820070828.

Miller, Matthew, and David Hemenway. "Guns and Suicide in the United States." *New England Journal of Medicine* 359, no. 10 (September 4, 2008): 989–91. https://doi.org/10.1056/nejmp0805923.

National Partnership for Women and Families. "Gun Violence: A Threat to Women and Families." March 2018. http://www.nationalpartnership.org/our-work/resources/health-care/gun-violence-a-threat-to-women-and-families.pdf.

National School Safety and Security Services. "ALICE & Run-Hide-Fight Training: Teaching Students to Attack Gunmen." Last modified 2019. Accessed November 22, 2019. https://www.schoolsecurity.org/trends/alice-training/.

Oostendorp, S. E., E. C. T. H. Tan, and L. M. G. Geeraedts Jr. "Prehospital Control of Life-Threatening Truncal and Junctional Haemorrhage Is the Ultimate Challenge in

Optimizing Trauma Care; a Review of Treatment Options and Their Applicability in the Civilian Trauma Setting." *Scandinavian Journal of Trauma, Resuscitation and Emergency Medicine* 24, no.110 (2016). https://doi.org/10.1186/s13049-016-0301-9.

Puri, Lakshmi. "It Is Time for Action to End Violence Against Women: A Speech by Lakshmi Puri at the ACP-EU Parliamentary Assembly." UN Women. Last modified June 19, 2013. Accessed November 14, 2019. https://www.unwomen.org/en/news/stories/2013/6/it-is-time-for-action-to-end-violence-against-women-a-speech-by-lakshmi-puri.

Silver, James, Andre Simmons, and Sarah Craun. "A Study of Pre-Attack Behaviors of Active Shooters in the United States Between 2000 and 2013." US Department of Justice, Federal Bureau of Investigation. June 20, 2018. https://www.fbi.gov/file-repository/pre-attack-behaviors-of-active-shooters-in-us-2000-2013.pdf/view.

Snortland, Ellen. *Beauty Bites Beast: Awakening the Warrior within Women and Girls.* Sunland, CA: B3 Books, August 2001.

Teixeira, Pedro, et al. "Civilian Prehospital Tourniquet Use Is Associated with Improved Survival in Patients with Peripheral Vascular Injury." *Journal of the American College of Surgeons* 226, no. 5 (September 2017): 769–76. https://doi.org/10.1016/j.jamcollsurg.2018.01.047.

Thompson, Andrew G., et al. "Autonomic Response to Tactical Pistol Performance Measured by Heart Rate Variability." *Journal of Strength and Conditioning Research* 29, no. 4 (April 2015): 926–33. https://doi.org/10.1519/jsc.0000000000000615.

University of Washington, Department of Epidemiology (EPI). "Study: 3 Million Americans Carry Loaded Handguns Daily." Last modified October 19, 2017. Accessed December 1, 2019.

https://epi.washington.edu/news/3-million-americans-carry-loaded-handguns-daily.

US Department of Homeland Security (DHS). *Active Shooter: How to Respond.* Last modified May 28, 2019. Accessed November 22, 2019. https://www.dhs.gov/publication/active-shooter-how-to-respond.

World Health Organization (WHO). "Violence Against Women." Last modified November 29, 2017. Accessed November 18, 2019. https://www.who.int/news-room/fact-sheets/detail/violence-against-women.

Chapter 4

Abbey, Antonia, et al. "Alcohol and Sexual Assault." *Alcohol Research & Health: The Journal of the National Institute on Alcohol Abuse and Alcoholism* 25, no. 1 (2001): 43–51.

Aggeler, Madeleine. "What Is the Red Zone? These Six Weeks Are the Most Dangerous Time for Campus Sexual Assault." Bustle. Last modified August 26, 2017. Accessed November 22, 2019. https://www.bustle.com/p/what-is-the-red-zone-these-6-weeks-are-the-most-dangerous-time-for-campus-sexual-assault-79177.

American Association of University Professors (AAUP). "Campus Sexual Assault: Suggested Policies and Procedures." Last modified November 2012. Accessed November 22, 2019. https://www.aaup.org/file/Sexual_Assault_Policies.pdf.

Busch-Armendariz, N. B., C. Sulley, and K. Hill. *The Blueprint for Campus Police: Responding to Sexual Assault.* Austin: Institute on Domestic Violence & Sexual Assault, University of Texas at Austin, 2016.

Cantor, David, et al. *Report on the AAU Campus Climate Survey on Sexual Assault and Sexual Misconduct.* Prepared for the University of Pennsylvania. Rockville, MD: Westat, September 21, 2015.

End Rape on Campus (EROC). "Action Now: Reclaiming the Red Zone." End Rape on Campus. Accessed November 22, 2019. https://endrapeoncampus.org/action-to-reclaim-red-zones.

Hoffman, Jan. "LGBT Students Three Times More Likely to Have Been Raped." *Boston Globe.* Last modified August 11, 2016. Accessed November 22, 2019. https://www.bostonglobe.com/news/nation/2016/08/11/gay-and-lesbian-high-school-students-report-heartbreaking-levels violence/i4QqZu2WyjQSj1c2D10MIN/story.html.

Kimble, Matthew, et al. "Risk of Unwanted Sex for College Women: Evidence for a Red Zone." *Journal of American College Health* 50, no. 3 (December 2008): 331–37.

Kingkade, Tyler. "The University of Texas Has a Blueprint to Stop Campus Cops from Blaming Rape Victims." Huffington Post. Last modified February 26, 2016. Accessed November 22, 2019. https://www.huffpost.com/entry/university-of-texas-sexual-assault_n_56d-4e61de4b0871f60ec9151.

Klein, L. B., et al. *Addressing Alcohol Role in Campus Sexual Assault: A Toolkit by and for Prevention Specialists.* Chapel Hill, NC: Campus Advocacy and Prevention Professionals Association and Prevention Innovations Research Center, 2018.

Lazard, Lisa. "Here's the Truth About False Accusations of Sexual Violence." The Independent. Last modified November 27, 2017. Accessed December 1, 2019. https://www.independent.co.uk/voices/false-sexual-violence-assault-rape-allegations-truth-rare-international-day-for-the-elimination-of-a8077876.html.

McClanahan, Kimberly K., et al. "Prevention: Sexual Violence Against Adolescent and Young Adult Women." In *Children, Violence and Bullying: International Perspectives,* edited by Joav Merrick, Isack Kandel, and Hatim A. Omar, 265–70. Hauppauge, NY: Nova Science Publishers, 2014.

Michigan Resource Center on Domestic Sexual Violence. "Male Survivors of Sexual Violence." Accessed November 23, 2019. https://www.michigan.gov/documents/datingviolence/DHS-DatingViolence-MaleSurvivors_198439_7.pdf.

National Alliance to End Sexual Violence. "Male Victims." Last modified 2017. Accessed November 26, 2019. https://www.endsexualviolence.org/where_we_stand/male-victims/.

National Institute of Justice. "Most Victims Know Their Attacker." Last modified September 30, 2008. Accessed November 23, 2019. https://nij.ojp.gov/topics/articles/most-victims-know-their-attacker.

National Institute on Alcohol Abuse and Alcoholism. "Alcohol Alert: National Institute on Alcohol Abuse and Alcoholism." Alcohol Alert. Last modified October 2000. Accessed November 22, 2019. https://pubs.niaaa.nih.gov/publications/aa38.htm.

National Research Council. *Estimating the Incidence of Rape and Sexual Assault.* Washington, DC: National Academies Press, 2014.

National Sexual Violence Resource Center (NSVRC). "Sexual Assault Statistics." Last modified 2018. Accessed December 1, 2019. https://www.nsvrc.org/node/4737.

———. "Statistics About Sexual Violence." Last modified 2015. Accessed December 1, 2019. https://www.nsvrc.org/sites/default/files/publications_nsvrc_factsheet media-packet statistics-about-sexual-violence_0.pdf.

Newman, Sandra. "What Kind of Person Makes False Rape Accusations?" Quartz. Last modified May 11, 2017. Accessed December 1, 2019. https://qz.com/980766/the-truth-about-false-rape-accusations.

Palmer, Rebekka, et al. "Coercive Sexual Experiences, Protective Behavioral Strategies, Alcohol Expectancies and Consumption Among Male and Female College Students." *Journal of Interpersonal Violence* 25, no. 9 (September 2010): 1563–78.

Pereda, N., et al. "The Prevalence of Child Sexual Abuse in Community and Student Samples: A Meta-Analysis." *Clinical Psychology Review* 29, no. 4 (June 2009): 328–38.

Rape, Abuse and Incest National Network (RAINN). "Perpetrators of Sexual Violence." Accessed December 5, 2019. https://www.rainn.org/statistics/perpetrators-sexual-violence.

———. "Victims of Sexual Violence: Statistics." Last modified 2019. Accessed November 27, 2019. https://www.rainn.org/statistics/victims-sexual-violence.

Rennison, Callie M. *Rape and Sexual Assault: Reporting to Police and Medical Attention, 1992–2000.* Washington, DC: US Department of Justice, Office of Justice Programs, Bureau of Justice Statistics Selected Findings, NCJ 194530, August 2002.

Ronken, Carol, and Hetty Johnston. *Child Sexual Assault: Facts and Statistics.* Arundel, Queensland: Bravehearts, 2012.

Shukman, Harry. "Half of Sexual Assaults on Campus Take Place in Freshman Dorms, New Figures Show." The Tab. Last modified 2017. Accessed November 22, 2019. https://thetab.com/us/2017/09/07/a-third-of-all-campus-sexual-assaults-happen-in-freshman-dorms-according-to-a-new-71446.

State of California Department of Justice, Office of the Attorney General. "Myths and Facts About Sexual Assault." State of California Department of Justice, Office of the Attorney General. Accessed November 22, 2019. https://www.meganslaw.ca.gov/Education_MythsAndFacts.aspx.

Thomas, Emily. "Rape Is Grossly Underreported in the U.S., Study Finds." Huffington Post. Last modified November 21, 2013. Accessed November 28, 2019. https://www.huffpost.com/entry/rape-study-report-america-us_n_4310765.

Wisconsin Coalition Against Sexual Assault. "Teen Sexual Assault and Abuse." Information Sheet Series, no. 2CAS (2000).

Chapter 5

Ali, Russlynn. "Dear Colleague—April 4, 2011." US Department of Education. Last modified September 25, 2018. Accessed December 12, 2019. https://www2.ed.gov/about/offices/list/ocr/letters/colleague-201104.html.

American Civil Liberties Union (ACLU). "Doing the Math: What the Numbers Say about Harassment of Gay, Lesbian, Bisexual, and Transgender Students." American Civil Liberties Union. Last modified 2019. Accessed December 2, 2019. https://www.aclu.org/other/doing-math-what-numbers-say-about-harassment-gay-lesbian-bisexual-and-transgender-students.

Beswick, Emma. "In Which Country Do Women Experience the Most Street Harassment?" Euro News. Last modified November 20, 2018. Accessed December 12, 2019. https://www.euronews.com/2018/11/20/in-which-country-do-women-experience-the-most-street-harassment.

Bidwell, Allie. "Study: Sexual Harassment Frequent Among Middle School Students." *U.S. News & World Report*. Last modified April 6, 2014. Accessed December 12, 2019. https://www.usnews.com/news/articles/2014/04/06/study-sexual-harassment-frequent-among-middle-school-students.

Bolger, Dana. "9 Things to Know About Title IX." Know Your IX. Last modified 2016. Accessed March 23, 2016. http://knowyourix.org/title-ix/title-ix-the-basics.

———, and Mahroh Jahangiri. "Title IX in High School: The Basics." Know Your IX. Last modified 2016. Accessed March 22, 2016. http://knowyourix.org/title-ix-in-high-school-the-basics.

Brown, Christia S. "The Majority of Girls Face Sexual Harassment with No Hashtag." *Psychology Today*. Last modified October 30, 2017. Accessed December 12, 2019. https://www.psychologytoday.com/us/blog/beyond-pink-and-blue/201710/the-majority-girls-face-sexual-harassment-no-hashtag.

Cheung, Kylie. "Proposed Title IX Policy Changes Could Hit K–12 Students Hardest." Brit + Co. Last modified November 21, 2018. Accessed December 12, 2019. https://www.brit.co/proposed-title-ix-policy-changes-could-hit-k-12-students-hardest.

Crouch, Margaret. "Sexual Harassment in Public Places." *Social Philosophy Today* 25 (2009): 137–48.

Dragan, Edward F. "Private School Sexual Abuse and Harassment: Professional Standard of Care." Education Expert. Last modified October 11, 2017. Accessed December 12, 2019. http://education-expert.com/2017/10/sexual-abuse-and-harassment-in-private-schools-professional-standard-of-care/.

Espelage, Dorothy L. "Understanding Types, Locations, & Perpetrators of Peer-to-Peer Sexual Harassment in U.S. Middle Schools: A Focus on Sex, Racial, and Grade Differences." *Children and Youth Services Review* 71 (December 2016): 174–83. https://doi.org/10.1016/j.childyouth.2016.11.010.

———, et al. *Bullying, Sexual, and Dating Violence Trajectories from Early to Late Adolescence.* Washington, DC: US Department of Justice, no. 246830. April 21, 2014.

Feldblum, Chai R., and Victoria A. Lipnic. *Select Task Force on the Study of Harassment in the Workplace: Report of Co-Chairs Chai R. Feldblum & Victoria A. Lipnic.* Washington, DC: US Equal Employment Opportunity Commission, June 2016.

Fogarty, Kate. "Teens and Sexual Harassment: Making a Difference." University of Florida IFAS Extension. Last modified 2018. Accessed October 29, 2018. http://edis.ifas.ufl.edu/fy850.

Golshan, Tara. "Study Finds 75 Percent of Workplace Harassment Victims Experienced Retaliation When They Spoke Up." Vox. Last modified October 15, 2017. Accessed December 9, 2019. https://www.vox.com/identities/2017/10/15/16438750/weinstein-sexual-harassment-facts.

Gordon, Claire. "By the Numbers: Sexual Violence in High School." Aljazeera America. Last modified November 14, 2014. Accessed December 2, 2019. http://america.aljazeera.com/watch/shows/america-tonight/articles/2014/11/14/by-the-numbers-sexualviolenceinhighschool.html.

Guarino, Ben, and Neel V. Patel. "An Academic Reported Sexual Harassment: Her University Allegedly Retaliated." The Verge. Last modified November 12, 2018. Accessed December 12, 2019. https://www.theverge.com/2018/11/12/18080876/une-university-new-england-sexual-harassment-retaliation-paul-visich.

Hill, Catherine. "Crossing the Line: Sexual Harassment at School." American Association of University Women. Last modified 2019. Accessed December 2, 2019. https://www.aauw.org/research/crossing-the-line.

———, and Holly Kearl. *Crossing the Line: Sexual Harassment at School.* Washington, DC: AAUW, 2011.

———, and Elena Silva. *Drawing the Line: Sexual Harassment on Campus.* Washington, DC: AAUW, 2005.

Jahangiri, Mahroh, and Dana Bolger. "Title IX in High School: FAQs." Know Your IX. Last modified 2016. Accessed July 13, 2016. http://knowyourix.org/title-ix-in-high-school-in-detail.

Kamenetz, Anya, and Cory Turner. "Trump and Transgender Rights: What Just Happened?" National Public Radio. Last modified February 23, 2017. Accessed November 22, 2019. https://www.npr.org/sections/ed/2017/02/23/516837258/5-questions-about-the-trump-administrations-new-transgender-student-guidance.

Kopels, Sandra, and David R. Dupper. "School-based Peer Sexual Harassment." *Child Welfare* 78, no. 4 (July–August 1999): 435–60. https://www.ncbi.nlm.nih.gov/pubmed/10418115.

Mackler, Laura. "Betsy DeVos Releases Sexual Assault Rules She Hails as Balancing Rights of Victims, Accused." *Washington Post*. Last modified November 16, 2018. Accessed December 12, 2019. https://www.washingtonpost.com/local/education/betsy-devos-releases-sexual-assault-rules-she-hails-as-balancing-rights-of-victims-accused/2018/11/16/4aa136d4-e962-11e8-a939-9469f1166f9d_story.html.

National Center for Transgender Equality. "The Trump Administration Says Trans Protections Are 'Fake News.' Federal Courts Disagree." Last modified 2019. Accessed December 2, 2019. https://transequality.org/federal-case-law-on-transgender-people-and-discrimination.

National Sexual Violence Resource Center (NSVRC) and Pennsylvania Coalition Against Rape. *Sexual Harassment & Bullying of Youth: Sexual Violence & Individuals Who Identify as LGBTQ*. Last modified September 2012. Accessed December 12, 2019. https://www.nsvrc.org/publications/nsvrc-publications-information-packets/sexual-violence-individuals-who-identify-lgbtq.

Parker-Pope, Tara. "Sexual Harassment at School." *New York Times*. Last modified May 1, 2008. Accessed December 12, 2019. https://well.blogs.nytimes.com/2008/05/01/sexual-harassment-at-school/.

Pennsylvania Coalition Against Rape (PCAR). *Sexual Harassment Prevention in the Schools: A Facilitator's Manual and Curriculum for Grades 1 through 12*. Harrisburg, PA: Pennsylvania Coalition Against Rape, 2009.

Rinehart, Sarah, Namrata Doshi, and Dorothy Espelage. *Sexual Harassment and Sexual violence Experience Among Middle School Youth*. Presented at AERA (American Education Research Association) 2014 Annual Meeting, April 6, 2014. Last modified 2014. Accessed December 12, 2019. http://www.aera.net/Newsroom/Recent-AERA-Research/Sexual-Harassment-and-Sexual-Violence-Experiences-Among-Middle-School-Youth.

Sanzi, Erika. "With Title IX Rewrite, DeVos Gets Right for Accusers and Accused." The Hill. Last modified November 22, 2018. Accessed December 12, 2019. https://thehill.com/opinion/education/417762-with-title-ix-rewrite-devos-gets-it-right-for-accusers-and-accused.

Simmons, Rachel. "When Middle Schoolers Say #MeToo." Huffington Post. Last modified December 15, 2017. Accessed December 12, 2019. https://www.huffpost.com/entry/sexual-harassment-in-schools_b_5a32b145e4b00dbbcb5bb530.

Stop Street Harassment. *The Facts Behind the #MeToo Movement: A National Study on Sexual Harassment and Assault*. Reston, VA: Stop Street Harassment, Raliance, and UC San Diego Center on Gender Equity and Health. February 2018.

———. "What Is Street Harassment." Last modified 2019. Accessed December 12, 2019. http://www.stopstreetharassment.org/about/what-is-street-harassment/.

———. *Unsafe and Harassed in Public Spaces: A National Street Harassment Report*. Spring 2014.

US Department of Education. "Know Your Rights: Title IX Prohibits Sexual Harassment and Sexual Violence Where You Go to School." Last modified September 25, 2018. Accessed December 12, 2019. https://www2.ed.gov/about/offices/list/ocr/docs/title-ix-rights-201104.html.

———. *Title IX of the Education Amendments of 1972*. Docket ID: ED-2018-OCR-0064-000, Federal Register Number: 2018-25314. November 29, 2018.

———. Office of Civil Rights. *Sexual Harassment: It's Not Academic.* September 2008.

———. Office of Innovation and Improvement. *State Regulation of Private Schools.* Washington, DC: US Department of Education. July 2009.

United Educators (UE)/EduRisk. "Student Sexual Harassment in Independent Schools: Is Title IX the Standard for Responding?" Last modified 2015. Accessed December 12, 2019. https://www.ue.org/uploadedFiles/Student%20Sexual%20Harassment%20in%20Independent%20Schools.pdf.

University of Illinois at Urbana-Champaign. "Sexual Harassment Common Among Middle School Children, Study Finds." Science Daily. Last modified December 9, 2016. Accessed December 12, 2019. www.sciencedaily.com/releases/2016/12/161209184825.htm.

Vagianos, Alanna. "Betsy DeVos' New Title IX Guidelines Prioritize Schools Over Sexual Assault Survivors." Huffington Post. Last modified November 16, 2018. Accessed December 12, 2019. https://www.huffpost.com/entry/besty-devos-new-title-ix-guidelines-prioritize-schools-over-sexual-assault-survivors_n_5beede5fe4b0510a1f3037cf.

Vinik, D. Frank. "Why Independent Schools Need to Act on Student-on-Student Assault." Gallagher Education. Arthur J. Gallagher & Co. February 2015.

Warkov, Esther. "Sexual Abuse in Elite Private Schools: What the Spotlight Team Asked Us." Huffington Post. Last modified May 09, 2016. Accessed December 1, 2019. https://www.huffpost.com/entry/sexual-abuse-in-elite-pri_b_9865768.

Younge, Ellie L., Betty Y. Ashbaker, and Bryan K. Young. *Sexual Harassment: A Guide for School Personnel*. Bethesda, MD: National Association of School Psychologist, 2010.

Zande, Irene van der. "Stopping Sexual Harassment in Schools." Kid Power. Last modified June 16, 2016. Accessed December 12, 2019. https://www.kidpower.org/library/article/sexual-harassment-schools/.

Chapter 6

Brody, Liz. "Meet Ashley Reynolds, the Woman Fighting 'Sextortion'." *Glamour*. Last modified July 7, 2015. Accessed December 2, 2019. https://www.glamour.com/story/ashley-reynolds-the-woman-fighting-sextortion.

Daily Mail. "Man Who 'Sextorted' 155 Teenage Boys into Sending Him Nude Pictures Gets Two Years Wiped From 40-Year Prison Sentence . . ." Last modified November 30, 2019. Accessed December 2, 2019. https://www.dailymail.co.uk/news/article-3987414/Man-ran-sextortion-ring-targeted-155-boys-jailed-38-years.html.

Hinduja, Sameer. "Sextortion." Cyberbullying Research Center. Last modified June 28, 2016. Accessed December 2, 2019. https://cyberbullying.org/sextortion.

Interpol. *Sextortion—Questions and Answers.* International Criminal Police Organization. September 16, 2015.

KSWO. "Special Report: 'Sextortion.'" American Broadcast Corporation. Last modified June 15, 2011. Accessed December 2, 2019. https://www.kswo.com/story/13367404/special-report-sextortion/.

National Center for Missing & Exploited Children. *Trends Identified in CyberTipline Sextortion Reports.* Last modified 2016. Accessed December 2, 2019. http://www.missingkids.com/content/dam/missingkids/pdfs/ncmec-analysis/sextortionfactsheet.pdf.

Reynolds, Ashley. "Sextortion: I Want People to Remember My Story." Thorn. Last modified October 3, 2017. Accessed December 3, 2019. https://www.thorn.org/blog/sextortion-remember-my-story/.

US Department of Education, Office of Safe and Healthy Students, Readiness and Emergency Management for Schools (REMS). *Incorporation Sextortion Prevention Response, and Recovery into School EOP Planning.* https://rems.ed.gov/docs/Resources/Incorporating_Sextortion_in_School_EOPs_Presentation_508C.pdf.

US Department of Justice. *The National Strategy for Child Exploitation Prevention and Interdiction: A Report to Congress.* Washington, DC: US Department of Justice, April 2016.

Wittes, Benjamin, et al. "Sextortion: Cybersecurity, Teenagers, and Remote Sexual Assault." Brookings Institution. Last modified May 11, 2016. Accessed December 2, 2019. https://www.brookings.edu/research/sextortion-cybersecurity-teenagers-and-remote-sexual-assault/.

Wolak, Janis, and David Finkelhor. *Sextortion: Findings from a Survey of 1631 Victims.* Crimes Against Children Research Center. Durham: University of New Hampshire, June 2016.

Chapter 7

Baker, Kelsey. "Maybe He Doesn't Hit You, but He Makes You Apologize for Getting Upset After Something He Did to Hurt You." Love What Matters. Accessed December 11, 2019. https://www.lovewhatmatters.com/maybe-he-doesnt-hit-you-but-he-makes-you-apologize-for-getting-upset-after-something-he-did-to-hurt-you/.

Baum, Katrina, Shannan Catalano, and Michael Rand. *Stalking Victimization in the United States.* US Department of Justice, Bureau of Justice Statistics, NCJ 224527, January 2009. http://www.opdv.ny.gov/professionals/abusers/coercivecontrol.html.

Break the Cycle. "The Myth of Mutuality." Teen Dating Violence Technical Assistance Center. Issue Brief no. 6, July 2016. https://www.breakthecycle.org/sites/default/files/pdf/ta-issue-brief-10-09-n6.pdf.

Bri. "Playing Their Part: How the "Good Behavior Is Part of the Act." Loveisrespect, National Domestic Violence Hotline. Last modified April 6, 2017. Accessed December

10, 2019. https://www.loveisrespect.org/content/good-behavior-abusive-partner.

British Broadcasting Company (BBC). "Alex Skeel: Domestic Abuse Survivor Was 'Days from Death.'" Last modified April 17, 2018. Accessed December 11, 2019. https://www.bbc.com/news/uk-england-beds-bucks-herts-43799850.

Catalano, Shannan. *Stalking Victims in the United States—Revised.* US Department of Justice, Bureau of Justice Statistics, NCJ 224526, September 2012. https://www.bjs.gov/content/pub/pdf/svus_rev.pdf.

Centers for Disease Control and Prevention (CDC). "Teen Dating Violence." Last modified June 11, 2018. Accessed November 16, 2018. http://www.cdc.gov/violenceprevention/intimatepartnerviolence/teen_dating_violence.html.

Children's Safety Network (CSN). "Teen Dating Violence as a Public Health Issue." Last modified February 2012. Accessed December 11, 2019. https://www.childrenssafetynetwork.org/sites/childrenssafetynetwork.org/files/TeenDatingViolenceasaPublicHealthIssue.pdf.

Domonoske, Camila. "CDC: Half of All Female Homicide Victims Are Killed by Intimate Partners." National Public Radio. Last modified July 21, 2017. Accessed December 11, 2019. https://www.npr.org/sections/thetwo-way/2017/07/21/538518569/cdc-half-of-all-female-murder-victims-are-killed-by-intimate-partners.

Emerge! Center Against Domestic Abuse. *Myths and Realities of Domestic Abuse.* Last modified November 2009. Accessed November 29, 2019. https://law.arizona.edu/sites/default/files/myths_and_realities_of_domestic_abuse.pdf.

Futures Without Violence. "The Facts on Women, Children and Gun Violence." Accessed November 23, 2019. https://www.futureswithoutviolence.org/userfiles/Gun%20Fact%20Sheet_FINAL%2003%20 03%2013.pdf.

Indiana Coalition Against Domestic Violence (ICADVINC). "Teen Dating Violence Facts." Last modified 2017. Accessed April 2017. http://www.icadvinc.org/prevention/for-youth-workers/teen-dating-violence-facts.

Iris Domestic Violence Center. "EBR District Attorney Reports: 14 Domestic Violence-Related Homicides in 2017." Last modified 2017. Accessed December 2, 2019. http://stopdv.org/index.php/.

Jeltsen, Melissa. "Who Is Killing American Women? Their Husbands and Boyfriends, CDC Confirms." Huffington Post. Last modified July 23, 2017. Accessed December 11, 2019. https://www.huffpost.com/entry/most-murders-of-american-women-involve-domestic-violence_n_5971fcf6e-4b09e5f6cceba87.

Karakurt, Günnur, and Kristin E. Silver. "Emotional Abuse in Intimate Relationship: The Role of Gender and Age." *Violence and Victims* 28, no. 5 (2013): 804–21. DOI:10.1891/0886-6708.vv-d-12-00041.

Liz Caliborne Inc., and TRU. *Teen Dating Abuse 2009 Key Topline Findings.* San Francisco, CA: Family Violence Prevention Fund, 2009. http://nomore.org/wp-content/uploads/2014/12/teen_dating_abuse_2009_key_topline_findings-1.pdf.

Loveisrespect. "Dating Abuse Statistics." Accessed December 11, 2019. http://www.loveisrespect.org/wp content/uploads/2015/02/Dating_Abuse_Statistics.pdf.

———. "Types of Abuse." Last modified 2017. Accessed December 11, 2019. https://www.loveisrespect.org/is-this-abuse/types-of-abuse/.

———. "What Is Stalking?" Last modified 2017. Accessed December 11, 2019. https://www.loveisrespect.org/is-this-abuse/types-of-abuse/is-this-abusetypes-of-abusewhat-is-stalking/.

Missouri Coalition Against Domestic and Sexual Violence (MCADSV). "What Is Teen Dating Violence (TDV)?" Accessed November 22, 2019. https://www.mocadsv.org/What-is-Teen-Dating-Violence-TDV/.

Mulford, Carrie, and Peggy C. Giordano. "Teen Dating Violence: A Closer Look at Adolescent Romantic Relationships." *NIJ Journal*, no. 261 (October 2008): 34–40. https://www.ncjrs.gov/pdffiles1/nij/224089.pdf.

Murphy, Clare. "Gender: How Men and Women Experience Domestic Violence Differently." SpeakOutLoud. Accessed December 12, 2019. https://speakoutloud.net/intimate-partner-abuse/domestic-violence-gender.

National Coalition Against Domestic Violence (NCADV). "Quick Guide to Stalking: 16 Important Statistics, and What You Can Do About It." Last modified January 30, 2017. Accessed December 11, 2019. https://ncadv.org/blog/posts/quick-guide-to-stalking-16-important-statistics-and-what-you-can-do-about-it.

———. "Statistics." National Coalition Against Domestic Violence. Last modified 2017. Accessed December 11, 2019. https://ncadv.org/statistics.

National Teen Dating Violence Prevention Initiative. *Teen Dating Violence Facts.* Last modified 2006. Accessed December 10, 2019. https://cdn.atixa.org/website-media/atixa.org/wp-content/uploads/2015/12/12193514/Teen-Dating-Violence-Facts-from-Clothesline-Project.pdf.

New York State Office for the Prevention of Domestic Violence. "Understanding Domestic Abusers: Coercive Control." Last modified 2013. Accessed December 11, 2019. http://www.opdv.ny.gov/professionals/abusers/coercivecontrol.html.

No Domestic Violence Los Angeles (NODVLA). "Teen Dating Abuse." Last modified 2016. Accessed December 11, 2019. http://nodvla.org/what-is-domestic-violence/teen-dating-abuse/.

Offenhauer, Priscilla, and Alice Buchalter. *Teen Dating Violence: A Literature Review and Annotated Bibliography.* Washington, DC: US Department of Justice, no. 235368, July 2011. https://www.ncjrs.gov/pdffiles1/nij/grants/235368.pdf.

One Love Foundation. "11 Reasons Why People in Abusive Relationships Can't 'Just Leave.'" Last modified 2017. Accessed December 11, 2019. https://www.joinonelove.org/learn/why_leaving_abuse_is_hard/.

Pelly, Lauren. "Leaving Relationship Is 'Most Dangerous Time' for Domestic Violence Victims, Experts Say." Canadian Broadcasting Corporation. Last modified December 8, 2019. Accessed December 10, 2019. https://www.cbc.ca/news/canada/toronto/domestic-violence-victims-1.3885381.

Pensak, Rebecca. "Must Be 18 or Older: How Current Domestic Violence Policies Dismiss Teen Dating Violence." *William & Mary Journal of Women and the Law* 21, no. 2 (2015): 499–523. http://scholarship.law.wm.edu/cgi/viewcontent.cgi?article=1406&context=wmjowl.

Petrosky, Blair E., et al. "Racial and Ethnic Differences in Homicides of Adult Women and the Role of Intimate Partner Violence—United States 2003–2004." *Morbidity and Mortal Weekly Report* 66, no. 28 (July 21, 2017): 741–46. http://dx.doi.org/10.15585/mmwr.mm6628a1.

Start Strong Idaho. *Navigating Teen Dating Relationships.* Boise, ID: Center for Healthy Teen Relationships, 2006. https://idvsa.org/wp-content/uploads/2013/01/High-School-Parent-Handbook.pdf.

Taylor, Bruce G., Elizabeth A. Mumford, and Weiwei Liu. *The National Survey of Teen Relationships and Intimate Violence (STRiV).* Washington, DC: US Department of Justice, no. 250292. October 2016. https://www.ncjrs.gov/pdffiles1/nij/grants/250292.pdf.

Thomson, Amy. "Verbal Abuse Is Just as Bad." Break the Silence. Last modified January 30, 2017. Accessed December 11, 2019. https://breakthesilencedv.org/verbal-abuse-is-just-as-bad/.

Thurrott, Krista. "'Maybe He Doesn't Hit You, But . . .': Woman's Viral Post about Emotional Abuse." Yahoo Finance. Last modified October 10, 2018. Accessed December 11, 2019. https://finance.yahoo.com/news/maybe-doesnt-hit-womans-viral-post-emotional-abuse-163005982.html.

US Department of Health and Human Services, Office on Women's Health. "Emotional and Verbal Abuse." Last modified September 13, 2018. Accessed December 11, 2019. https://www.womenshealth.gov/relationships-and-safety/other-types/emotional-and-verbal-abuse.

US Department of Justice, Office of Justice Programs, National Institute of Justice (NIJ). "Effective School Level Interventions to Prevent Teen Dating Violence." Last modified February 12, 2014. Accessed November 22, 2019. https://nij.ojp.gov/topics/articles/effective-school-level-interventions-prevent-teen-dating-violence.

———. "Relationship Characteristics and Mutual Violence." National Institute of Justice. Last modified January 5, 2015. Accessed December 11, 2019. https://nij.ojp.gov/topics/articles/relationship-characteristics-and-mutual-violence.

———. "Risk and Protective Factors, Psychosocial Health Behaviors and Teen Dating Violence." National Institute of Justice. Last modified January 5, 2015. Accessed December 11, 2019. https://nij.ojp.gov/topics/articles/risk-and-protective-factors-psychosocial-health-behaviors-and-teen-dating-violence.

Vagianos, Alanna. "30 Shocking Domestic Violence Statistics That Remind Us It's an Epidemic." Huffington Post. Last modified December 6, 2017. Accessed December 11, 2019. https://www.huffpost.com/entry/domestic-violence-statistics_n_5959776.

Ybarra, Michele, and Jennifer Langhinrichsen-Rohling. "Stalking-Like Behavior in Adolescence: Prevalence, Intent, and Associated Characteristics." *Psychology of Violence* 7, no. 2 (2017): 192–202.

Youth.gov. "Prevalence." Last modified 2018. Accessed November 29, 2019. https://youth.gov/youth-topics/prevalence-teen-dating-violence.

Chapter 8

Aubrey. "Teen Uses His Love of Baseball to Create a Positive Digital Footprint." Use Tech 4 Good. Last modified January 8, 2018. Accessed December 11, 2019. https://usetech4good.com/positive-digital-footprint.

Career Builder. "More Than Half of Employers Have Found Content on Social Media That Caused Them NOT to Hire a Candidate, According to Recent Career Builder Survey." Last modified August 9, 2018. Accessed December 11, 2019. http://press.careerbuilder.com/2018-08-09-More-Than-Half-of-Employers-Have-Found-Content-on-Social-Media-That-Caused-Them-NOT-to-Hire-a-Candidate-According-to-Recent-CareerBuilder-Survey.

Greene, David. "We Don't Need New Laws for Faked Videos, We Already Have Them." Electric Frontier Foundation. Last modified February 13, 2018. Accessed December 11, 2019. https://www.eff.org/deeplinks/2018/02/we-dont-need-new-laws-faked-videos-we-already-have-them.

Heid, Markham. "You Asked: Is Social Media Making Me Miserable?" *Time.* Last modified August 2, 2017. Accessed December 11, 2019. https://time.com/4882372/social-media-facebook-instagram-unhappy.

Kaplan Test Prep. "College Admissions: The Complete Guide to Social Media." Accessed December 11, 2019. https://www.kaptest.com/study/college-admissions/college-admission-the-complete-guide-to-social-media/.

———. "Kaplan Test Prep Survey Finds Colleges and Applicants Agree: Social Media Is Fair Game in the Admissions Process." Kaplan Test Prep. Last modified April 17, 2018. Accessed December 11, 2019. https://www.kaptest.com/blog/press/2018/04/17/kaplan-test-prep-survey-finds-colleges-applicants-agree-social-media-fair-game-admissions-process/.

Mahnken, Kevin. "The Rise of 'College Admissions Sabotage': When HS Seniors Use Social Media to Rat Out Their Classmates." The 74. Last modified July 11, 2017. Accessed December 11, 2019. https://www.the74million.org/article/the-rise-of-college-admissions-sabotage-when-hs-seniors-use-social-media-to-rat-out-their-classmates.

Suler, John. "The Online Disinhibition Effect." True Center Publishing. Last modified August 4, 2004. Accessed December 11, 2019. http://truecenterpublishing.com/psycyber/disinhibit.html.

Wallace, Kelly. "Surprise! Social Media Can Help, Not Hurt, Your College Prospects." Cable News Network. Last modified February 10, 2017. Accessed December 11, 2019. https://www.cnn.com/2017/02/10/health/college-admissions-social-media-parents/index.html.

Chapter 9

Anderson, Monica. "Teens, Social Media & Technology 2018." Pew Research Center. Last modified May 31, 2018. Accessed December 12, 2019. https://www.pewresearch.org/internet/2018/05/31/teens-social-media-technology-2018.

Davis, Gary. "Why Software Updates Are So Important?" McAfee. Last modified September 19, 2017. Accessed December 12, 2019. https://www.mcafee.com/blogs/consumer/consumer-threat-notices/software-updates-important/.

Gregoire, Carolyn. "Why Are Teens So Moody and Impulsive? This Neuroscientist Has the Answer." Huffington Post. Last modified December 6, 2017. Accessed November 27, 2018. https://www.huffingtonpost.com/2015/06/14/teeage-brain-neuroscience_n_7537188.html.

Hamm, Catharine. "Airport Wi-Fi Can Be a Security Nightmare: Here's What You Can Do to Stop Cyber Criminals." *Los Angeles Times*. Last modified December 3, 2018. Accessed December 12, 2019. https://www.latimes.com/travel/la-tr-spot-cyber-security-threats-20181202-story.html.

Identity Theft Resource Center (ITRC). "What Are Security Patches and Why Are They Important?" Last modified July 22, 2019. Accessed December 12, 2019. https://www.idtheftcenter.org/what-are-security-patches-and-why-are-they-important/.

Jenkins, Jeffery L. et al. "More Harm Than Good? How Messages That Interrupt Can Make Us Vulnerable." *Information Systems Research* 27, no. 4 (2016): 880–96. https://doi.org/10.1287/isre.2016.0644.

Norton Life Lock. "The Risks of Public Wi-Fi." Last modified 2019. Accessed December 12, 2019. https://us.norton.com/internetsecurity-privacy-risks-of-public-wi-fi.html.

Quinn, Dave. "Maine Lobster Festival Strips Sea Goddess, 18, of Crown Over 'Inappropriate' Social Media Photos." *People.* Last modified August 4, 2018. Accessed December 12, 2019. https://people.com/human-interest/maine-lobster-festival-replaces-sea-goddess-social-media-photos/.

Rogers, Katie. "Mark Zuckerberg Covers His Laptop Camera: You Should Consider It, Too." *New York Times*. Last modified June 22, 2016. Accessed December 12, 2019. https://www.nytimes.com/2016/06/23/technology/personaltech/mark-zuckerberg-covers-his-laptop-camera-you-should-consider-it-too.html.

Taylor, Stephanie. "10 Ways to Make Your Phone Safer, According to Security Experts." Business Insider. Last modified September 25, 2019. Accessed December 12, 2019. https://www.businessinsider.my/how-to-make-phone-safe-security-tips-2019-9/.

What Is My IP Address. "11 Ways People Can Spy on Your IP Address." Last modified 2018. Accessed October 27, 2018. https://whatismyipaddress.com/get-ip.

Chapter 10

American Sociological Association. "Youth Cyberbullying Most Common Among Current or Former Friends and Dating Partners." Last modified August 20, 2016. Accessed December 12, 2019. https://www.asanet.org/press-center/press-releases/youth-cyberbullying-most-common-among-current-or-former-friends-and-dating-partners.

Anderson, Monica. "A Majority of Teens Have Experienced Some Form of Cyberbullying." Pew Research Center. Last modified September 27, 2018. Accessed December 12, 2019. https://www.pewresearch.org/internet/2018/09/27/a-majority-of-teens-have-experienced-some-form-of-cyberbullying.

Cable News Network (CNN). "Police Arrest a 15-Year-Old Girl Accused of Cyberbullying in Florida." Last modified November 7, 2013. Accessed December 12, 2019. https://www.cnn.com/2013/11/07/justice/florida-cyberbullying-arrest/index.html.

Carter, Margaret Anne. "Third Party Observers Witnessing Cyber Bullying on Social Media Sites." *Procedia—Social and Behavioral Science* 84 (July 9, 2013): 1296–1309. https://doi.org/10.1016/j.sbspro.2013.06.747.

Cyberbullying Research Center. Bullying and Cyberbullying Laws Across America." Last modified 2018. Accessed December 14, 2019. https://cyberbullying.org/bullying-laws.

——. "Cyberbullying Facts." Last modified 2018. Accessed December 12, 2019. https://cyberbullying.org/facts.

Delete Cyberbullying. "Why Do People Cyberbully." Accessed December 12, 2019. http://endcyberbullying.net/why-do-people-cyberbully/.

Ditch the Label. *The Annual Bullying Survey, 2017.* Last modified 2017. Accessed December 12, 2019. https://www.ditchthelabel.org/wp-content/uploads/2017/07/The-Annual-Bullying-Survey-2017-1.pdf.

Do Something. "11 Facts about Cyberbullying." Accessed December 12, 2019. https://www.dosomething.org/us/facts/11-facts-about-cyber-bullying.

Edgington, Nicole. "The Girl Who Got Even: A True Cyberbullying Story." Last modified February 2012. Accessed June 6, 2016. https://choices.scholastic.com/story/girl-who-got-even-true-cyberbullying-story.

Eluna. "Cyber-bullying Awareness." Tulane University, School of Social Work. Last modified 2018. Accessed December 12, 2019. https://elunanetwork.org/resources/cyber-bullying-awareness.

Florida Atlantic University. "Nationwide Teen Bullying and Cyberbullying Study Reveals Significant Issues Impacting Youth." Science Daily. Last modified February 21, 2017. Accessed December 12, 2019. https://www.sciencedaily.com/releases/2017/02/170221102036.htm.

Gay, Lesbian & Straight Education Network (GLSEN). "Out Online: The Experiences of LGBT Youth on the Internet." Gay, Lesbian & Straight Education Network. Last modified July 10, 2013. Accessed December 12, 2019. https://www.glsen.org/news/out-online-experiences-lgbt-youth-internet.

Hannah, Scott. "The Great American No Bull Challenge." *Global Education Magazine.* Last modified December 10, 2013. Accessed December 12, 2019. http://www.globaleducationmagazine.com/great-american-bull-challenge/.

Hinduja, Sameer, and Justin W. Patchin. *Cyberbullying: Identification, Prevention & Response, October 2014.* Cyberbullying Research Center. Last modified October 2014. Accessed December 12, 2019. https://cyberbullying.org/Cyberbullying-Identification-Prevention-Response.pdf.

———. *Cyberbullying: Identification, Prevention & Response, 2018.* Cyberbullying Research Center. Last modified 2018. Accessed December 12, 2019. https://cyberbullying.org/Cyberbullying-Identification-Prevention-Response-2018.pdf.

———. *Cyberbullying: Identification, Prevention & Response, 2019 Edition.* Cyberbullying Research Center. Last modified 2019. Accessed December 12, 2019. https://cyberbullying.org/Cyberbullying-Identification-Prevention-Response-2019.pdf.

———. "State Bullying Laws." Cyberbullying Research Center. Last modified 2018. Accessed December 12, 2019. https://cyberbullying.org/Bullying-and-Cyberbullying-Laws.pdf. Kowalski, R. M., and Limber S. P. "Electronic Bullying Among Middle School Students." *Journal of Adolescence Health* 41, no. 6, supplement 1 (December 2007): S22–30. https://www.ncbi.nlm.nih.gov/pubmed/18047942.

Lenape Regional High School District (LRHSD). "Why Do Kids Cyberbully Each Other?" Last modified May 3, 2011. Accessed December 12, 2019. https://www.lrhsd.org/Page/3157.

Lucie. "Lucie's Cyberbullying Story." Cybersmile Foundation. Last modified August 24, 2017. Accessed December 12, 2019. https://www.cybersmile.org/blog/lucies-cyberbullying-story.

Multi-State Information Sharing and Analysis Center (MS-ISAC). *The Parents Guide to Cyberbullies.* State of Michigan, Department of Information Technology. Accessed December 12, 2019. https://www.michigan.gov/documents/cybersecurity/Parent_Guide_to_Cyberbullies2010_293897_7.pdf.

National Women's Law Center. "Cyberbullying and Sexual Harassment: FAQs about Cyberbullying and Title IX." Last modified February 20, 2012. Accessed December 12, 2013. http://www.nwlc.org/resource/cyberbullying-and-sexual-harassment-faqs-about-cyberbullying-and-title-ix.

Patchin, Justin. "Millions of Students Skip School Every Year Because of Bullying." Cyberbullying Research Center. Last modified January 3, 2017. Accessed December 14, 2019. https://cyberbullying.org/millions-students-skip-school-year-bullying.

———. "Student Experiences with Reporting Cyberbullying." Cyberbullying Research Center. Last modified May 15, 2018. Accessed September 15, 2018. https://cyberbullying.org/students-experiences-with-reporting-cyberbullying.

Peebles, Erin. "Cyberbullying: Hiding Behind the Screen." *Pediatric & Child Health* 19, no. 10 (December 2014): 527–28. https://doi.org/10.1093/pch/19.10.527.

Pew Research Center. "YouTube, Instagram and Snapchat Are the Most Popular Online Platforms among Teens." Last modified May 29, 2018. Accessed December 12, 2019. https://www.pewresearch.org/internet/2018/05/31/teens-social-media-technology-2018/pi_2018-05-31_teenstech_0-01/.

Rivers, Ian, et al. "Observing Bullying at School: The Mental Health Implications of Witness Status." *School Psychology Quarterly* 24, no. 4 (2009): 211–33. https://doi.org/10.1037/a0018164.

Schneider, Shari Kessel. "Cyberbullying, School Bullying, and Psychological Distress: A Regional Census of High School Students." *American Journal of Public Health* 102, no. 1 (January 2012): 171–77. https://www.doi.org/10.2105/AJPH.2011.300308

StopBullying.gov. "Facts about Bullying" Accessed December 12, 2019. https://www.stopbullying.gov/resources/facts.

Tampa Bay Times. "15-Year-Old St. Pete Girl Charged with Stalking in Cyberbullying Case." Last modified November 13, 2013. Accessed December 12, 2019. https://www.tampabay.com/news/publicsafety/crime/15-year-old-st-pete-girl-charged-with-stalking-in-cyber-bullying-case/2151342.

Toner, Kathleen. "A Brother's Plight Inspires an Anti-Bullying Mission." Cable News Network. Last modified October 14, 2016. Accessed December 12, 2019. https://www.cnn.com/2016/10/13/us/cnn-hero-matthew-kaplan-be-one-project/index.html.

Chapter 11

British Broadcast Company (BBC). "Selfie Deaths: 259 People Reported Dead Seeking the Perfect Picture." Last modified October 4, 2018. Accessed December 12, 2019. https://www.bbc.com/news/newsbeat-45745982.

Celizic, Mike. "Her Teen Committed Suicide over 'Sexting." Today. Last modified March 06, 2009. Accessed December 12, 2019. https://www.today.com/parents/her-teen-committed-suicide-over-sexting-2D80555048.

Cyber Civil Rights Initiative (CCRI). "End Revenge Porn Infographic." Cyber Civil Rights Initiative. Last modified January 3, 2014. Accessed December 12, 2019. https://www.cybercivilrights.org/revenge-porn-infographic/.

Dokur, Mehmet, Emine Petekkaya, and Mehet Karadag. "Media-Based Clinical Research on Selfie-Related Injuries and Deaths." *Turkish Journal of Trauma and Emergency Surgery* 24, no. 2 (2007): 129–35. https://www.doi.org/10.5505/tjtes.2017.83103.

Eaton, Asia A., Holly Jacobs, and Yanet Ruvalcaba. *2017 Nationwide Online Study of Nonconsensual Porn Victimization and Perpetration.* Cyber Civil Rights Initiative, Florida International University Department of Psychology, June 2017. https://www.cybercivilrights.org/wp-content/uploads/2017/06/CCRI-2017-Research-Report.pdf.

Gabriel, Erin. "1 in 4 Young People Has Been Sexted, Study Finds." Cable News Network. Last modified March 1, 2018. Accessed October 21, 2018. https://cnn.com/2018/02/26/health/youth-sexting-prevalence-study/index.html.

Hinduja, Sameer. "Revenge Porn Research, Laws, and Help for Victims." Cyberbullying Research Center. Last modified 2018. Accessed December 12, 2019. https://cyberbullying.org/revenge-porn-research-laws-help-victims.

Huffington Post. "Jessica Logan Suicide: Parents of Dead Teen Sue School, Friends Over Sexting Harassment." Last modified December 6, 2017. Accessed December 12, 2019. https://www.huffpost.com/entry/jessica-logan-suicide-par_n_382825.

Johnson, Annysa. "Fallout Continues for White Male Students at Wisconsin High School Accused of Giving Nazi Salute." First Coast News. Last modified November 14, 2018. Accessed December 12, 2019. https://www.firstcoastnews.com/article/news/nation-now/fallout-continues-for-white-male-students-at-wisconsin-high-school-accused-of-giving-nazi-salute/465-a15fb2a3-c358-48ed-9835-c5b2eeb1c93a.

Levy, Sandra. "More Teens Are Sexting and Are Unaware of Legal Ramifications, Says Study." Health Line. Last modified June 23, 2014. Accessed December 12, 2019. https://www.healthline.com/health-news/youth-sexting-more-prevalent-unaware-criminal-implications-062314#1.

Madigan, Sheri, Anh Ly, and Christina L. Rash. "Prevalence of Multiple Forms of Sexting Behavior Among Youth: A Systematic Review and Meta-Analysis." *JAMA Pediatrics* 172, no. 4 (2018): 327–35. http://doi.org/10.1001/jamapediatrics.2017.5314.

McKay, Tom. "Researchers Identify Hundreds of 'Selfie Deaths' from Media Reports." Gizmodo. Last modified October 4, 2018. Accessed December 12, 2019. https://gizmodo.com/research-ers-identify-hundreds-of-selfie-deaths-from-med-1829513496.

Minutaglio, Rose. "Photo of Wisconsin High School Boys Giving Nazi Salute Before Junior Prom Is Going Viral." Yahoo Lifestyle. Last modified November 12, 2018. Accessed December 12, 2019. https://www.yahoo.com/lifestyle/photo-wisconsin-high-school-boys-184400334.html.

Ocklenburg, Sebastian. "Men Die More Often Than Women When Taking a Selfie." *Psychology Today*. Last modified July 24, 2019. Accessed December 12, 2019. https://www.psychologytoday.com/us/blog/the-asymmetric-brain/201907/men-die-more-often-women-when-taking-selfie.

Patchin, Justin. "Youth Sexting in the U.S.: New Paper in Archives of Sexual Behavior." Cyberbullying Research Center. Last modified July 17, 2019. Accessed July 19, 2019. https://cyberbullying.org/youth-sexting-archings-sexual-behavior.

Pattani, Aneri. "Sexting Linked to Anxiety, Depression, and Substance Use in Teens." *Philadelphia Inquirer*. Last modified June 21, 2019. Accessed December 12, 2019. https://www.inquirer.com/health/sexting-sex-teens-adolescents-mental-health-depression-anxiety-birth-control-drugs-alcohol-20190621.html.

Shannon, William. "The Deadly Waterfall in the Instagram Age." *New York Times*. Last modified August 4, 2018. Accessed December 12, 2019. https://www.nytimes.com/2018/08/14/nyregion/kaaterskill-falls-catskills-deaths-instagram.html.

Sliver, Kate. " Checklist for Taking Safe Seflies." *Washington Post*. Last modified May 13, 2019. https://www.washingtonpost.com/lifestyle/travel/a-checklist-for-taking-safe-self-ies/2019/05/10/768c3b02-71d1-11e9-9f06-5fc2ee80027a_story.html.

Smith, Belinda. "Chart of the Day: Nearly Half of Selfie-Related Deaths Are Caused by Drowing." ABC Science. Last modified July 29, 2018. Accessed December 12, 2019. https://www.abc.net.au/news/2018-07-30/selfie-deaths-chart-of-the-day/10029708.

Strohmaier, Heidi, Megan Murphy, and David DeMatteo. "Youth Sexting: Prevalence Rates, Driving Motivations, and the Deterrent Effect of Legal Consequences." *Sexuality Research and Social Policy* 11, no. 3 (September 2014): 245–55. http://doi.org/10.1007/s13178-014-0162-9.

Union Pacific (UP). "Selfie Tragedy Forever Impacts Those Left Behind." Inside Track. Last modified December 8, 2016. Accessed December 12, 2019. https://www.up.com/aboutup/community/inside_track/selfie-tragedy-12-7-2016.htm.

Wells, Charlie. "Family of Jessica Logan, Who Hanged Herself after Nude-Picture Sexting Led to Bullying, Awarded $154,000 in Settlement." *New York Daily News*. Last modified October 9, 2012. Accessed December 12, 2019. https://www.nydailynews.com/news/national/teen-bullying-victim-family-settlement-article-1.1178783.

WLWT5. "2 Sexting Investigations May Involve Hundreds of Students in Madeira." WLWT5 Cincinnati. Last modified February 28, 2013. Accessed December 12, 2019. https://www.wlwt.com/article/2-sexting-investigations-may-involve-hundreds-of-students-in-madeira-1/3529284.

Index

Acknowledgments

There are so many people who helped me in meaningful ways as I wrote this book. For the time, insights, and assistance they provided, I am in their debt. Many thanks to:

The attorneys who lent their expertise:

- Alec Scott Rose, law office of Alec Rose, PC
- Andrew Miltenberg, law offices of Nesenoff and Miltenberg
- Brad Shear, Shear Law
- Jerry Coleman, Special Assistant Deputy District Attorney for the San Francisco District Attorney's Office and Adjunct Professor of Law, USF Law School
- Judge Thomas A. Jacobs, author of *What Are My Rights?*
- Steve Katz, Head Deputy District Attorney, Los Angeles County District Attorney's Office (also a super brother-in-law!)
- Michael DeRose, Deputy District Attorney, LA County District Attorney's Office
- Payal Sinha, Esq., Managing Attorney Legal Advocacy Project
- William Goren, attorney/consultant on the American with Disabilities Act (ADA), williamgoren.com

The academics and authorities in their respective fields:

- Alan Katzman, social media strategist, socialassurity.com
- Alicia Kozakiewicz, The Alicia Project
- Bruce Anderson, Cyber Investigations Services, LLC
- Cindy Miller, LCSW, Paramus Public Schools
- Connie J Kirkland, MA, NCC, CTTS, Director of Sexual Assault Services, Northern Virginia Community College
- Danielle Brooks, MA, LMFT, Brooks Psychological Group
- David Finkelhor, professor of sociology, University of New Hampshire and Director of the Crimes Against Children Research Center

- Dr. Michael Pittaro, associate professor of criminal justice at American Military University and East Stroudsburg University
- Dr. Bianca Fileborn, lecturer in criminology, University of Melbourne (I have yet to meet an Aussie that I haven't liked and Bianca kept my streak alive in spades. So thank you for that too!)
- Ellen Friedrichs, health educator and author of *Good Sexual Citizenship: How to Create a (Sexually) Safer World*
- Elizabeth Englander, PhD, professor and the Director of the Massachusetts Aggression Reduction Center at Bridgewater State University and author of *Bullying and Cyberbullying: What Every Educator Needs To Know*
- Enrique Dans, PhD, professor of innovation at IE Business School
- Evan Gerstmann, professor of political science, Loyola Marymount University
- Geoffrey Luurs, assistant professor, Department of Organizational Communication, Murray State University
- Glen Pounder, CEO, Child Rescue Coalition, Inc.
- Jedidiah Bracy, Editorial Director at the International Association of Privacy Professionals (IAPP)
- Joe Ryan, Education Coordinator (former), Internet Crimes Against Children Task Force, scsafetynet.com
- Joel Levin, PhD, Director of Programs, Co-Founder stopsexualassaultinschools.org
- Josh Ochs, SmartSocial.com
- Justin W. Patchin, professor of criminal justice, University of Wisconsin-Eau Claire, and Co-director of the Cyberbullying Research Center
- Kate Fogarty, PhD, associate professor, University of Florida, Dept. of Family, Youth & Community Sciences
- Kami Kosenko, associate professor, Department of Communication, North Carolina State University
- Kevin Ripa, President, Computer Evidence Recovery, Inc.
- Larry Magid, CEO: ConnectSafely.org and Founder SafeKids.com

- Lisa Lawrence, media relations, National Domestic Violence Hotline and loveisrespect.org
- Melissa Davis, CEO, goennounce.com
- Patti Giggans, M.A., Executive Director, Peace Over Violence
- Rich Matta, CEO, ReputationDefender
- Rosemary Rade, Director of Digital Services, National Domestic Violence Hotline and loveisrespect.org
- Stacey A. Jeleniewski, senior research specialist, National Center for Missing and Exploited Children (NCMEC)
- Sheri Bauman, professor, College of Education, University of Arizona
- Sue Thotz, Senior Program Manager, Los Angeles, Common Sense Media Education
- Sunitha Menon, Director, Training & Consultation Services, Rape, Abuse & Incest National Network (RAINN)
- Terry M. Evans, CEO Cybersleuth Investigations, Inc.
- Tim Lynch, adjunct scholar at the Cato Institute

Some of the brave men and women of law enforcement:
- Lieutenant Alisha Jordan, LAPD
- Cedric Alexander, Psy.D, Chief of Police, Rochester Police Department (Ret.)
- Senior Lead Officer Gary Verge, LAPD
- Detective Geoff Chavez, LAPD
- Detective Jason Ames, Los Angeles County Sheriff's Department and instructor/founder of Swifttactical.net
- Jason Hanson and his aide Lisa Hutter
- John Torres, Special Agent in Charge (SAC), Ret., Bureau of Alcohol, Tobacco, Firearms, and Explosives (ATF) and now the Systemwide Director of Investigations at the University of California Office of the President

The people who helped in many different ways:

- Ali Norman-Franks, intervention counselor, Beverly Hills High School
- Anthony Locke, Upper School Dean, Crossroads School for Arts & Sciences
- Ali Myers—thanks for your belief in the mission and continued support
- Capri Maddox, Esq., Executive Director, LA Dept. of Civil and Human Rights
- Carly Myers
- Avery Kaplan
- Bella Echols
- Betsy, Kevin, and Sam Dill—each of you, in your own ways, did something really cool for me. Thank you.
- Brett Levine, MD—thank you for your friendship and your belief from day one
- Brian Arechiga
- Brian Michael, Esq., and Jennifer Gilbert—thanks for your support and the warm introduction to A.L.
- Cara Natterson, MD
- Carol Todd, amandatoddlegacy.org
- Cathy Gordon, L.C.S.W., Head of Religious School, Wilshire Boulevard Temple
- Dan Whitley, Esq.
- Darcie Rowan, my publicist, darcierowanpr.com
- Darin Greenblatt
- David Rosenblum, Esq., thanks for your thoughtful edits and many years of friendship
- Dolly Klock, MD, Adolessonsla.com, it's such a pleasure working with you on our events and thanks for your continued support
- Emily Brown
- Literary Agent Felicia Eth—thank you for your early interest in the book

- Georgia Bryan—wise beyond your years!
- Girl Scout Troop No. 02545: Gabriella Wahlig, Livia Rosenmayr, Tonya Yermilova, Lulu Gourrier, Ella Tabachnikoff
- Jenny and Jacque Forman
- Jaguar Bennett, Quill Driver Books
- Jeff Fishman, JSF Financial
- Caroline Geller
- Jordan Geller, MD—my oldest friend, who was one of the first people I told about the concept of the book. He loved the idea and told me to get off my butt and start writing. Thank you.
- Julie Sandor
- To the Katzes, my family by marriage, thank you all for your love and support
- Kent Sorsky, my editor at Quill Driver Books, who immediately recognized the relevance and importance of the book and gave me the extended time I needed to get the job done
- Kevin Wittenberg, PhD, thank you for the support and encouragement, my friend
- Lianne Barnes, PhD, Assistant Professor-in-Residence, University of Nevada, Las Vegas—thank you for all you did for the book, Lianne. Congrats to you on your recent accomplishments.
- Lisa Solomon, Regional Manager, Los Angeles, Common Sense Media
- Talent Agent Mickey Berman, UTA
- Marisa LaDuca Crandall, Ph.D., Director of Educational and Counseling Services, Marlborough School
- Maryl Georgi
- Mattimore Cronin from Noble Growth Marketing
- Michele Wahlig
- Mimi Cristall, for your love and support
- Miranda and Jake Tollman
- Nancy Moscatiello
- Nancy Wu

- Nima Asghari, web consultant
- Randi Michel, nanager at Artists First
- Ruth Fragoso, Shireen Rafat, and Manja Lenkin from Santa Monica High School PTSA
- Sara Bowman, Los Angeles Regional Director, Common Sense Media
- Sohaila Abdulali, author, sohailaink.com
- Steve Gold, Esq.
- Steve Stokdyk, Esq., and Evan Stokdyk
- Tamar Galatzan, Esq.
- Tamara White
- Tamberley Much
- Tedra Smedley
- Temple Isaiah and Rabbi Zoë Klein
- Tom Brennan, Horse Sense Media
- Wendy "Weniki" Heller-Stein
- Whitney Giancola

My parents:

Barbara Cristall, for your love, support, and always doing your very best.

Robert Cristall, for your love, doing your part when I was a teen headed in the wrong direction, and for encouraging me to write the book.

The Magnificent Three…

I am certainly in the debt of all of those mentioned above, but there are three people who helped me at almost every turn along the way:

Kimberly Combs and Mickey Mandelbaum, thank you for your friendship and all of your help and support. Being able to turn to you both when I was spinning my wheels on the book was invaluable. Your edits and suggestions made this book unquestionably better.

No one contributed more to this project than my incredible wife Lisa. This book would not exist without your sacrifice and never-ending love and support. Thank you for your patience, belief in me, and top-notch editing skills!

About the Author

Jonathan Cristall, Esq., spent his own teen years taking unnecessary risks and getting into avoidable trouble. Now a veteran prosecutor for the City of Los Angeles, he went from disregarding laws to enforcing them.

Cristall is a certified sexual violence prevention instructor who works extensively with teenagers, their families, and schools to teach physical, digital, emotional, and legal life skills.

What They Don't Teach Teens is his first book. Cristall lives in Los Angeles with his wife and three sons.